MILLENNIAL DREAMS AND MORAL DILEMMAS

Seventh-day Adventism and contemporary ethics

Courtesy of the Ellen G. White Estate

MILLENNIAL DREAMS AND MORAL DILEMMAS

Seventh-day Adventism and contemporary ethics

MICHAEL PEARSON

*Principal Lecturer in
Christian Philosophy and Ethics,
Newbold College*

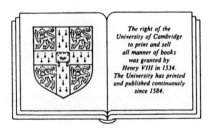

The right of the
University of Cambridge
to print and sell
all manner of books
was granted by
Henry VIII in 1534.
The University has printed
and published continuously
since 1584.

CAMBRIDGE UNIVERSITY PRESS

Cambridge
New York   Port Chester
Melbourne   Sydney

BJ1251
.P38
2008x
024476 7792

CAMBRIDGE UNIVERSITY PRESS
Cambridge, New York, Melbourne, Madrid, Cape Town, Singapore, São Paulo, Delhi

Cambridge University Press
The Edinburgh Building, Cambridge CB2 8RU, UK

Published in the United States of America by Cambridge University Press, New York

www.cambridge.org
Information on this title: www.cambridge.org/9780521365093

First published 1990
This digitally printed version 2008

A catalogue record for this publication is available from the British Library

Library of Congress Cataloguing in Publication data

Pearson, Michael, 1947–
Millennial dreams and moral dilemmas: Seventh-Day Adventist
responses to some contemporary ethical issues / Michael Pearson.
p. cm.
Bibliography.
ISBN 0 521 36509 0
1. Christian ethics. 2. Social ethics. 3. Seventh-Day
Adventists – Doctrines. 4. Adventists – Doctrines. I. Title.
BJ1251.P38   1989
241'.046732 – dc20   89-9772   CIP

ISBN 978-0-521-36509-3 hardback
ISBN 978-0-521-09148-0 paperback

For Helen
sine qua non

Contents

Acknowledgements

It is as important to express one's gratitude to those who have helped to bring a book like this to its final form as it is impossible to discern the extent of one's indebtedness to others. The book is based on the foundation of an education made possible by my mother, Jessie, and my late father, Sidney. Without their constant encouragement and willingness to forgo those things which would have made life a little easier for themselves, I would never have pursued my academic interests. This is the kind of debt one can acknowledge but never repay; one can only try to do the same for one's own children. And yet I am in debt to my children too. Emma and Martin have played no small part in this work. They have done much to try to keep me human and in touch with the realities of life when I might easily have retreated into an academic ivory tower. More than that, they have borne with a father who was sometimes distracted, tired and irritable, with remarkable cheerfulness and understanding. I owe them a great deal though they may not yet understand precisely why. I should also like to thank my parents-in-law, Rhona and Victor Cooper, for their constant encouragement and valuable insights into the nature of Seventh-day Adventism.

I owe much to the Board of Governors of Newbold College and to its administrators for generously granting me the opportunity to complete this research. The staff of the College library were enormously co-operative in making their resources available to me, and I am also extremely grateful to the staff both of the Ellen G. White – SDA Research Centre at Newbold College and of the Ellen G. White Estate in Washington, DC, for allowing me free access to the manuscripts and correspondence. My colleagues at the College consistently encouraged me with the thought that I was doing something which was worthwhile. If my work has some practical value for the Seventh-day

Adventist church then that will in some measure repay the debt I owe to Newbold College.

A special vote of thanks must go to Harry Leonard of Newbold College and Dennis Porter of the Bodleian Library in Oxford for reading the manuscript in various forms and for making invaluable suggestions as to how to improve it. I owe a great deal to Bryan Wilson of All Souls College, Oxford, who supervised the present work in its original form as a D.Phil. thesis. His clear understanding of the religious impulse at work in people, and his constant availability for consultation were invaluable. In his use of the English language he set the highest of examples. His graciousness was oil on the wheels of the research process.

A number of people at various stages have helped me to prepare the manuscript. Particular thanks are due to Jonquil Hole, Alethea Mustard, Helen Savage and Margit Fuhrmann for their expert and willing help. More than that, I should like to thank them for their patience and amazing cheerfulness. I should also like to thank Ulrike Hellen, Alex Wright and Mary Baffoni of Cambridge University Press for their invaluable assistance in the final preparation of the copy.

Lastly, and most importantly, I want to thank my wife, Helen. She acted as a sounding board for new ideas. She gave comfort in times of discouragement. She kept our home on an even keel when I was distracted by the job in hand. She showed me new ways of looking at the world. But more than all that, she has helped me to *be* — I can think of no better way to describe her role in helping me to become capable of completing such an undertaking. Without her the book simply would not have been written, and I want to express my deep gratitude by dedicating it to her.

My indebtedness is great, the *et alii* includes many more people. Ultimately, of course, the judgements contained herein are my own. I trust that they will benefit the church about which they are written.

I

INTRODUCTION

1 · Confrontation with the issues

General context of the research

Even the most cursory examination of publishers' lists from the last two decades will reveal an enormous upsurge of interest in matters of private and public morality. Other media reflect the same trend. While the reasons for this are no doubt extremely complex, two factors must figure prominently in any attempt to explain it. Recent and rapid technological developments on many fronts have placed us in some extraordinarily difficult moral predicaments. Previous generations have not had to face the dilemmas posed, for example, by the availability of safe abortions, sperm banks, and prostaglandins. They have not had to come to terms with the fact that new industrial processes, modern farming techniques, and unchecked exploitation of natural resources may precipitate an ecological crisis of unimaginable proportions. Worst of all, only in the current generation have human beings had to recognize that they have the capacity to destroy themselves and their environment. Such issues have provoked endless discussion and the formation of numerous pressure groups.

By no means unrelated to this first factor is the second, the rapid erosion of traditional Christian morality. For example, homosexuality has become a tolerated sexual option where once it was not even considered a fit subject for private conversation. The indiscriminate use of violence by terrorist organizations is something to which we have become increasingly accustomed but which strikes at the very heart of the Christian ethic. The feminist movement is one important manifestation of the breakdown of traditional lines of authority. Any institution, group, or individual purveying a set of values today must expect to have to render account for it.

The Christian church has faced the stark alternative of framing a positive response to these changes in the moral climate, or becoming an irrelevance in contemporary society. The Church of England has dealt with such issues through its Board for Social Responsibility, formerly the Moral Welfare Council. Other religious organizations either have similar agencies, or establish committees with specific terms of reference. American churches have typically set up 'task forces' to deal with such matters. Such a reaction normally comes, however, only in response to an issue which has already become contentious, and on which a secular literature already exists. Formal institutional deliberations are frequently preceded, or even provoked, by contributions from those within the church farsighted enough to want to meet the secular challenge head-on.

Among the most valuable of such publications have been those that have sought to formulate an opinion on some aspect of moral theology only after having set the contemporary situation in historical context. One of the earliest and best examples of this approach was D. Sherwin Bailey's *Homosexuality and the Western Christian Tradition*. Another similar work of seminal importance was A. R. Winnett's *Divorce and Remarriage in Anglicanism*. The latter concerned itself primarily with the political history of the issue within the church, while the former provided an historical analysis of biblical, extra-canonical, and traditional pronouncements. Both, in their different ways, attempted to inform and shape the church's response to the rising tide of moral relativism, by, as it were, staking out the territory. Other Christian writers have since built moral theologies on the important foundation which they laid.

The present volume is somewhat in the tradition of Winnett's publication, and his later *The Church and Divorce*, inasmuch as it seeks to trace developments in moral thought, policy, and behaviour, in a limited area and within a particular communion. Surprisingly little work of this sort has been attempted. Kenneth Boyd, in *Scottish Church Attitudes to Sex, Marriage and the Family 1850–1914*, analysed the changing position of four major churches in Scotland to such issues as sexuality, marriage, divorce, venereal disease, and housing conditions. John Noonan's *Contraception: A History of its Treatment by the Catholic Theologians and Canonists* was in the same general category, although it concerned itself less with actual practice. And there are a number of other volumes which to some extent overlap with the concerns of such analytical historical works, but fewer than one might expect. This territory, then, is not entirely unexplored, but much of it remains to be charted.

The Seventh-day Adventist context

The Seventh-day Adventist church has also found it necessary to address the kinds of moral issues mentioned above, not only because members encountered them in the wider world, but because they were finding themselves personally in moral difficulty. Inevitably the spirit of the age, in some measure, percolated down into the church. The present work attempts to illuminate the moral dilemmas within contemporary Seventh-day Adventism by reference to its past.

The church's moral theology is best understood, of course, in the light of its general history. A good deal has been written about the history of Seventh-day Adventism, and this is not the place to repeat it.[1] However, it may well prove worthwhile to digress briefly at the outset in order to provide the reader with a basic historical framework with which to work.

The first four decades of the nineteenth century witnessed an enormous amount of religious activity and revivalism in certain parts of the United States, which became known as the 'Second Great Awakening'.[2] To most native Americans and immigrants this was the land of promise; reform movements and utopian ventures mushroomed. Many Americans believed that theirs was the land where the kingdom of God was to be established; a stable, moral and devout Republic was to be the fulfilment of the millennial dream.[3]

However, a section of the population – and by no means simply an eccentric fringe – rejected such optimism. William Miller, a leading figure among them, attracted large audiences from various denominational backgrounds with his apocalyptic preaching. On the basis of his study of Bible prophecy, he believed that something eschatologically significant would happen around 1843. As the time approached, the Millerites found themselves increasingly ostracized by the religious establishment, as their own proclamations became more strident. Finally, attention focused on 1844 as the year when Christ would return triumphantly to the earth to collect his people. If the passing of the spring date for the advent caused dismay among the believers, the disappointment of 22 October dealt a mortal blow to the Millerite movement, and many left it disillusioned.

Of the various rationalizations for the apparent failure of prophecy, the most enduring was that on that date Christ had in fact passed, not from heaven to earth, but from one part of a sanctuary in heaven to another, there to begin a work of 'investigative judgement'. This gave new vitality to a minority among the adventists, who also soon came to believe that God was calling them to observe the seventh-day Sabbath. Confirmation of this came, they believed, in a vision granted to a young woman in their midst, Ellen Gould Harmon, who had earlier been deprived of membership of the Methodist church because of her adventist beliefs.

So strongly convinced was this core of sabbatarian adventists that Christ's return was still imminent that they held to a 'shut-door' theory, that is, that the 'door of salvation' was now closed to all except those who had passed through 'the great disappointment' of 1844. However, the view that these were the only ones to whom sabbatarian adventists should bear witness soon crumbled as others, not involved in the events of 1844, sought to ally themselves with them. The group grew considerably, and, for various administrative reasons, the General Conference of Seventh-day Adventists was founded in May 1863, even though the original Millerites had eschewed all forms of religious organization. The new church prospered particularly under the charismatic influence of Ellen Harmon, now Ellen White after her marriage to one of the staunchest of the Millerites, James White. Although she never had any formal authority in the organization, she, and others, believed that God had chosen her to be the recipient of visions and divine instruction. She it was who held the movement together in the face of considerable turmoil in various phases of the first fifty years of its existence.

The leaders of the fledgling church – once of the opinion that their mission to proclaim 'the truth' was restricted to 'the world' as represented in the melting pot of American society – soon lifted their sights higher. Adventist literature sent by immigrant converts back to their relatives in Europe soon created interest and a demand for a visit by a representative of the church. In 1874, John Nevins Andrews became the first official Seventh-day Adventist foreign missionary when he began work in Switzerland. So began over a

6

century of Seventh-day Adventist missionary activity on a world-wide scale. By the time of Ellen White's death in 1915, the church had grown to a membership of 125,000[4] scattered throughout the world, although as yet the majority was still resident in the United States.

Since then, the church has involved itself in an enormous range of educational, medical, welfare, and evangelistic ventures. It has invested huge sums of money in the erection of all kinds of institutions besides churches, from bush clinics to universities, from health-food restaurants to publishing houses, and in the provision of myriad services from 'stop-smoking' clinics to disaster relief, from 'dial-a-prayer' telephone networks to mobile open-heart surgery teams. The power base of the church remains in the United States although by 1984 only about 15 per cent of its 4.5 million membership was American.[5]

It is now over 140 years since the Millerites earnestly anticipated the return of their Lord in 1844, and more than 120 years since the official foundation of the church in 1863. As the expected advent has failed to materialize, and as the experience of the Seventh-day Adventist pioneers becomes increasingly remote from that of their modern heirs, the church has faced some major problems in the area of faith and practice. At the level of doctrine, some members have difficulty in sustaining a lively adventist expectation in the face of an apparently indefinite postponement of the parousia. Debate continues as to the extent to which Adventists should emphasize their distinctive features. The controversial book *Seventh-day Adventists Answer Questions on Doctrine*, published in 1957, was seen by many as a conscious attempt to lead the church away from the backwaters of sectarian religion into the mainstream of evangelical Protestantism. Some members were offended by what they saw as its betrayal of the uniqueness of Adventism. In this regard, the doctrines of the heavenly sanctuary and the investigative judgement,[6] which are peculiar to Seventh-day Adventism, have recently been the focus of a debilitating internal struggle, partly because, according to some, they can be substantiated only from Ellen White's writings, and not from biblical sources. Indeed, the authority of her pronouncements on matters of faith and practice is currently under severe scrutiny (see below, pp. 46–7).

Any religious group operating in the modern world and boasting a prophet from the Victorian era will face the problem that rising generations of members will find the prophetic word, in part at least, outmoded. Furthermore, any religious group whose members move relatively freely in the wider world, will have to respond to issues which are current in that society, and seek to resist the forces of secularism while maintaining its credibility. The Seventh-day Adventist church is no exception. In the last two decades, it has encountered serious difficulties over the representation of ethnic minorities at all levels of church government. It has witnessed among its members an increase in the incidence both of divorce and what it considers to be illicit sexual behaviour. It has faced legal charges of sexual discrimination from its employees. It has had to confront accusations of mismanagement of large amounts of church funds. And so on. All this has produced in the denomination a ferment of ideas which is still in process. Membership of the church, however, continues to grow rapidly, particularly in the Third World.

The purpose of the research

The primary purpose of this work is to break new ground in the chronicling and analysis of significant developments in Seventh-day Adventist moral thought. The bulk of the book seeks to provide a detailed chronology, from the church's beginnings to the present day, of Seventh-day Adventist responses, official and unofficial, to certain ethical problems which attract considerable attention in contemporary society. The five issues are all bound up in some way with human sexuality: contraception, abortion, the role of women, divorce, and homosexuality. To facilitate a thorough analysis of these responses, the account of Seventh-day Adventist thinking and behaviour in these matters has been set in historical and social context. The responses of other Christian denominations have been recorded to lend a further perspective. The historical background provided is by no means exhaustive; for that, the reader must go to volumes cited in the notes. It merely provides, as it were, a series of 'still images' against which the continuing account of developments within Seventh-day Adventism can be viewed. The earlier chapters attempt to identify the mainsprings of Seventh-day Adventist moral decision-making, by examining matters of broader ethical and socio-political concern before the focus narrows to issues related to human sexuality.

A further objective of this research is to probe beyond mere pronouncements, official or otherwise, on these issues, to discover something of the actual practice of Adventists. The subjects under discussion are, of course, highly sensitive ones about which it is extraordinarily difficult to gather reliable data. Where it exists, this has been used. Efforts to add to it for the purposes of this research have proved relatively unsuccessful. Elsewhere, it has been possible only to offer informed speculation on the basis of certain empirical indicators. Important among these are denominational publications. It is difficult to gauge accurately the extent to which the published opinion of church leaders influences the behaviour of the rank and file, or indeed reflects it. Since, as will be argued later, Adventists manifest considerable pragmatism, and since Adventist publications address a predominantly Adventist readership, it seems a reasonable assumption that denominational literature addresses certain issues only, or mainly, when there exists a practical problem of some significance in denominational life. Impressionistic evidence confirms this assumption.

While the research may contribute, if only obliquely, to the growing self-understanding of Seventh-day Adventists, it is hoped that it will allow the disinterested observer a fuller appreciation of the ethos of Adventism. Beyond the sphere of Seventh-day Adventism the work has perhaps two main values. First, since Adventism is in many ways representative of other conservative Christian organizations, this study offers a general guide to their probable thinking about sexual matters. It also draws together information about Christian responses to these issues which is perhaps not elsewhere available in one place. In this respect, it may serve a useful bibliographical function.

The scope of the research

The focus of this study is Seventh-day Adventism in the United States, for, as will be argued in a later chapter, Adventism is essentially an American phenomenon. Although approximately 75 per cent of the current world membership now resides in the Third World,[7] the ethos of the movement is unmistakably American. It may well be that, in time, the emergent nations will come to dominate church structures; as yet, that process is not advanced. Although Europeans have served widely and with distinction in the movement, they have not, for a variety of reasons, succeeded in diminishing American domination of it.

The study covers the years between the middle of the nineteenth century and the present day. The period has been divided into two, 1840–1915, and 1915–85, both to make the material more manageable, and to facilitate comparison between what might be called 'primitive' and 'modern' Seventh-day Adventism. The choice of the actual year 1915 as the dividing point is somewhat arbitrary, as most such divisions are. The period around that date, however, is of significance not only in the development of Seventh-day Adventism but in the history of the wider world. It was in 1915 that Ellen White died, and the church had to begin to learn to live without an oracle. By 1915, the total membership outside North America was rapidly approaching the level of that within,[8] a fact which would inevitably affect the nature of Seventh-day Adventism. The wider world, of course, was involved in hostilities on a vast scale, which created social dislocation of enormous proportions, and in time provoked a reappraisal of traditional values.

Sources

A major concern here, then, is to trace and analyse the attitudes, policies, and values of the Seventh-day Adventist establishment. One sometimes hesitates to describe these as 'official', since a major finding of this research is that the church has often avoided committing itself irrevocably to a fixed position on such issues. Part of what might be described as the genius of Adventism is its pragmatism, as a later chapter will argue.

The general church paper, *The Adventist Review*, is the principal vehicle for establishment views.[9] Between 1973 and 1979, its masthead described it as the 'official organ of the church'; usually it has been regarded as its 'general paper'. It regularly carries news of General Conference decisions, and articles printed therein must conform to certain standards of orthodoxy, and may thus be regarded as having semi-official status.[10] It has recently had a weekly circulation of 75,000, with individual copies tending to be widely shared.

A more self-critical analysis of developments in Seventh-day Adventism is provided by *Spectrum*, a journal produced by Adventist intellectuals since 1969, which provides very valuable commentary on various aspects of denominational life and history. Together with the *Review*, it constitutes the main periodical source for this study.

The church produces a large range of periodicals which cater for various special interests. For example *Ministry*, a magazine for clergy, and *Insight*, designed for Seventh-day Adventist youth, both reflect trends of thinking within the denomination. All have to meet certain criteria of orthodoxy, although some scope for divergence of opinion exists. The climate of opinion within the church can also be deduced from numerous unpublished manuscripts which the church has commissioned at one time or another to inform its decisions. These are housed in the General Conference headquarters in Washington, DC. The same archives contain a vast quantity of correspondence to and from leaders of the denomination throughout its history, some of which illuminates the present study.

A dominant feature of the book is the counsel of the church's prophetic leader, Ellen White, whose writings have exercised, and continue to exercise, an enormous influence on the faith and practice of Seventh-day Adventists. It is contained in innumerable books, articles, unpublished manuscripts, and a vast correspondence to members great and small. Her whole literary output contains detailed counsel on doctrinal, devotional, moral, and practical matters.

Correspondence between the author and administrators in various Adventist institutions throughout the world has yielded valuable information, particularly about recent developments. Further insight into contemporary trends within Adventism is provided by ephemera produced by special interest groups, of which there are a considerable number. *SDA Kinship Connection*, newsletter of the organization of Adventist homosexuals, is a well-produced example.

Much of the information used to reconstruct the historical context in which Seventh-day Adventists were operating when making their responses to moral dilemmas, comes from secondary sources. Further insights into the functioning of sectarian groups in general, and of Seventh-day Adventism in particular, are provided by the work of sociologists which, it is hoped, will lend a measure of objectivity to the research.

Objectivity

It is important to consider whether a piece of research such as this is best done by an 'outsider' or an 'insider'. The 'outsider' may succeed in achieving a certain objectivity but fail to understand the real heart of the movement, in spite of making serious efforts to remedy this by meeting members of all ranks, over a long period of time, in a variety of milieux. An 'insider' will have the advantage of having a finger on its pulse as a matter of regular devotional, and perhaps occupational practice, but faces two main dangers. On the one hand, out of a perhaps unconscious concern to vindicate a movement with which one's own identity is inextricably bound up, one may produce research which tends to be apologetic in nature. On the other hand, familiarity may breed contempt, with the result that the analysis becomes unduly cynical. A conscious effort has been made to steer a middle course between the Scylla of special pleading and the Charybdis of cynicism.[11]

Terminology

One or two terminological points ought perhaps to be made clear at the outset. The term 'Seventh-day Adventist' has been abbreviated to 'Adventist' in many places, treating of developments after the official foundation of the General Conference in 1863. The groups of believers are referred to as 'sabbatarian adventists' in the period between the beginning of observance of the seventh-day Sabbath in 1844 and official organization in 1863. The term 'adventist' is used to describe all who were expecting Christ's imminent return.

The reader will also find that the terms 'church', 'sect', 'denomination', and their derivatives, are frequently used to refer to Seventh-day Adventism. This is not done out of ignorance of, or indeed, to indicate rejection of, various typologies which sociologists have employed to analyse religious movements. On the contrary, a number of these classifications are exceedingly helpful. The rather loose usage of these terms is justified on two grounds: first, it relieves the text of a

12

certain heaviness which would result from a fastidious adherence to one epithet; second, Seventh-day Adventism is extremely difficult to categorize on the basis of these typologies. While it manifests definite sectarian tendencies, it is also a good example of a religious movement where the process of denominationalization is well advanced. There are even certain island communities in the Caribbean and Pacific regions where Adventism is the religious preference of the majority and might loosely be called the 'established Church'. However unimportant that may be, the movement certainly claims to be a church.

Conclusion

No attempt has ever been made by Seventh-day Adventists to produce a comprehensive and clearly articulated moral theology consistent with their faith. Various influences have combined to produce that set of moral commitments peculiar to Adventists. The cultural context in which Adventism first developed exercised an important formative influence, of course. A child of this milieu, Ellen White, has been a major source of moral authority in the church. However, she has remained somewhat elusive inasmuch as her voluminous counsels were often addressed to specific situations, and required caution on the part of any wishing to make general application of them. Paradoxically, her unwillingness to be entirely explicit concerning moral behaviour, typical of the more restrained age in which she lived, has added to the sense of elusiveness, as did the fact that her counsels were not always immediately available to a wide audience. However, her influence on Adventist moral thought must not be underestimated. Where the Bible writers and Ellen White have been thought to speak unequivocally, the Adventist moral code has been absolute. In those areas of ethical concern where questions have not been readily resolved by reference to an authority, Adventist positions have reflected and refracted the currents of opinion prevailing in the wider society. Values have been forged in the market-place of Adventist public opinion and practice. In this connection, the remarkably wide range of periodical literature which Adventists have produced assumes great importance, since it both reflects and shapes the behaviour of members.

This volume, then, is not an attempt to produce a moral theology consistent with the Seventh-day Adventist faith. It is rather an exercise in historical ethics, an attempt to discover what moral postures Adventists have adopted on a range of issues which are very much alive in contemporary society. It further attempts to discover why they have reacted thus, both from an ideological and sociological point of view. This research may be of value in the attempt to develop a consistent moral theology; it does not itself seek to provide it.

II

MAJOR INFLUENCES IN ADVENTIST MORAL THOUGHT

2 · Advent and remnant: two major doctrinal influences

Advent and remnant

It goes without saying that our view of the way in which the world is constituted will profoundly affect our behaviour and our perception of our status in that world. The doctrinal structure of Adventism has thus inevitably influenced the way in which its adherents have sought to discharge their moral responsibilities in the world. On the other hand, the ethical consequences of a complex doctrinal system such as that to be found in Adventism may not be at all self-evident. They may need to be uncovered by careful theological excavation. Those ethical consequences will certainly change in response to developments in the larger society.

Adventists have, like other Christians in recent years, given increasing attention to the business of formulating a mature moral response to the many dilemmas which present themselves. Adventists have become less comfortable about defining morality in terms of a set of traditionally acceptable behaviours. Times are undoubtedly changing within the church. However, there are perhaps two fundamental doctrinal positions which have always exercised, and continue to exercise, a profound influence on Adventist moral thought and action. Both concern the dimension of time. The belief in an imminent second advent emphasizes the transitory nature of our present existence. Earthly life is but a prelude to life in heaven to which the faithful will ultimately pass when Christ returns. In the intervening time, and particularly in the end time, there must exist a rallying point for the faithful. The 'remnant church' then must function as a bridge between the present moment and the second advent.

Belief in an imminent second advent

Seventh-day Adventism has its immediate roots in the revivalism which swept the north-eastern part of the United States in the 1830s and 1840s. It would be wrong, however, to see this revivalism as all of one piece; certain sociological patterns can be discerned, and various doctrinal differences detected. Of the latter, a major source of disagreement was the millennium. There were those, like Charles G. Finney, who believed that the thousand-year period of peace and plenty, described in the book of Revelation, would precede the restoration of God's kingdom. Finney expected that, if the momentum towards social reform and greater piety were sustained, the millennium might begin in a matter of a few years. Many believed, with Lyman Beecher, that America was 'in the providence of God, destined to lead the way in the moral and political emancipation of the world'.[1] For such post-millennialists, the millennium was to be the climax of the American dream. Since the millennium was to be ushered in by human instrumentality, the motivation for reform on both a personal and social level was strong.

Another prominent revivalist grouping, the pre-millennialists, viewed this sort of optimism as a gross deception. They believed that the millennium would *follow* the second advent of Christ, who would come 'as a thief in the night' (1 Thessalonians 5:2). No steady, humanly inspired progress in social justice and morality could be anticipated; on the contrary, the scriptures, they believed, indicated that further decline would be halted only by God's merciful intervention in earthly affairs. The millennium could begin only after judgement had taken place, after the divine purging of corrupt human society.

Followers of William Miller, a leading exponent of this view, came to focus their adventist expectations on 21 March 1844, on the basis of his exegesis of the prophecies of Daniel. The date was revised to 22 October 1844; to those who had left their crops unharvested in their fields, the dawn of 23 October came as a great shock.[2] Many withdrew from the movement, disillusioned; others sought various rationalizations for the disappointment.

A core of believers remained convinced, however, that, while they had miscalculated the date, and even been wrong in setting it, the advent could not long be delayed. Yet, even under the pressure of such a strong belief in the dissolution of all things temporal, the adventists were unable for long to dissociate themselves from normal social arrangements. Having criticized two young adventists who announced in 1845 their intention to marry, James White, a leading adventist, himself married less than a year later. His own marriage in turn unsettled some believers, who saw it as an indication of waning faith in an imminent advent.[3] While the Whites were able to satisfy believers on this point (see below, p. 58), their marriage was a tacit acknowledgement of the fact that adventist expectations did not put man beyond the power of sexual drives, that sexual activity had to be regulated, and that adventists continued to support the institution of the family, as traditionally conceived, rather than the alternatives of celibacy or communitarianism, alternatives espoused by the contemporary Shakers, the Amana Society, and numerous utopian sects. The fact that Ellen gave birth to a child a year after their marriage confirms the view that the Whites believed that normal social arrangements should continue until the advent.[4] Ellen White's criticism of those believers who thought it unnecessary to work substantiates this position.[5]

The tension between sustaining a lively expectation in an imminent advent, and maintaining more or less normal social arrangements, became evident in other areas of believers' lives. At first, attempts to extend the scope of the movement met with determined opposition from those who believed that the door of opportunity had been shut against all but those believers who had passed through the disappointment of 1844.[6] Ultimately, a renewed drive to proselytize demanded that a strategy be devised. A broadsheet, the *Second Advent Review and Sabbath Herald*, began publication in 1850, while prominent leaders travelled the countryside organizing sabbath-keeping adventists into bands. Incipient organization, however, raised a serious dilemma. Some, arguing that a major impulse of adventism had been the rejection of the formalism which they found in the mainstream churches, vehemently opposed any form of organization.[7] Others, however, perceived the practical advantages of organization,[8] principal of which perhaps was the question of ownership of property. By 1861, a brick publishing building had been constructed, and a number of meeting places erected. These properties, although financed by groups, were registered in the names of individuals. In the event of their death, properties would have reverted to next of kin, and so the sabbatarian adventists stood to lose considerable assets. James White, emerging as one of the leaders of the group, suggested corporate ownership as a solution to the problem. Incorporation, however, required the creation of a formal organization with which the state could deal. Consequently the General Conference of Seventh-day Adventists was organized in May 1863. The new church now stood in official relationship to the state, which twenty years earlier adventists had regarded as a demonic agency. According to the theory of H. Richard Niebuhr, these would have been the first steps towards the ethical compromise inevitably generated by the act of organization.[9]

The organization of the church came at a time when the nation was in the midst of a fearful civil war, in which a central issue was the institution of slavery. This threw the Adventists into considerable confusion. Since members were then located entirely in the northeastern corner of the country, they were almost exclusively abolitionists. Ellen White, whose claims to prophetic authority were now widely acknowledged by Adventists, regarded it as a profoundly important moral issue:

There are a few in the ranks of Sabbathkeepers who sympathize with the slaveholder. When they embraced the truth, they did not leave behind them all the errors they should have left ... The colored race are God's property. Their maker alone is their master, and those who have dared chain down the body and the soul of the slave, to keep him in degradation like the brutes, will have their retribution.[10]

Indeed, one member who had publicly expressed his approval of the slave trade was threatened with expulsion from the church.[11] Some leading Adventists, like John Byington, sought to conform their actions to their convictions by helping runaway slaves to freedom, in defiance of the law.[12]

Other Adventists, however, believed such activity to be ill-advised and short-sighted. Joseph Bates, a prominent Adventist, and once heavily involved in social reform, reasoned thus:

I have no less interest in temperance and in freeing of the slave than before; but I am come face to face with a tremendous enveloping cause. When

Christ comes, liquor will be forgotten and the slave will be free. The lesser causes are swallowed in the greater.[13]

He clearly believed that slavery was one symptom of the much larger disease of sin, which would shortly be remedied at the second advent. Believers would be better employed proclaiming news of the overall cure rather than merely treating a single symptom.

Like other evangelical Christian groups, Seventh-day Adventists experienced then, and continue to experience, the tension produced by the dual imperatives, 'Prepare to meet thy God', and 'Occupy till I come' (Amos 4:12 and Luke 19:13). The tension is, however, heightened by a third duty, the fulfilment of which characterizes the time of occupation, that is, the duty to preach the 'everlasting gospel' to 'every nation, and kindred, and tongue, and people' (Revelation 14:6). With the broadening of the scope of the mission which Adventists perceived to be theirs, the advent became located in a more remote future. On the other hand, the vitality of the hope in the second advent has been maintained by portentous events in the world which are deemed, by Adventists, to herald the apocalypse.

Such tensions in the Adventist world view have, not surprisingly, produced certain paradoxes in behaviour. There is something odd, at first sight anyway, about an organization which, on the one hand, proclaims that Christ's return is imminent, and, on the other, regularly engages in the construction of institutions costing untold millions of dollars. One can understand Gaustad's observation that, while Adventists were 'expecting a kingdom of God from the heavens, they worked diligently for one on the earth'.[14] If this has been true of the organization itself, it has also been true of individual members, who have been shown to display a high attachment to material possessions.[15] The force of Wilson's claim must be acknowledged:

What Seventh-day Adventism does in effect is not to set men alight, perhaps not even to make them impatient about the advent. It provides a framework of orderly life in which many of the principal needs for social security are met.[16]

The longer the delay in the fulfilment of the advent hope, the greater is the emphasis on occupation rather than preparation. The longer the occupation, the greater is the tendency towards concerns of this world and diversification of interests. The increasing demand

21

among rising generations of Adventists that their church address itself to issues of a socio-political and ethical nature[17] is part of a pursuit of relevance in face of an advent which appears reluctant to materialize. On the other hand, some Adventists attribute the apparent delay to the fact that Adventists have not 'finished the work', have not been faithful in the proclamation of the 'everlasting gospel', and thus have kept Christ, as it were, waiting in the wings.[18] According to this account, ironically, the church controls, rather than awaits, the advent.

James Walters, an Adventist ethicist at Loma Linda University, has argued that

Because Adventists keenly anticipate a soon-coming, perfect world, they are typically not so concerned with how persons ought to relate to one another here and now, but with how to reach future goals or ends.[19]

While such an attitude has undoubtedly characterized traditional Adventist approaches to moral issues, it has never been entirely so, and there are signs of change. Sensing that Adventism is 'a Victorian Protestant subculture sustaining itself long after the host society has disappeared',[20] Jonathan Butler, formerly professor of history at Loma Linda University, has argued that modern generations of Adventists must find their own 'present truths' as did their forebears. Devotion to peace or conservationist movements may be no more incompatible with a lively belief in the second advent than a concern for dress reform or temperance, but the greater the distance from the original adventist expectation, the greater perhaps is the danger that secondary interests will predominate.

However, as Wilson has pointed out,[21] it must be borne in mind that the teaching of an advent was only part of the charter of the movement. Adventism by no means conformed perfectly to the model of a revolutionist sect. Specific views concerning the conditions for the advent emerged, and a complex denominational infrastructure began to develop quite early. Herein, perhaps, lies the root of Adventist ambivalence over the relationship between advent and ethics.

The preservation of the remnant church

Seventh-day Adventists, like many other religious groups, have always regarded themselves as having a unique place in human, even cosmic history. They have viewed themselves as God's 'remnant Church',[22] a minority which, in the end-time, will remain faithful when all other Christians accommodate to the secular world. They believe that Adventism will be the refuge of all true believers in the midst of public opprobrium, and hostility from secular and ecclesiastical monoliths. The 'remnant' will be the focus of the last battle in 'the great controversy between Christ and Satan',[23] immediately prior to the advent. That is not to say that salvation is thought to be available only within the Adventist church, although some conservative members may come perilously close to such a view. Rather, it is held that Adventism is, so to say, the grit in the oyster around which the pearl of the remnant church will be formed.

Such a self-understanding demands above all else that the Adventist church be preserved inviolate to perform its vital role. The implications of this view for engagement in ethical and socio-political matters have been enormous. A principal conclusion which Adventists have drawn is that their overriding responsibility to preach 'the everlasting gospel' demands political neutrality. The Civil War provided a serious test of priorities for the fledgling Seventh-day Adventist Church. Seventh-day Adventists had declared themselves to be unequivocally opposed to slavery, and some felt it only consistent to accept conscription into the army when it came. Others argued that involvement in the military campaign would involve violation of the commandments concerning murder and sabbath-keeping. *Review* editor, Uriah Smith, was criticized for being less than overtly abolitionist. He believed that biblical evidence indicated that slavery would still exist at the second advent, and that it was therefore either useless or impious to seek to overthrow the system.[24] James White's ambiguous editorial, 'The Nation',[25] seemed to argue that Adventists could not participate in the war, and yet it advised against resisting the draft, a classic example of the pursuit of an elusive neutrality.

The sometimes heated debate, which threatened to cause serious division, was settled in 1862, when the authoritative voice of Ellen

White was heard above the indecisive murmurings of the church's male leadership. She maintained that members could not, in all good conscience, bear arms, honourable though the cause might be. And the cause was not, in her opinion, entirely honourable; she believed that the principal inspiration behind the campaign was a political concern about secession rather than a humanitarian concern about human rights. Members were therefore to continue to oppose the institution of slavery while dissociating themselves from the violent attempt to overthrow it. They were to confine themselves to preaching the gospel.[26] This, however, was extremely difficult with the country involved in hostilities on such a wide scale. Paradoxically, therefore, Adventists longed for normality to return to a situation which they were not materially influencing, so that they could warn of the apocalypse, a prelude to which, they believed, was the manifest failure of the American dream.[27] The priority of Seventh-day Adventists during the Civil War was to keep their church intact and ready to preach 'the everlasting gospel' when hostilities ceased. As will be shown later, such a policy has left the church awkwardly placed when it has encountered the moral dilemmas posed by existence under various forms of totalitarian government.

If Adventists have sometimes pursued political neutrality as a means of preserving the integrity of their church, they have, on other occasions, used the machinery of politics to achieve the same ends. The prime example of this lies in the area of religious liberty. While the Adventist church was yet young, the radical Protestant organization, the National Reform Association, had attempted to introduce legislation which would regulate public behaviour on Sundays. Adventists, seeing this as a threat to their religious liberty, appeared, for the first time in the 1880s, in various legislative halls to defend their rights. In 1886, they began publication of *The American Sentinel*, and, in 1889, formed the Religious Liberty Association, to defend the interests of members, some of whom had been arrested for engaging in work on Sundays, particularly in the southern states.[28] One of the justifications offered by Ellen White for the removal of church headquarters from Battle Creek to the capital in 1903 was that Adventists would be better able to prosecute the cause of religious liberty.[29] They continue to maintain a presence on Capitol Hill and at the United Nations.

Adventists have also been politically active over the issue of membership of trade unions which, they believe, threaten to compromise individual conscience. The history of this is long and complex.[30]

The Adventist concern to protect the civil liberties of members, while entirely understandable, has created difficulties in the minds of some observers. The principal difficulty perhaps is that the desire to protect the 'remnant church' is based on an ethic of self-interest, that Adventists have been politically active primarily only in so far as they have wanted to protect the interests of organization and members. Other worthy but non-sectarian causes have sometimes failed to attract Adventist support, and the church, it is felt, has thereby been morally compromised.[31] Some see the church's silence on the issue of human rights in the 1960s as a prime example.[32]

Adventists, viewing themselves as the guardians of Christian doctrine in its refined and absolute form, have tended to believe that they must generally occupy positions which are final and unalterable. Yet many contemporary ethical questions are so elusive that it becomes extraordinarily difficult to settle on ultimate solutions. Adventists have often resolved this problem, at an official level, by avoiding corporate ethical commitment. As a consequence, regarding matters of contemporary ethical concern, individual members have enjoyed considerable freedom but sometimes lacked direction, and perhaps even interest.

The tendency of Adventists to regard themselves as constituting a reform movement within Christianity,[33] has perhaps diminished their inclination to achieve a sense of brotherhood with other Christians.[34] As will be shown below, Adventists were reluctant to participate in interdenominational city missions at the turn of the century. Similarly, Adventists have always been cautious in their relationships with the ecumenical movement.[35] This has protected Adventism from becoming identified with some of the alleged excesses of the World Council of Churches but has perhaps neutralized its capacity to respond to large-scale social problems requiring a co-ordinated Christian response.

Adventism contains within it a strain of perfectionism.[36] Members have traditionally sought to follow behaviour patterns which were beyond reproach. Some have undoubtedly believed that moral impurity would decline in a church preparing to meet its Lord. An increasing divorce rate, and other evidence of the fragility of members and leaders at the ethical level, offer a confusing prospect to them, even to the point of unsettling in their minds the whole notion of 'the remnant'. The survival of 'the remnant' has been ensured by the mechanism of institutionalization, but that which has survived appears to some to bear little resemblance to the original.[37] In the last decade or so, there has come, by way of reaction, an effort to 'preserve the landmarks',[38] to re-establish the primary identity of Adventism, the search for which has, perhaps inevitably, brought with it much introspection. In the eyes of more than one observer, it is precisely this preoccupation with itself which constitutes the principal ethical failure of contemporary Adventism.[39]

In the world − of the world: a tension

These two important doctrinal beliefs combine to create a major tension within Adventism. The idea that Christ is due to return very soon to this earth to bring salvation to those who are faithful, and judgement to those who are not, lends great urgency to the missionary task. It becomes the immediate responsibility of the church to penetrate the world in order to maximize other people's opportunities for finding salvation. The doctrine of the remnant, on the other hand, demands that a pure and faithful community exists to which the redeemed can repair. The ideal is that the church influences the world without itself being influenced; the reality is otherwise.

Troeltsch observed that, as Christians seek to discharge their ethical responsibilities, they try to reconcile the demand to show brotherly love with the effort to sanctify themselves by detachment from the world; they constantly renew both the search for this compromise and opposition to the spirit of compromise.[40] It is an apt description of a 'remnant' which seeks to protect its moral integrity from external threat while attempting to communicate the 'everlasting gospel' to a secular world. On the one hand, Adventism is 'world-rejecting'[41] in that it encourages men to abjure the pleasures, goals, and values of a transitory world. On the other hand, it is 'world-affirming' in that it recognizes the world as a determining factor in the soteriological equation. Further evidence of its attachment to this world is the creation of a vast organization, the erection of numerous institutions, the presence of many members who are upwardly mobile, a commitment to a rational rather than a spiritual approach to healing, and so on. It was precisely this kind of ambivalence towards the world which, as we have seen, encouraged Gaustad to observe that, while Adventists were 'expecting a kingdom of God from the heavens, they worked diligently for one on the earth' (see note 14).

The early Adventists experienced the tension with regard to their place of domicile. Ellen White urged these people, who were mainly of farming stock,[42] to live outside the cities, lest they become infected with the evils thereof. Her counsel regarding the establishment of institutions was the same. The salvation of the urban masses was to be effected by evangelistic sallies into the cities.[43] Today, small numbers of Adventists attempt to remain faithful to the letter of Ellen White's counsel by establishing working communities in rural locations, independently of the official church organization. The principal means of achieving a measure of insulation from the modern world, however, is through the establishment of Adventist communities. A large number, though not a majority, of members,[44] live in communities clustering around medical or educational institutions. This is a paradigm of Adventist attempts to be in the world but not of it.

This 'insulationist' strategy found one of its greatest opponents in the history of the church in the person of John H. Kellogg. In the 1890s, Kellogg channelled enormous energy and resources into the foundation of city missions to serve the slum-dwellers particularly of Chicago, which had a huge floating immigrant population. For a time, Adventist mission centres offered simple medical treatments, served 'penny dinners', distributed clothes, ran dispensaries and laundries, provided child-care facilities for working mothers, operated sanctuaries for orphans, old people, and prostitutes, offered simple courses in health and nutrition, and so on.[45]

The mission to the urban poor faltered, however, largely through a conflict of ideals between Ellen White and Kellogg, who was gradually becoming alienated from Adventism. Ellen White certainly regarded favourably the work being done in the city missions,[46] but she felt that Kellogg's schemes in Chicago were absorbing too many of the denomination's slender resources, both financial and human.

Classes other than the urban poor, cities other than Chicago, and programmes other than medical missions were being neglected. Moreover, Kellogg's venture was non-denominational, and Ellen White felt that resources were sufficient only to support distinctively Adventist endeavours; the Life Boat Mission was the sole part of Kellogg's whole enterprise to maintain a traditional evangelistic approach. She evidently felt that the 'in the world – of the world' tension was not being properly sustained. Furthermore, Kellogg was an empire-builder; his other institutions were large, and autonomous, a real threat to the denomination.

In engaging in social-welfare work, Adventists clearly felt that they ran the risk of being deflected, almost unawares, from fulfilling their mission to proclaim the 'everlasting gospel'. Ellen White commented:

The Salvation Army workers are trying to save the neglected, downtrodden ones ... Let them do that class of work by their own methods and in their own way. But the Lord has plainly pointed out the work that Seventh-day Adventists are to do. Camp meetings and tent meetings are to be held. The truth for this time is to be proclaimed. A decided testimony is to be borne.[47]

By 1910, Adventist city missions had largely ceased to function. Of the many contributing factors, the principal was undoubtedly the desire to remain faithful to the primary task of the church, which was to declare to 'every nation, kindred, tongue, and people' that they should 'fear God and give glory to him' for 'the hour of his judgement' had come, and that they should 'worship him that made heaven, and earth, and the sea, and the fountains of waters' (Revelation 14:6–7). Kellogg was finally disfellowshipped in 1907, but the excesses of the Chicago mission long discouraged Adventists from participating in large-scale social-welfare enterprises.

Memories fade, however, and there has developed in Adventism today a situation not altogether dissimilar, involving two of the church's humanitarian enterprises. Adventist Development and Relief Agency International (ADRA) feeds and clothes hundreds of thousands of the world's poor, organizes agricultural projects in inhospitable regions of the world, operates numerous clinics, and so on. It functions principally as an agency through which national governments channel their resources. In 1984, ADRA's annual budget of 24 million dollars contained very little denominational money.[48]

The expansion of ADRA's activities has been sudden;[49] in the past few years, ADRA has undertaken work which was previously beyond the financial reach of the church. Strict governmental controls ensure that public funds are not used for narrowly sectarian ends, but the church clearly derives benefit from administration of these resources. However, the constraints imposed by governments, together with the diversification of denominational interests, even of a humanitarian kind, generate fears of secularization. While some would see such humanitarian endeavour as a preliminary to a more specifically evangelistic end, others fear that the mission of the church will become obscured. All welfare programmes have traditionally been viewed by Adventists as 'pre-evangelistic', and,

worthy as they may be, if they do not lead to the new-birth experience in Christ and acceptance of the doctrinal tenets of God's remnant church, they consume the time, attention and money of the church and its working force without achieving God's ultimate objective of saving a man for eternity.[50]

The danger exists also of the rise of another 'empire'; with economic recession producing a decline, in real terms, in members' contributions,[51] large government grants to ADRA strengthen its influence within the denomination.

A still greater threat, however, is posed by the Adventist Health System (AHS), now one of the nation's leading health-care corporations. Adventists have continued to acquire new clinical facilities despite a recent national decline in hospital admissions.[52] The annual budget of AHS of 2 billion dollars[53] far exceeds that of the General Conference for the operation of the church world-wide. Similarly, the total indebtedness of AHS is many times greater than that of the General Conference, which, nevertheless, assumes ultimate liability for it; the failure of AHS might well devastate denominational finances. Nor is the threat only financial. The higher salaries offered by AHS may attract gifted members away from regular denominational employ. Increasingly large numbers of non-Adventists will work in the denomination's hospitals, which will tend to employ personnel on the basis of their professional qualifications rather than their religious commitment. The professionalization of medical personnel will hasten the same process in other parts of the denominational structure, and professionalization is a major vehicle of secularization.

Some Christians with a developed social conscience would invoke the words of the Israelite prophets and of Christ himself to argue that God is the champion of oppressed peoples. They would further contend that, while medical and social welfare programmes might be valuable in the short term, they serve only to perpetuate existing social structures which are the real sources of oppression. Liberation theologians would therefore advocate greater social and political involvement, even the use of violence, to fight such oppression. On a theological level, Adventists regard such action as futile since they believe that human structures will remain corrupt until the advent. On a practical level, they find it difficult enough to preserve their distinctive ethos within the limited range of humanitarian activities they now sponsor. Extension of denominational concern to a wider range of social welfare activities would further jeopardize the Adventist *raison d'être*.

The dilemma which Adventists face at an institutional level, they also face in their personal lives. Having refused the communitarian option, they must maintain a distinct identity while living 'in the world'. Among Ellen White's reasons for opposing adoption of the new style of dress popularized by Amelia Bloomer was the desire to dissociate Adventism from feminist concerns. Another was the need for women members to distinguish themselves from Spiritualists, who favoured the dress.[54]

Opinions vary widely among Adventists, even within the same culture and the same generation, about numerous matters of moral comportment, not least concerning the wisdom of venturing into the world for the purposes of social concourse. Some would regard this as a threat to religious commitment; others would say that in order to evangelize the world one first must know it. A common compromise is to replicate existing secular arrangements; a relatively broad experience can therefore be offered in a controlled situation. The vast educational network operated by the church affords an obvious example of this.

An incident from Ellen White's experience further illustrates this point. After being stricken with paralysis in 1865, James White, together with his wife and two other weary Adventist pioneers, retired to a non-Adventist health-reform institution, a stay from which they derived great benefit. Ellen White, however, opposed the resident doctor's view that amusements were a necessary diversion from introspection, and a prerequisite for regaining health. Ultimately the Whites withdrew, but they were sufficiently impressed to be instrumental in establishing a similar Adventist institution, the Western Health Reform Institute, within a year.[55]

A community relatively thickly populated with Adventists located close to a denominational institution is, then, a paradigm of Adventist attempts to be in the world but not of it. Yet, the dangers of this arrangement quickly became apparent to Ellen White, who frequently warned against the tendency to congregate in one place.[56] Such communities readily became self-sufficient. Degeneration of the church into a self-servicing organization is just as great a threat to its mission as over-extension of itself in social-welfare activities. As one senior administrator observed:

The cries of neglected children in the slums, the despair of unemployed fathers who live only a few blocks from our comfortable homes and campuses, cry out for us to do justice and to seek truth.[57]

If, in the past, Adventists sometimes failed to sustain the ethical tension of which Troeltsch spoke, it was because, in the quest for a sanctified life, they opposed zealously the 'spirit of compromise' with the world. Among rising generations of members, the impulse to show brotherly love threatens the priority traditionally afforded to the pursuit of sanctification by detachment from the world. According to Wilson, the tension only becomes harder to sustain with the passage of time, but Adventists appear not to flinch from the task:

As social relationships transcend the communal level, as they now so quickly do, even in the life of the child, so the moral commitment of the separated groups may be harder to sustain since its moral precepts were forged with face to face relations in mind. In the modern world, it appears to me to be more difficult than ever to be in but not of the world. But Seventh-day Adventists appear to be continuing to wage that struggle – and not without success.[58]

However, it has been observed that most new Adventists come from a Christian background; only about 5 per cent are unchurched. This raises a question about which 'world' precisely Adventists are in.[59]

3 · Keeping the family together: stable homes and a united church

Maintaining church unity

If, as the previous chapter has suggested, the church has always been concerned to protect itself against external threat, it has also sought to minimize the danger posed by internal divisions. In this it has been very successful; although there have been groups of disenchanted members who have hived themselves off at various times from the main body,[1] Adventism has suffered no major schism in its 120-year history.

Seventh-day Adventism is a world-wide organization drawing its membership of well over 4 million from a wide variety of cultural backgrounds. Unity is ensured through a number of mechanisms. Perhaps the most important is, as Wilson has observed, that an Adventist's religious affiliation 'is the single most significant fact about him'.[2] Such a strong religious commitment serves as a powerful, internal regulator of behaviour. In addition, the denomination employs a full-time ministry which nurtures and catechizes the local church membership, and is highly esteemed by it. Representatives from each of the administrative levels of the denomination maintain regular contact with the churches. Still more significant, perhaps, is the denominational emphasis on creating institutions; employing, as it does, such a high proportion of its members,[3] the church has been able to maintain a relatively clear consensus on standards of moral comportment among them. The situation is not, however, without its dangers. Centralized authority may stifle the moral imagination.[4] The central organization of religion is a movement, albeit unconscious, in the direction of secularization. As Adventism grows, it faces the prospect of becoming increasingly impersonal and fundamentally amoral like the society of which it is a part.[5]

A large number of periodicals, and the universally distributed *Sabbath School Lessons*, contribute much to group cohesion, as does the similarity of worship forms. As has already been suggested, Ellen White's influence has been a largely unifying one, although the claims to authority made on her behalf have sometimes had the effect of alienating some members.[6] Such mechanisms have successfully held together an organization, the members of which differ enormously in cultural, educational, and occupational background. Nationalism and alleged discrimination have caused some difficulties but indigenization of the church work-force and the movement towards equal representation have generally remedied major problems. Adventists can justifiably claim that, in certain important respects, their large organization retains a strong 'family atmosphere'.

The traditional Adventist theological perception of a threat to its integrity from external monolithic sources has undoubtedly strengthened group unity. Recently, however, the major threat to Adventist unity has been internal. In 1976, Ronald Numbers argued in a scholarly volume called *Prophetess of Health* that Ellen White's counsel on health reform had its origin in temporal rather than divine sources. In 1982, Walter Rea accused the prophetess of wide-scale plagiarism in books which she said were written under divine inspiration. Although the attack was cynical and ill-constructed, it fired a major debate about Ellen White's authority. The intervening years witnessed a major controversy surrounding a prominent Australian theologian, Desmond Ford, who challenged the church's traditional understanding of the heavenly sanctuary and investigative judgement.[7] Adventist morale was dealt a further severe blow, in the early 1980s, by an episode involving the misappropriation of denominational funds, which became known as the 'Davenport affair'.[8] Prior to these disturbances in church life, great denominational energy had been expended over the efforts of ethnic minorities to gain representation on decision-making bodies at all levels.[9] The turmoil of the last decade has posed so serious a threat to Adventist unity that some have expressed fears about schism.[10] It has coincided with a greater public awareness of social and ethical issues. Church leaders have sought to contain any threat to denominational stability by proceeding extremely cautiously with ethical issues of a highly contentious nature. Decisions on church policy with regard to divorce and remarriage have been deferred, and attempts have been made to achieve some *modus vivendi*. Similarly, the church has approached the potentially divisive issue of the ordination of women very charily. Maintaining the unity of the movement is a clear administrative priority.

The church has, however, been outspoken about those moral issues which do not threaten Adventist unity. Recently, it has unequivocally condemned homosexual behaviour, since, it claims, there is clear scriptural support for so doing, and since it could undoubtedly count on the support of the vast majority of Adventist members. Neither has the church been reluctant to raise its voice on the subject of temperance. Indeed, in the nineteenth century, members were exhorted to use their vote to promote the prohibitionist cause,[11] they petitioned various government agencies, and participated in numerous rallies. There is even the interesting case of W. C. Gage, an Adventist minister, who, with the approval of the church leaders, successfully sought election to the mayorship of the Adventist headquarters town of Battle Creek, specifically to promote the prohibitionist cause.[12] It is clear that, since abstinence from alcohol was inextricably bound up with the ethos of Adventism, the believers were unanimous, division did not threaten, and thus mild political activism could be encouraged.

Where the issue at stake was less clear-cut, Adventists were counselled to be more cautious. All were permitted to use their vote. Church employees, if they did vote, were enjoined to keep their political preferences strictly to themselves. Members generally were urged to keep the excitement of the hustings entirely away from church life, thus avoiding possible division in the churches.[13]

The desire to maintain unity among such a diverse membership, where varying moral positions sometimes obtain, has made the denomination slow to respond to ethical issues. Conservative churchmen in Latin America might well hold views on abortion widely diverging from those of executives in the health-care corporations of North America. It is politic to inspect any issue from the perspective of major interested parties, and a consensus may only slowly be achieved. An important consequence is that, when Adventist spokesmen do pronounce on ethical issues, they address only their own community. The response is usually too slow in coming to allow Adventists to exercise moral authority in the wider world.[14]

Theobald has observed that Adventism is 'a curious blend of intellectually disciplined ascetic protestantism' and 'populist adventist fundamentalism'.[15] As such, it attracts a wide variety of individuals, even within a particular culture; many of them are of independent mind, unlikely to conform uncritically to the moral judgements of their leaders. The leaders may therefore think it prudent to confine themselves to addressing issues which are more intimately and traditionally bound up with good membership, like abstention from alcohol. Furthermore, as Glock, Ringer, and Babbie have pointed out, most church organizations perform the dual functions of 'comforting' and 'challenging' their members. Some Adventists, seeking refuge from an impersonal and hostile world, would not welcome the disturbance created by debate on issues they deemed not to be central to Adventist concern.[16]

The understandable desire to foster the unity of 'the remnant' has had the perhaps unforeseen effect of muting the Adventist response to contemporary ethical problems. Underlying this desire is the intuition that preoccupation with popular causes may separate members from each other, and, indeed, from their primary cause. The case of John H. Kellogg is a precedent which is still alive in the Adventist folk memory.

The protection of the nuclear family

Perhaps even more essential to the continued healthy existence of Adventism than the institutional community is the stability of the Adventist family unit.[17] The estimate of Adventist missiologist, Gottfried Oosterwal, that second-generation members represent 75 per cent of accessions, is probably accurate, although precise statistics are impossible to obtain.[18] If this is so, Adventist ethical values and organization can be expected to reflect a deep concern to protect the nuclear family.

Later chapters will attempt to demonstrate this. There is a strong presumption in favour of child-bearing, thus generating a future membership of the church. Yet Adventists encourage careful contraceptive practice so as to protect the nuclear family from undue strain.

Sentiment against abortion is somewhat muted by a readiness to weigh the interests of the existing family against the rights of a prospective new member of it. A major objection to homosexual practice is the destabilizing effect it has on the institution of the nuclear family. The church has refused to admit women to the ordained ministry partly because this might appear to endorse contemporary gender-role changes, and to accede to feminist demands. Finally, the continued hesitancy of the church to act decisively on the issue of divorce is an indication of its concern to protect the sanctity of marriage, while minimizing the wounds inflicted on those trapped in unhappy marriages.

There are many other evidences of concern to protect the Adventist family unit. The strong presumption in favour of marriage has tended to assign an inferior status to those who remain single. As in most Christian communions, women are over-represented, and a proportion have to choose between remaining single, marrying a non-Adventist, or attempting to introduce a prospective partner into the church. Not until very recently has it been acknowledged that singleness might be a vocation. Presumably, it was felt that single people, having made fewer commitments of various types, represented a greater potential destabilizing factor in the church. Until recently, marriage has been a prerequisite for ordination to the ministry in some parts of the United States.[19] It has now been recognized, however, that perhaps as many as one third of adult Adventists in North America may be unattached.[20] In response to this hitherto undetected need, the *Review* periodically carries a feature called 'Single Life',[21] the Home and Family Service of the General Conference has generated considerable resources,[22] and, in some regions, a ministry to single persons has been initiated.

Nevertheless, some efforts are made to introduce single Adventists to suitable spouses. 'Adventist Contact' describes itself as a 'computer dating service' which seeks to establish levels of compatibility between unattached adult Adventists in North America.[23] 'Philosda' is an organization which operates in some local churches to arrange social events for single people; it appears to attract a high number of divorcees. These are tokens of the high premium placed upon the married state. An examination of the departmental structure of the church and its calendar of events shows how much Adventist activity centres upon the nuclear family.

At the other end of the spectrum, Adventists have had considerable difficulty in addressing the issue of polygamy ever since they broadened the scope of their missionary endeavours to Africa. Ellen White roundly condemned polygamy.[24] Although her clearest denunciations were contained in later works, *Patriarchs and Prophets* (1890), and *Prophets and Kings* (1916), both were published before Adventist missionaries had encountered polygamous cultures on a wide scale.

The kinship patterns of many traditional African societies have been impossible to reconcile with the Adventist norm, as expressed below:

In the social order there stands before us at the beginning of time, and continuing through all ages, the prime, basic institution of the ... Occidental family ... Parenthood and the family are a mirror of the life and government of God.[25]

Where marriage is traditionally bound up with complex kinship ties, domestic economy, and the production of descendants, childlessness becomes an enormous burden. Thus it is normal to employ the mechanisms of plural marriage, levirate marriage, and surrogacy. Since whole lineage groups are affected by marriage arrangements, the absence of institutionalized forms of divorce has reduced the risk of conflict.

A General Conference policy statement issued in 1926, having enunciated the monogamous ideal, went on to recognize the likely disturbance to the domestic arrangements of polygamists seeking baptism. It reached a rather uneasy compromise in a provision to allow such to be admitted to church fellowship provided that they held no office requiring ordination, and that they married if circumstances permitted.[26] A modification of policy, in 1930, introduced the category of 'probationary members'; individuals would be admitted to full membership only when they had a sole spouse. Anyone who contracted a polygamous marriage subsequent to baptism would be disfellowshipped as an adulterer. Where circumstances permitted a man to repudiate a wife without bringing hardship upon her, he was free to choose which of his wives he retained.[27] In 1941, a more rigorous code required a man to be monogamous before being admitted to the church. He was to make provision for a repudiated wife and her children; she was free to marry again.

Baptism was available to wives of polygamists.[28] Subsequent actions have left this policy substantially intact.[29]

The problem of polygamy poses an enormously difficult dilemma for Adventism and other missionary organizations. The biblical witness appears to be less than unequivocal, for, while the New Testament upholds the monogamous ideal, the Old Testament cites a number of polygamists as examples of faith. The church, in upholding the monogamous ideal, may appear to fail to bear testimony to the permanence of the family by multiplying divorces and generating internecine strife. Furthermore, it faces the prospect that some women, finding themselves without economic support, will turn to prostitution as a means of subsisting. Third World Adventists might well object that the practice of divorce among western Adventists is nothing more than serial polygamy.

Given the crucial importance of the stable family unit to Adventism, it is not surprising that there is a heavy emphasis on group endogamy. Warnings of the dangers of being 'unequally yoked with unbelievers' are commonplace in Adventist literature.[30] Research suggests that about 75 per cent of Adventists marry within the denomination. In the United States, Adventist schools and colleges provide the setting in which nearly 40 per cent of Adventists meet their mates.[31] Clearly, the Adventist church wants to elicit a high level of commitment from its members; exogamous marriages are perceived to dilute that commitment and thus to pose a threat to the church, even perhaps where a non-Adventist spouse might in time become a member. On the other hand, the pressure to marry a church member may sometimes produce ill-advised liaisons, which end in inflicting wounds on the individuals concerned and on the church.

The loosely organized Adventist community frequently provides support in times of individual need, and thus functions as a kind of extended family. There are, no doubt, many reasons why Adventists have rejected fully fledged communitarianism. It seems probable that the desire to protect the exclusivity of intimate relationships is one, since communitarianism raises important issues concerning the regulation of intimacies. The following words from Ellen White suggest something of the ethos of the Adventist home:

There is a sacred circle around every family which should be preserved. No other one has any right in that sacred circle. The husband and wife should be all to each other. The wife should have no secrets to keep from her husband and let others know, and the husband should have no secrets to keep from his wife to relate to others ... Never should either the husband or wife in sport or in any other manner complain of each other to others, for in frequently indulging in this foolish and what may seem perfectly harmless joking, it [sic] will end in trial with each other and perhaps estrangement.[32]

She was clearly concerned to protect the family from all external threat, however innocent it might first appear.

All this is not to say that evidence of communitarianism proper within Adventism is entirely lacking. In recent years, a number of community projects have begun in North America and elsewhere, initiated by conservative Adventists eager to follow the counsels of Ellen White more rigorously. Agricultural, horticultural, medical, or educational activities absorb the energies of community members. The official church organization has tended to keep a discreet distance from such groups, while generally seeming to approve of their activities.

Wilson has observed that '... only the family shares with religion the idea of the community as an end in itself, and the modern family, now nucleated, is too small to fulfil the functions of a community'.[33] As the modern family has relinquished traditional functions, 'declined in size, and in the duration of its intense associations, so, at least in the West, the assumption that a family would be united within one religion has been eroded'.[34] Curiously but inevitably, the church, in assuming functions once performed by the family, has undermined that institution which it has most sought to protect.

Individualism

It is perhaps worthwhile adding a concluding note here concerning individualism and the church. An individualistic spirit would, of course, be regarded as a desirable quality in an Adventist to the extent that it permitted him to swim against the social current as members inevitably have sometimes to do. When the same individualistic spirit is exhibited in the life of the church, it may, on occasion, become a threat to unity.

39

H. Richard Niebuhr observed that

The ideas of sin, righteousness, and salvation which flourish in the middle-class milieu are profoundly influenced ... by the sense of individual worth and responsibility. Sin is not so much a state of soul as a deed or a characteristic; it is not so much the evil with which the whole social life and structure is infected as it is the personal failure of the individual.[35]

Certain features of Adventist belief serve to exaggerate the general Protestant emphasis on individual responsibility before God. The idea that God is now in the 'heavenly sanctuary' carrying out a work of 'investigative judgement' to determine the eternal destiny of each human being, is likely to lend a great deal of urgency to matters of personal piety and morality.[36] Adventists believe, with all heirs of the Reformation, that they are justified before God by faith alone, but that there follows a process of moral growth, or 'sanctification', made possible by the transforming presence of Christ. Such a doctrinal position may, on occasion, degenerate into a sterile legalism as adherents attempt to win divine approbation.

The emphasis on individual responsibility is illustrated, perhaps even caricatured, by the following extract from an Adventist publication:

If you should see an unfortunate specimen of humanity lying in the gutter, would you accuse his mother of giving birth to a derelict of society? Of course not. When that man was a baby, he was as pure and sweet as any other baby. As he grew to manhood, he chose to do evil. He made a derelict out of himself.[37]

The book in question was published a quarter of a century ago, and there would now exist a greater reticence among Adventists to analyse the situation in such a facile manner. Nevertheless, Adventist theological and devotional literature places much emphasis on the role of the will in human behaviour.[38] There may indeed be something to the view that such teaching initially attracts strong-minded people.[39]

The consequences of a firm emphasis on individual behaviour are several; on the whole, it will tend to reduce appeals to promote social justice. One commentator judged that probably the most conspicuous factor underlying traditional Adventist hostility to trade unionism is 'a commitment to the ideal of self-sufficient individualism'.[40] Ellen White frequently warned that union membership would inevitably violate individual conscience.[41] It has also been argued that the strong emphasis on individual salvation permitted racist policies to persist in the church. The idea that sin was an entirely private affair between God and his individual creatures obscured the sinfulness of certain denominational structures.[42] Another alleged failure of Adventists to accept corporate responsibility was its unwillingness to adjust its investment practices to effect social change; it was held that, generally, the church sought the best returns on its investments, to maximize its resources for proclaiming the gospel, regardless of larger questions of social justice.[43]

Adventists remain sceptical about the exhortations to promote social justice which are to be found in contemporary Christian literature. The risk of generating internal strife, the prohibitive cost of social action, the dangers of political activism, together with the underlying belief that human structures are irreparably evil make the Seventh-day Adventist church slow to engage in the search for social justice. Ultimately, Adventists hold that social change is realized only through the transformation of individuals. A decisive factor here is the way in which Ellen White perceived Christ's reaction to the dilemma:

The government under which Jesus lived was corrupt and oppressive; on every hand were crying abuses, − extortion, intolerance, and grinding cruelty. Yet the Saviour attempted no civil reforms. He attacked no national abuses, nor condemned the national enemies. He did not interfere with the authority or administration of those in power. He who was our example kept aloof from earthly governments. Not because he was indifferent to the woes of men, but because the remedy did not lie in merely human and external measures. To be efficient, the cure must reach men individually and must regenerate the heart.[44]

More cynically, it could be argued in accordance with Weber's model that emphasis on individual responsibility before God has eventuated in social mobility which has generated a contentment with the *status quo*, diminishing interest in matters of social justice.

Speaking of the middle-class religious ethic, Niebuhr also observed that an 'interest in family morals may also be due to the threat to stable family relations which arises out of this same individualism'.[45] Any religious group which encourages its members to accept full personal responsibility before God faces possible difficulty in establishing a consensus on moral matters. The vigorous and expanding network of independent Adventist institutions bears eloquent witness to that, as does the Association of Adventist Forums, an influential organization of the denomination's intellectuals. The threat to Adventist identity is countered by the erection of specific behavioural norms, as the following section will show. But an expanding organization with an international membership living in an increasingly secularized world can expect to find its control over the moral lives of its adherents diminishing.[46]

Adventism clearly stands for the view that good men make good social institutions, rather than that good institutions make men good. The paradox is that Adventists have expended so much effort to create good institutions.

4 · A cultural legacy: Victorian and American

Ethics and taboos

Schwartz has rightly observed that Adventism, unlike Pentecostalism, provides its members with a highly developed ethical sub-system.[1] Inasmuch as the pioneers considered Adventism to be a refined form of Reformation Christianity, Adventist moral teaching constituted, in some measure at least, a 'fine-tuning' of traditional Christian morality. In early Adventist literature, one was more likely to read about the evils of dancing and tea-drinking, for example, than about respecting property or keeping promises. These highly specific prohibitions, or taboos, included the consumption of alcohol, coffee, condiments, and meat (especially pork), the use of tobacco and cosmetics, the wearing of immodest dress and jewellery, card-playing, gambling, the theatre, and other forms of worldly entertainment. They related to easily observable behaviour and provided convenient criteria for distinguishing the 'good' member from the less faithful, the Adventist from the non-Adventist. They functioned, together with Sabbath observance, as powerful markers of Adventist identity, and as such were strongly endorsed by Ellen White.[2] Many of these prohibitions remain quite firmly in place, while others have been subject to some erosion.

Some of these prohibitions can be seen as a reflection of Victorian concerns; others are not so easily explained. Adventists see the provision of a clearly defined behavioural code as a divine providence; certainly, modern research on the hazards of smoking, the consumption of alcohol, and even meat, has confirmed its benefits to the health of the Adventist community.[3]

On the other hand, Adventists face the prospect that they have allowed their value system to become petrified. According to

43

Jonathan Butler, Adventist attitudes on a whole range of ethical issues 'show Adventism to be a Victorian Protestant subculture sustaining itself long after the larger host society has disappeared'.[4] The danger exists that Adventists come to believe that the observance of highly specific legislation absolves them from wider moral responsibility; it may even obscure the larger questions from view. An example is instructive here. Adventists, notably in the United States, have debated at length the propriety not simply of wearing jewellery but even wedding rings,[5] some believing that Ellen White recommended rejection of the wedding-ring tradition.[6] Her major concern, however, seems to have been the conservation of funds for the gospel cause.[7] Adventists might therefore have done greater justice to the spirit of Ellen White's counsel by considering the greater temptations which a consumer society has to offer.

The simplicity of the ethical subsystem has clearly yielded enormous benefits for Adventism, but to the extent that it has encouraged members to operate at the level of taboos and avoid more complex ethical reasoning, it has produced a certain failure of the Adventist moral imagination. There are distinct signs, however, that Adventists are seeking to remedy the weakness. The extent and sophistication of discussion of ethical issues in Adventist circles has increased enormously of late. Perhaps the most concrete symbol of this development was the foundation of the Loma Linda University Center for Christian Bioethics in 1984.[8] Indeed, rather than simply coming to terms with the ethical problems posed by a secular technological society, the Adventist church has itself recently placed an important item on the agenda of bioethicists. The attempt by staff at Loma Linda University Medical Center, in 1984, to sustain the life of an ailing infant by the transplantation of a baboon's heart attracted media attention world-wide, and posed a new set of moral questions.[9]

The role of Ellen White

The profound influence of Ellen White on all areas of Adventist thought will become increasingly evident and will not therefore be dealt with in great detail at this point. Her influence has been particularly strong in North America, where she travelled as guest speaker for half a century, in Australia, where she spent the entire

1890s, and in the Third World, where the simple behavioural code outlined by her has been enthusiastically received by people not unfamiliar with the figure of a prophet. The reception of her work has, perhaps, been less enthusiastic in parts of Europe, although she did visit there between 1885 and 1887. The unavailability of much of her work in translation until recently, the feeling that this was a gift particularly to the American church,[10] and her conflict with the prominent German Adventist leader, L. R. Conradi[11] have all contributed to the lack of response.

Her charismatic leadership has had an undoubted stabilizing and unifying effect on the movement. That is not to say that her role has not given rise to controversy fairly consistently, even in the United States. It was not unusual for malcontents to circulate rumours in an attempt to discredit her,[12] and she was inclined to believe that certain church leaders had manipulated her into going to Australia in order to rid themselves of her discomforting presence.[13]

The authority of her pronouncements has always been a contentious issue, of course. She consistently claimed divine legitimation for them[14] while asserting, 'In regard to infallibility, I never claimed it; God alone is infallible.'[15] She further acknowledged that when she addressed 'common' rather than 'sacred' matters she merely expressed her own opinion.[16] In practice, however, members often found it difficult to regard her as less than oracular. They feared that to ignore her counsel was to oppose God. It has been suggested that the criticism frequently suffered by James White was provoked by his wife's words because, unlike her, he was regarded as a legitimate target.[17]

Arthur Spalding observed in his history of Adventism:

She never claimed infallibility. The setting up of an infallible human authority is the recourse of unsure followers, who cannot think for themselves, and require an oracle.[18]

While Ellen White never claimed infallibility for herself, there has always existed the temptation for others to thrust it upon her:

She received revelations from the Holy Spirit who *is* infallible, and her messages written in human language reflect as accurately as human language can the mind and will of an infallible God.[19]

It was not unknown for the prophetess herself to castigate church leaders for using her as an oracle rather than making decisions themselves.[20]

Prior to her death, Ellen White indicated that believers should expect no new prophet to arise, and that the counsel given through her would suffice God's people for 'the rest of the journey'.[21] In the seventy years since her death, the White Estate has supervised publication of many anthologies of her writings,[22] which have been used to nurture and catechize members. Ellen White continues, to a considerable extent, to establish the parameters of Adventist moral thought. While this has provided a ready measure of discipline, it has not been without its problems. Since extracts from her writings are usually published without any respect for chronology or reference to context, her words may sometimes appear extreme or equivocal. James White himself recognized that her counsels sometimes had the opposite effect to that which she had intended:

What she may say to urge the tardy, is taken by the prompt to urge them over the mark. And what she may say to caution the prompt, zealous, incautious ones, is taken by the tardy as an excuse to remain too far behind.[23]

The temptation exists for all Adventists to use Ellen White citations to endorse their own predilections without engaging in the arduous process of distilling the wisdom of many years to achieve a balanced understanding of her views. There exists the danger that in 'having so many Ellen Whites ... the Adventist church may soon have no Ellen White at all'.[24]

The desire to revise traditional views about Ellen White has been strong in Adventism for a decade or more. Ronald Numbers claimed that she was dependent on human rather than divine sources for her counsels on health;[25] Walter Rea sought to demonstrate the same regarding her devotional writings,[26] and others have represented her as a classical Victorian figure.[27] Such views are not new; she had at various times faced accusations that she was unduly reliant on James and her son, Willie, for her counsels.[28] A few Adventists, like Rea, discovering Ellen White to be less than they had thought her to be, have dismissed her as an impostor. Others, believing that Adventism will lose something of its essential nature when it ceases to take her seriously, have attempted more modest revisions of their ideas; one writer has concluded that Ellen White was at her most reliable and mature as a messenger in her later years.[29]

A church confronting the modern world with a nineteenth-century mentor faces the challenge of applying perennially sound moral principles to contemporary dilemmas; it confuses Victorian applications of those principles with the principles themselves only at its own cost. Ellen White's influence on the church has thus been beneficial to the extent that it has provided generations of members with clear moral directions, and debilitating to the extent that Adventists have permitted it to inhibit, rather than stimulate, serious moral thinking.

Americanism

There have appeared recently several studies of the theological and historical roots of Adventism. Bryan Ball has demonstrated the continuity of Adventism with seventeenth-century English Puritanism in *The English Connection*. Geoffrey Paxton has identified important links with the magisterial Reformation in *The Shaking of Adventism*. Meanwhile, in *The Reformation and the Advent Movement*, W. Leslie Emmerson has argued that Adventism has roots deep in the soil of the Anabaptism. Accurate and helpful though such insights may be, it remains undeniable that Adventism is American in its ethos. The main events in the church's formative years were played out on the soil of New England, New York State, and Michigan. The church's prophet, born in Maine, did not venture abroad until she was in her mid fifties. Adventist interpretations of apocalyptic literature were set boldly in an American context; major eschatological events were related to the failure of the Republic.[30] Adventist educational institutions the world over have tended to follow American patterns closely.[31] The church headquarters is in Washington, DC, and only once, in 1975, has the church held a General Conference session outside the United States. The host nation not surprisingly supplies a large proportion of the staff at headquarters. While there has been a genuine attempt to grant other divisions a higher degree of autonomy, and to indigenize work-forces, Americans still hold key positions around the world. Significantly, North Americans provide

almost three-quarters of the annual budget of the church.[32]
Although the membership outside the United States first, around
1920, exceeded that within, and although today only 15 per cent are
American, the American flavour of the movement has not been
dramatically diluted. The opinion is popular among Adventists that
'It was in the wise providence of God that the last gospel message
was based, in human terms ... in the United States of America.'[33]
And it is probably true that American soil was alone capable of
yielding a harvest of 75,000 members by the turn of the century, from
seed of just 3,500 in 1863.[34]

A major legacy of the close identification of Adventism with
Americanism has been in the area of church–state relations, where
separation has become the model for the church the world over.
However, the church takes seriously the Pauline exhortation to submit
to civic authority, except where to do so would be to violate conscience. Thus the church chooses to support the government of the
day, at least passively, by refraining from any activities which might
threaten national stability. Adventists thereby seek to foster peaceful
conditions which will permit open evangelistic endeavour. Furthermore, it is believed that such a demonstration of civic responsibility
will allay any suspicions which authorities might harbour concerning
the activities of the church.

While the church's chosen posture may have secured a stable
relationship with government in the United States and other liberal
democracies, it has created difficulties elsewhere, especially where the
church operates under a totalitarian regime. Adventists, like many
other Christians, found themselves placed in extraordinarily difficult
moral circumstances in Nazi Germany.[35] Disagreement over the conduct of relationships with the state has created a long and sometimes
bitter schism among Adventists in the Soviet Union.[36] The official
Adventist church, having established a *modus operandi* with the
government there, has enjoyed a relatively peaceful existence. The
True and Free Adventists, believing that the price of such peace was
too high, have opposed co-operation with the government and have
experienced oppression. The church thus finds itself awkwardly placed
over the issue of human rights. If it seeks to protect the rights of those
regarded by the government as dissidents, it jeopardizes the welfare
of the majority of Adventists, and perhaps the continued existence of

the organization itself. If it ignores the plight of the True and Free
Adventists, it appears insensitive to the needs of a group of seemingly
very devout believers.

On another front, Schantz has observed that, in their missionary
endeavours, Adventists have tended to replace local patterns of leadership roles and organization with standard denominational structures.
Indeed, the importation of a life-style which has a marked American
flavour has, he believed, all too often resulted in the church being
viewed as a foreign presence. The effect may have been, at times, to
isolate individual Adventists from their culture, to restrict the church's
capacity to respond to local problems, and thus to reduce its general
appeal.[37] Furthermore, the receipt of substantial American government funds, through ADRA (Adventist Development and Relief
Agency) for example, may have made the church an 'agent of
American imperialism' in the eyes of some, particularly in the Third
World, with the result that the church may have suffered as American
fortunes have wavered in the world at large.[38] The temptation to
sacralize cultural accretions of the faith has faced Adventism like any
other missionary movement. However, a serious attempt to foster
respect for cultural diversity has characterized the preparation of
Adventist missionaries more recently.[39] Indeed, no less an authority
than Timothy Smith has suggested that more than all other religious
communities

Adventists have renounced with a special urgency the notion that the Christian
religion is to be identified with American culture, with any country's
nationalist policies, or with upper-class social ideals.[40]

Wilson has observed that

In the United States, with its high immigrant and highly mobile population,
churches have functioned as much more basic foci of community identity
than has been their role in settled societies.[41]

Marty went perhaps a little further when he observed that being
religious was synonymous with being a good American.[42] A major
consequence of this, according to Wilson, has been that 'in America
secularizing processes appear to have occurred *within* the church'.[43]

The American origins of Adventism have thus proved to be a mixed
blessing. The church would never have prospered as it has without

the energy, initiative, commitment, and resources provided by its American constituency. The church world-wide has suffered at times when cultural accretions of the faith have been confused with the faith itself.

Pragmatism

Perhaps one of the greatest gifts bequeathed to the Adventist church by its American origins has been a ready pragmatism.[44] The church showed early its ability to accommodate in order to survive. Millerite diatribes against organized religion notwithstanding, the official organization of the church in 1863 permitted Adventists to secure their properties and to avoid combat in the Civil War. Theobald has rightly noted the denomination's ability to 'come to terms' with the world, without allowing such acts of accommodation to threaten the essence of Adventism.[45] The 'Adventist genius for mixing otherworldly and this-worldly concerns'[46] permeates all aspects of the church's work, and is designed to facilitate efficient communication of the Adventist message in a particular context.

This pragmatic approach to problem-solving has, on occasion, created difficulties for the church; several examples illustrate the point. In 1894, the church accepted a gift of 12,000 acres of land from Cecil Rhodes, then prime minister of the Cape Colony, for the purpose of establishing a mission. Ellen White favoured acceptance, and found those who harboured fears about church identification with the state to be unduly fastidious.[47] The same kind of fear has surfaced periodically over the acceptance of federal aid for denominational educational institutions. Some see it as an opportunity to extend Adventist influence, while others fear a measure of government interference with curricula, and a violation of the principle of separation. Adventists regard this as a matter of policy rather than doctrine, and so act according to the context.[48] On quite a different issue, the church, in 1978, elected to replace denominational rates of pay with higher community rates for its medical workers in its hospitals in order to attract well-qualified staff. One observer thought the move

demonstrated again the church's willingness to solve administrative problems with pragmatic solutions, even if these modify significantly historically held positions, that, in the minds of many, are based on the writings of Ellen White.[49]

A pragmatic approach to affairs moral and administrative provides the flexibility necessary to an organization which is international in its membership and highly diversified in its interests. The major disservice of such an approach has been that the church has failed to demand of its scholars and leaders, until very recently, a careful investigation of ethical concerns, with the result that Adventist moral action has sometimes lacked consistency.

III

ISSUES OF HUMAN SEXUALITY

5 · Marital relations among Adventists: the pursuit of purity

Introduction

In October 1845, James White, a future leader of the Seventh-day Adventist church, made public his view that to marry at that particular time was to deny faith in the imminent second advent of Christ, which, he believed, would take place later that year.[1] It was, he said, 'a wile of the Devil'.[2] Although he soon renounced all time-setting, and within a year was himself married, it is clear that for him and his fellow believers the demands of human sexuality had to be strictly subordinated to the requirements of human spirituality.

Given this situation of tense expectation, it would not have been surprising had the sabbatarian adventists adopted an extreme teaching on marital relationships, as did some other religious groups developing at the same time. The Shakers, for example, held that, since the Bible taught that there would be no sexual relations after the resurrection of the just, they should abstain now by way of preparation. The practice of celibacy was an expression of unselfishness and a sign of triumph over sin. The exclusive attachments of normal family life were eliminated, and all energies devoted to the glory of God and the well-being of the community, which was rigidly segregated along sexual lines. While John Humphrey Noyes acknowledged the undesirability of exclusive emotional attachments, he advocated a rather different remedy. His experiment in community living, located at Oneida, New York, was based on a system of 'complex marriage', which, in principle, gave all males sexual privileges with all females, and vice versa. He was critical of unplanned procreation, and of full intercourse when there was no procreative motive. He therefore introduced a mechanism of sexual regulation called 'male continence' which required all male sexual activity to stop short of climax.

Different again was the Mormon experiment with plural marriage, which became more general and open after a pronouncement on the subject by Brigham Young, in 1852.

While Adventists needed to adopt a clear policy on marriage and the regulation of sexual activity less urgently than the various communitarian groups which mushroomed at that time, they nevertheless needed to give the matter consideration. They were obliged to encounter the effects of increasing industrialization, urbanization, and geographical mobility on their personal lives. As the century progressed, they had to judge whether, in the prevailing socioeconomic conditions, they would restrict the size of their families. Ultimately they had to decide whether it was morally acceptable to use artificial means to achieve this end. The decision was further complicated for Adventists by a belief in an imminent second advent, a far more radical social upheaval even than that then taking place in the nation.

Birth control in the United States

Charles Knowlton's *Fruits of Philosophy*, published in 1832, was the first serious discussion of birth control to appear in the United States. However, the issue attracted little attention for nearly half a century thereafter, in spite of evidence which suggests that contraceptive devices were quite widely available. This is confirmed by the enactment in 1873 of the Comstock bill, which provided for a maximum of five years' imprisonment and a $5,000 fine for anyone mailing 'paper, writing, advertisement or representation that any article, instrument, substance, drug, medicine, or thing may, or can be, used or applied, for preventing conception'.[3] In his capacity as a special agent for the New York Society for the Suppression of Vice, Anthony Comstock was responsible for the arrest of 3,873 persons, of whom 2,911 were convicted.[4] The ease with which the measure passed into law reflected the prevailing medical opinion of the day. The opposition of doctors to contraceptive practice stemmed from various beliefs: that it caused ill-health in women; that it encouraged sexual promiscuity or was associated with prostitution; that it could be equated with masturbation, opposition to which was an obsession with the Victorians.

Comstock legislation continued to be used in the campaign against the distribution of contraceptive literature and materials well into the new century. Theodore Roosevelt, Republican president between 1901 and 1909, denounced contraceptive practice as 'race suicide'; those who did not want children were, he said, 'the object of contemptuous abhorrence by healthy people'.[5] Cracks in the establishment consensus soon began to appear, however. Dr Abraham Jacobi caused a considerable controversy by recommending the use of contraceptive methods in his presidential address to the American Medical Association, in 1912. Dr Robert Dickinson, a president of the American Gynaecological Association, was influential in securing increased support for contraception from members of the medical profession. Margaret Sanger, a radical socialist and feminist, led a vigorous campaign to promote the use of birth control, while the National Birth Control League, founded in 1915, though less strident, pursued similar aims.

An examination of histories of contraception shows that the churches had little to say on the subject in the nineteenth century. It was a matter too delicate for most churchmen to want to tackle. By the last quarter of the century, the medical profession and the judiciary in the United States had set themselves against the practice strongly enough to relieve the clergy of any great burden in that direction. The first major pronouncement by an ecclesiastical body was made in Britain. The Lambeth Conference of 1908 urged all 'to discountenance the use of all artificial means of restriction as demoralizing to character and hostile to national welfare', and asserted that 'deliberate tampering with nascent life [was] repugnant to Christian morality'.[6]

Early Adventist philosophy and practice

Family size of the early adventists

While some religious groups emerging around the middle of the century saw fit to modify traditional family patterns, and to innovate with regard to the regulation of sexual activity, sabbatarian adventists made no such adjustments. It is true that, as late as 1868, Ellen and James White committed to print their opinion that the option of remaining single had to be considered seriously in view of the imminent advent.[7] Sabbatarian adventists, however, continued to establish normal family units. Ellen White herself gave birth to a child within a year of her marriage, and three other children were to follow. The size of the families of the group's leaders does not indicate that a belief in an imminent advent significantly lowered fertility rates. Indeed, one of the first sabbatarian adventists, William Farnsworth, fathered twenty-two children between 1830 and 1874 (in two marriages), in spite of the fact that he believed it unnecessary to educate them because of the imminence of the advent.[8] Generally, however, it seems that 'Adventists did not differ much from their neighbors in the number of children they had ...'.[9] Events surrounding the 'great disappointment' of October 1844 had no doubt alerted the leaders to the dangers of extreme behaviour. They saw it now as their duty to 'occupy' until Christ returned, which in practice meant that they went about their normal business, although devotional activity was heightened. Child-bearing and rearing were no doubt seen as an inevitable part of 'normal business'.

That is not to say that evidence of extreme behaviour among those early adventists was entirely lacking. Indeed, some of the believers were startled by the announcement of the forthcoming marriage of Ellen Harmon and James White,[10] seeing it as an expression of confidence in the relative permanence of the here-and-now, just as White had himself done a year before. The believers, however, were satisfied with the explanation that was offered: Ellen Harmon had been travelling beyond her home town relating the content of her visions. White had been functioning as her escort, and saw marriage as the best means of stopping the gossip about their relationship which had begun to spread.

Among those adventists who did not defect after the 'great disappointment' were some who believed that Christ had indeed come on 22 October 1844, but in a spiritual rather than a literal manner. He was, in their view, living within them in order to sanctify them perfectly. They attempted to demonstrate their holiness by, among other things, refusing to work (because they believed they had already entered into eternal rest), and by practising celibacy within marriage, as others later were also to do. A few believed that, having been sanctified, they were incapable of sinning; this led to some irregular sexual relationships.[11] Ellen and James White vigorously sought to curb these extreme practices.

At the time of the emergence of Seventh-day Adventism, knowledge of contraceptive techniques like the withdrawal method, the sheath, the vaginal sponge, and various types of douche was slowly filtering down to the populace. It is impossible to say precisely, however, how aware Adventists were of such information. Most lived in rural areas which are traditionally the most resistant to social change. As they became increasingly health-conscious under Ellen White's tutelage, they were more likely to be influenced by fears about the hazard to health posed, according to the medical profession, by the use of contraceptives. Given the conservative nature of early adventist thought on sexual matters generally, it seems likely that members remained either ignorant, or suspicious, of the use of contraceptive methods, and employed them very little. They did, however, believe in restricting family size and spacing children, an end probably effected mainly by strict sexual discipline and coitus interruptus, though not typically by total abstinence.

Ellen White's early counsel

As early as 1862, Ellen White advised that funds should not be used to give aid to poor people with large families. Apart from reducing the flow of money available for the proclamation of the gospel, this encouraged irresponsible behaviour both on an economic and sexual level, she felt.[12] In 1868, she particularly criticized the irresponsible sexual behaviour of men which kept some families in a perpetual state of poverty, damaged the health of the mother, and meant that the children often lacked education, affection, and spiritual discipline.[13] However, she also observed that childless couples easily lapsed into selfishness.[14] There emerged, then, at this early stage of her work, the principle of family limitation. In 1870, Ellen White expressed her views on sexual activity more fully. She attributed much of the suffering experienced by unwilling mothers and unwanted children to the unbridled passions of men 'who bear the name husband – more rightly could they be called brutes'.[15] Many women, she warned, were dragging out miserable existences because of repeated sexual exploitation and child-bearing. Significantly, she urged that believers

MILLENNIAL DREAMS AND MORAL DILEMMAS

consider the result of every privilege of the marriage relation, and sanctified principle should be the basis of every action. Before increasing their family they should take into consideration whether God would be glorified or dishonored by their bringing children into the world.[16]

The connection in her mind between the 'privilege of the marriage relation', her euphemism for intercourse, and an increase in family, is undeniably close. It seems reasonable to infer that she believed that all couples having sexual intercourse ran a high risk of starting a pregnancy. It was therefore incumbent on the husband to master his animal nature.

She advanced a good many other reasons for strict control by husbands over their sexual desire. Sexual activity was, she observed, very debilitating, and often encouraged the spread of disease, culminating even in 'paralysis of nerve and brain' and premature death.[17] More importantly, spiritual health was adversely affected by overindulgence; there were many whose 'polluted carcasses' would 'never pass the portals of the heavenly city'.[18] While she laid much of the blame on sensual husbands, she chided wives for complicity in the matter. They submitted to becoming 'slaves to lustful passion'. They allowed their 'godlike womanhood' to be 'consumed upon the altar of base passions'. Their passive submission was no virtue, since God had enjoined them to 'possess their bodies in sanctification and honor'. God had 'the first and highest claim upon [their] entire being'.[19] Passive submission by the wife to her husband's advances raised fears in each party about the faithfulness of the other. In resisting their husbands' frequent amorous advances, wives were performing an important religious duty.

Sexual excess will effectually destroy a love for devotional exercises, will take from the brain the substance needed to nourish the system, and will most effectively exhaust the vitality. No woman should aid her husband in this work of self-destruction.[20]

On the contrary:

If she possesses true love and wisdom, she will seek to divert his mind from the gratification of lustful passions to high and spiritual themes by dwelling upon interesting spiritual subjects. It may be necessary to humbly and affectionately urge, even at the risk of his displeasure, that she cannot debase her body by yielding to sexual excess.[21]

While she stopped short of calling for total sexual abstinence, she urged the strictest possible control of sexual desire. The 'nominal churches' were full of all manner of sexual excess which Seventh-day Adventists were to avoid. They 'above all other people in the world, should be patterns of piety, holy in heart and in conversation'.[22] This call for the strictest vigilance, she claimed, came from God.

'A Solemn Appeal'

1870 saw the publication of a substantial volume called *A Solemn Appeal Relative to Solitary Vice and the Abuses and the Excesses of the Marriage Relation.* Edited by James White, it was an unusual book in that it contained significant contributions from two non-Adventist physicians, besides much counsel from Ellen White. Much of Ellen White's contribution had already appeared in pamphlet form.[23]

Many of the same themes were present. Couples intending marriage gave more attention to romantic than financial and moral considerations (p. 104). The assumption that intercourse would probably be followed by pregnancy was clear (p. 105). She concluded that Adventists would engage in intercourse infrequently, and only when they were prepared to enlarge their families (pp. 105, 111, 139). Association between the sexes at too early an age resulted in a lack of tenderness between spouses (pp. 147–57). Husbands who were too sexually demanding of their wives during pregnancy were guilty of 'murdering' those children (p. 119). Briefly stated, all those who hoped soon to join the company of sinless angels should seek to avoid the least taint of sin (p. 139).

The passage cited from *The Cause of Exhausted Vitality*, by E. P. Miller, a non-Adventist, warned that frequent intercourse would result in a great loss of nervous energy which would eventuate in ill-health. Furthermore, such indulgence would, as it were, dilute the semen and result in an unhealthy child, just as it would transmit a sensual nature to it.

While the rest of *A Solemn Appeal* clearly echoed the general theme of 'self-denial and temperance in married life' (p. 178), the extract from *Amativeness*, by O.S. Fowler, another non-Adventist, was instructive in its specificity. He opined that for light-built, fine-skinned, fine-haired, spare-built, sharp-featured, light-eyed persons, of either sex, to indulge, even in wedlock, as often as the moon quarters, is gradual but effectual destruction of both soul and body. (p. 200)

He further believed that

Whoever indulges often, and weekly is often, in wedlock or out of it, will experience an unnatural heat, tension, tenderness, irritation, swelling, perhaps soreness in these organs, of course resulting from their inflammation.

(p. 205)

Thus, any who controlled their sexual nature only with difficulty should

Flee at once to *perfect continence* ... Oh! will you, for a low-lived animal gratification, sell the birth-right of your nature − all your intellectual power, all your moral endowments, all your capabilities of enjoyment ... TOTAL ABSTINENCE IS LIFE; animal, intellectual, moral. INDULGENCE IS TRIPLE DEATH. (p. 251)

On the subject of birth control Fowler was also enlightening:

A physician recently avowed his belief that if, by any secret means, however painful or dangerous, he could prevent progeny, he could make a princely fortune in a year. Thank God! No one has found out a specific preventive. Nor ever should; because this will throw open the floodgates of passion, and trample under the foot of unbridled lust nature's great ordinance, nature's great laws. (p. 182)

While he stopped short of recommending complete celibacy in marriage, his views tended to be extreme.

It is important to seek to establish whether Fowler's views were representative of those of the Adventist leadership. Since the book was published by Adventists, and James White described Fowler's views as 'timely admonitions' (p. 181), it seems a reasonable inference that leading Adventists concurred with them. A note of caution, however, must be introduced. The publication *How to Live* (1865), also a composite work, had contained a statement condoning the use of alcohol during pregnancy (no. 2, p. 50). On this matter, Ellen White would certainly have disagreed with her fellow contributor. It seems safe to assume, however, that the Adventists would have regarded *A Solemn Appeal* as a book whose credentials were endorsed by James White, and that therefore their sexual behaviour would have been influenced by it.

John Harvey Kellogg

Born in 1852, just when his father was embracing sabbatarian adventism, John Harvey Kellogg showed at an early age the boundless energy and ingenuity which was later to characterize his medical career. He attracted the attention of James and Ellen White, and, with their encouragement, enrolled for medical studies at Bellevue Hospital Medical College in New York, in 1873. He soon took over the editorship of the *Health Reformer* from James White and, in 1876, was appointed superintendent of the Adventist-run Western Health Reform Institute in Battle Creek, Michigan. The Battle Creek Sanitarium, as it later became known, developed an international reputation under the direction of this militant campaigner for health reform. He himself achieved prominence as he broadened his medical experience in the company of some of Europe's leading practitioners. The Sanitarium became the focus of an enormous range of medical, welfare, and educational projects. As his empire grew, Kellogg came into increasing and sometimes bitter conflict with the Adventist establishment until, in 1907, for a variety of reasons, he was deprived of his membership. Although he continued the same type of work after his link with the church was severed, he never rejoined, and thus his career loses its relevance for this study. He was undoubtedly the church's leading qualified spokesman on medical matters in the nineteenth century, and, as such, exerted a considerable influence: 'Dr Kellogg doubtless did as much as any man in the denomination, if not more, to bring the name and work of SDA's favorably before the world.'[24]

In addition to his other accomplishments, he was a prolific writer, and produced four works which are of significance in the present context: *Plain Facts about Sexual Life* (1877); *Plain Facts for Old and Young* (1879); *Ladies' Guide in Health and Disease* (1882); *Man the Masterpiece* (1885). Each tends to echo the other but their importance can be judged from the fact that the first volume is reputed to have sold half-a-million copies.[25]

He consistently argued that it was illegitimate to engage in intercourse for the sake of pleasure, insisting that 'the sexual function is for the purpose of producing new individuals'.[26] Thus it was wrong, in his opinion, to indulge during menstruation and pregnancy, or after the menopause. Over-excitement of the nervous system and frequent emission of 'life-giving fluid' produced all manner of illness from throat disease to consumption, from indigestion to uterine cancer. The over-demanding husband was responsible for 'legalized prostitution', even 'legalized murder', and for 'murdering self by degrees'. He believed, along with Ellen White, that couples ought to limit their children to a number they could adequately support.

Unlike her, however, he was prepared to address the subject of contraception directly. He reserved some of his most scathing criticism for the withdrawal method, which might suggest that it was a popular method in his own community. Incomplete intercourse he thought likely to cause cancer of the womb, and at least, to leave a wife feeling resentful. His greatest fear, however, was that this 'conjugal onanism' would result in an imperfectly formed child. He reasoned that, since the physical and personal characteristics of the foetus were transmitted via the ejaculate, an incomplete ejaculation would leave the transmission process unfinished. He was critical of the Oneida community for practising this 'double masturbation'. Similarly, he believed that when old men fathered children they invariably produced weak specimens because their seminal fluid had deteriorated in quality.

In *Plain Facts about Sexual Life*, he deemed it improper to describe mechanical devices available for thwarting conception, even in such 'a plain-spoken work'. He believed that to condemn them individually was to publicise them, and he had no wish to encourage men in their 'lewd imaginations'. Furthermore, he clearly welcomed the Comstock legislation and no doubt wished to avoid all possibility of falling foul of it.[27] Later, in *Plain Facts for Old and Young*, he was prepared to condemn 'cold ablutions', 'astringent infusions', and 'medicated washes' as causes of various uterine complaints. Condoms, or 'intermediate tegumentary coverings, made of thin rubber and gold beater's skin', were, in his opinion, a 'bulwark against love' and

produce a feeling of shame and disgust utterly destructive of the true delight of pure hearts and refined sensibilities. They are suggestive of licentiousness and the brothel and their employment degrades to bestiality the true feelings of manhood and the holy state of matrimony.   (p. 494)

Neither, he believed, were they really effective! He did not believe the sexual function to be essential to the maintenance of health, and recommended certain strategies to minimize resort to it. He believed that certain foods, a sedentary occupation, romantic literature, and theatre-going were all likely to encourage the habit of 'conjugal masturbation'. Separate bedrooms, or separate beds with intervening curtains would help to check the sexual instincts. He grudgingly allowed the use of the rhythm method while warning that it was unreliable. In fact, the version he gave maximized the prospect of conception. Those couples who did indulge, should limit their intimacy 'to the number of lunar months in the year'.[28]

He saw all methods as attempts to thwart a holy purpose, and, as such, inherently sinful. The only option remaining which was both natural and thus morally defensible, was total abstinence, although he recognized that it required a 'heroism ... equal to death at the stake'.[29] He believed it would be productive of greater married joy.

Kellogg was ahead of his time in his concern to protect the rights of the unborn child. The sperm and the egg were, in his view, embryonically human as soon as they met, and should instantly enjoy the full rights accorded to human beings. Any attempt to destroy the conceptus immediately, or prevent the union of sperm and egg, was morally reprehensible, and the agent incurred great guilt. He rejected the view that a foetus assumed special human significance only at quickening. He even went so far as to argue that intercourse should be avoided during pregnancy to protect the constitution of the new infant; sexual activity at this time would transmit a sensual disposition and might also result in epilepsy.

Kellogg's radical views on sex were no doubt in some measure a reflection of the entrenched attitudes of his profession, and of his own uncompromising personality. It may not be totally irrelevant that Kellogg and his wife produced no children of their own, although they adopted or fostered a total of forty-two children in the course of their marriage. He is said to have treated her with respect yet with no sense of intimacy. It is tempting to speculate that his puritanical views were also, in some degree, a matter of autobiography. Certainly a recent study has asserted that Kellogg's own marriage was never consummated.[30]

Several questions arise concerning Kellogg's role within the church at this time. To what extent did his views reflect Adventist thinking in general? This is impossible to determine with any accuracy. To what extent did he influence Adventist thinking? Again, this is difficult to ascertain, but the *Health Reformer* certainly served as a ready vehicle for his views. To what extent did he influence Ellen White in her counsel on the matter? This question will be treated below. The most one can say with any certainty is that, in a society which generally saw in sex something distasteful, Kellogg's work was calculated to encourage readers towards an extreme of sexual temperance.

Ellen White's later counsel

General philosophy

It has been alleged that, after the early 1870s, Ellen White's writings reveal a declining willingness to address sexual topics.[31] The evidence does not permit easy computation but, if the claim is true, the trend was no doubt occasioned partly by the increased demands made of her as the whole Adventist enterprise grew in scope. It would be more accurate to confine the observation to her published works; in her unpublished manuscripts and letters she not infrequently inveighed against various forms of licentiousness. The suggestion that she, like other female leaders of religious movements, addressed the subject less after she reached the menopause is plausible, but conclusive evidence is lacking.[32]

Writing from Europe in 1885, Ellen White observed that, in the interests of efficient proclamation of the gospel, missionaries should not have large families.[33] 1890 saw the publication of *Christian Temperance and Bible Hygiene* which made earlier testimonies on sexual behaviour more widely available. Similar warnings about the physical and spiritual dangers of frequent indulgence were completely lacking in her voluminous work on health and the home, *The Ministry of Healing*, published in 1905. In her later published works, she added very little to the exhortations of the earlier years.

In an unpublished manuscript written in 1888, she condemned those 'loathsome practices' which went on in many a bedroom,[34] although there are no grounds for equating these with the use of contraceptives. Other similar exhortations to purity of life appeared in the same year, emphasizing the function of the body as 'the temple of the Holy Spirit'.[35] Another document urged husbands to act considerately in sexual matters towards their wives who, in circumstances of exploitation, were justified in acting 'promptly and independently'.[36] To these can be added the many items of correspondence to specific individuals or groups which confronted the problem of improper sexual relationships. It may be that Ellen White viewed such matters with increasing distaste; it cannot be demonstrated that she avoided them altogether in her later years.

A disputed testimony

Mention must be made of the existence of several documents, allegedly from the pen of Ellen White, which criticized Adventist workers for increasing their families at a time when they should have been putting all their efforts into proclaiming the imminent advent. The writer was 'thoroughly disgusted' with the behaviour of such workers, whose course was judged to be at variance with the will of God. It was argued that, given the decaying state of the world, the birth of a child was 'more an occasion of grief than joy'. Church workers should be an example to others in such matters.[37] The letters seemed to oppose any further reproductive activity among Adventist workers, and could perhaps have been taken to recommend the same behaviour to ordinary members.

The letters seem to have a familiar ring to them, but the White Estate has disputed their authenticity. Certainly such documents could readily have been fabricated by a would-be detractor. If the documents were demonstrated to be genuine then they would represent a marked development in Ellen White's thinking, thereby placing Adventists in a real dilemma as far as their personal lives were concerned, and raising important questions concerning the authority of their prophetess.

The circumstantial evidence is conflicting. It is certain that this was an issue at the time the purported testimony was written, as an official biography has acknowledged. Two women confronted Ellen White with the question, 'Is it a sin to raise children? ... Ellen White referred them to her writings on each point, and told them that she was not commissioned to answer such questions ...'.[38] One witness has claimed that, in 1884, Ellen White advised a meeting of Adventist workers to refrain from having children, and that her counsel caused 'perplexity among the young married people'.[39] A *Review* article by Ellen White, published in 1885,[40] certainly demonstrates that her mind was running along these lines. She also clearly believed that the decision to rear children in the current social climate required great deliberation,[41] and further that it was a sin to become a parent without having made proper spiritual and mental preparation.[42] In her correspondence she commented that, 'The time has come when a sterile condition is not the worst condition to be in.'[43]

All of this, however, falls short of demonstrating that Ellen White believed that Adventists as a body of people should henceforth avoid child-bearing. The evidence seems, on balance, to suggest rather that Ellen White did indeed send letters to several missionary families advising them against having families, or criticizing them for having done so, when they had had a specific task assigned to them.[44] The content of some of those letters seems to have become public knowledge, thus creating a stir as it was assumed that the testimony had a general application. Ellen White clearly regretted the whole matter, chastising herself for perhaps assuming too much responsibility in the cause of God; she pronounced herself unwilling to enter that particular debate again.[45]

Material written by Ellen White after this episode in the mid 1880s, extolled the virtues of Christian parenthood.[46] It seems safe to conclude that Ellen White did not enjoin celibacy or childlessness on Adventist couples in general. At the same time, she counselled them against so enlarging their families that they had little time or energy for witness. However, the issue, which had first surfaced after the 1844 disappointment, refused to go away.

The Anna Phillips case

While in Australia in October 1893, Ellen White learned of visions which a certain Anna Phillips was purported to be experiencing in

Battle Creek. With the support of some church leaders, she was delivering testimonies rather in the style of Ellen White. To an Adventist married couple who hoped for a child Anna Phillips wrote, in 1892:

But the earth is about to pass away, only a very few short years, a very few at the most and the Lord will come again ... Then could you raise children to God's glory now? No, for they would soon be laid away, the time is past when children can be brought into the world for the glory of God, and God did not create woman for man's pleasure ... The time has come of which Paul spoke when he said, But this I say, brethren, the time is short; it remaineth that both they that have wives be as though they have none.[47]

Of their sexual relationship, she advised, 'Give it up for God.'[48] There is evidence that her advocacy of sexual abstinence was influential for a short time, and that it eventuated in considerable marital disruption in the somewhat ingrown Adventist community in the headquarters town of Battle Creek.[49]

Ellen White was thus placed in an extremely awkward situation. Silence might well be construed as an endorsement of these alleged visionary experiences. A vehement denunciation of these claims might have been interpreted as a blatant attempt to reinforce her authority from a distance. Moreover, she recognized that 'There is danger even in reproof, of causing minds to dwell upon topics that lead to sensuality.'[50] What was certain was that Anna Phillips' testimonies were creating confusion and division, as the following letter from Ellen White to a church leader indicated:

Young, unmarried women, would have a message for married men and in no delicate words would tell them to their face of their abuse of the marriage privilege. Purity was the burden of the messages given, and for a while everything appeared to be reaching a high state of purity and holiness. But the inwardness of these matters was opened to me: I was shown what would be the outcome of this teaching. Those who were engaged in this work were not a superficial, immoral class, but persons who had been the most devoted workers. Satan saw an opportunity to take advantage of the state of things, and to disgrace the cause of God. Those who thought themselves able to bear any test without exciting their carnal propensities, were overcome, and several unmarried men and women were compelled to be married. I am afraid of those who feel so great a burden to labor in this direction. Satan works upon the imagination, so that impurity is the result, instead of purity.[51]

69

When the undesirable consequences of this teaching on abstinence became evident, Anna Phillips submitted to Ellen White's judgement without rancour.[52]

The 'holy flesh' movement

The doctrine of 'holy flesh' developed among Adventists in Indiana around the turn of the century, reaching its peak in the pentecostal frenzies of the state camp meeting in September 1900. Subscribers to the doctrine believed that, just as Christ had possessed 'holy flesh' in Gethsemane prior to his death, so those who were 'baptized by the Spirit' received a 'translation faith', and would not see death. Such faith was evidenced in ecstatic and convulsive experiences. The movement arose at a time when there was much talk in the church about the 'outpouring of the latter rain'.

It was but a short step from this view to the idea that

the affections of the sanctified were never in danger of leading astray. The result of this belief was the fulfilment of the evil desires of hearts which, though professedly sanctified, were far from purity of thought and practise.[53]

The meetings of the movement were emotionally charged, with much physical contact between participants; similar manifestations among believers in New Hampshire led to 'free-lovism'.[54] Such doctrines created considerable confusion in a certain section of the church as far as sexual intimacy was concerned. Some believed that it was a missionary duty to raise as many children as possible to fill the ranks of the saintly 144,000 (of the Book of Revelation) with Adventists. Others believed that 'social purity' or abstinence was an integral part of the sanctified life. Rumours about Ellen White's teaching on the matter were rife.[55] These doctrines relating to the imminence of Christ's second advent generated problems of 'large proportions', according to Ellen White, in Maine, New York, Massachusetts, New Hampshire and parts of the south.[56]

Conclusions

It has been demonstrated above that the prophetic leader of the Adventist church, Ellen White, believed in the principle of family limitation, while rejecting abstinence as the sole means of achieving that goal. Furthermore, she refused to say that the procreative motive should be present in all true Christian love-making. One is left, however, with an enigmatic silence as to how these values were to be reconciled, since she never pronounced on the matter of birth control. Although she never endorsed the use of contraceptives, it is significant that, unlike Kellogg and many other members of the medical profession, she did not condemn the use of them. It is worthwhile considering the possible reasons for this.

It could be argued simply that she, like other church leaders, considered such matters too delicate to broach. Yet it must be remembered that she pronounced at some length on the habit of masturbation, although it is true that the subject was something of an obsession with the Victorians. Another possible explanation is that she felt insufficiently qualified to address the medical aspects of the problem. Generally, however, she did not seem to allow this sort of consideration to inhibit her. A view favoured by the White Estate is that she said nothing because she received no divine enlightenment on the subject.[57] Another possibility is that she kept silence because she wished to avoid all possibility of falling foul of the Comstock legislation.

Although such explanations may have their place, two others seem better candidates for our acceptance. It would seem possible that Ellen White did not view contraceptive devices as being evil in themselves. She would, however, have been hesitant to recommend them for fear of encouraging the very sexual abuses which she so often condemned. Furthermore, as has already been demonstrated, Adventists, in their zeal, on occasion took up positions on matters relating to sexuality extreme enough to cause strife and division. She probably judged that any statement, public or private, would have created more problems than it solved. She seems to have been content therefore to leave such decisions to the consciences of Adventist couples. It was fortunate, Adventists would say 'providential', that Ellen White did not pronounce on the subject in line with the views of her protégé Kellogg, and the medical establishment, for modern generations of believers would then have found themselves in precisely that dilemma which faces Roman Catholics.

6 · Adventists and intimacy: the celebration of sex

Acceptance of contraception in the United States

A readiness to accept birth control as an integral part of responsible parenthood gradually developed among Americans in the years after the First World War. By 1932, there were some eighty clinics in the nation offering counsel on contraception. At approximately the same time, Comstock legislation was effectively overturned by several legal judgements permitting the importation of contraceptive literature and devices. Although the campaign in Britain was somewhat in advance of that in America, by the outbreak of the Second World War major resistance in the United States to contraceptive practice was overcome. Since that time, control over fertility has had profound social and economic ramifications.

While the efforts of campaigners on both sides of the Atlantic no doubt served as catalysts in the process of change, the major influences were social and economic. In an increasingly industrialized and urbanized society, a large family was both costly and inconvenient. With the slackening of the influence of the Christian religion over the lives of an increasingly large proportion of the population, a desire for greater sexual freedom grew. Developments in contraceptive technology, particularly the advent of the pill in the 1950s, further facilitated the fulfilment of that desire.

Despite the public calls for a liberalization of attitudes made by individual churchmen, it came as something of a surprise that the 1930 Lambeth Conference declined any longer to condemn the use of contraceptive methods if conscientiously adopted.[1] Fears concerning depopulation, promiscuity, the loss of self-control, and the viewing of sexual union as an end in itself were no longer deemed sufficient to outweigh the obvious benefits to married life. The decision prompted a swift reaction from Rome by Pius XI, whose *Encyclical Letter on Christian Marriage, Casti Connubii* (1930) vehemently denounced contraception and made it a matter for the confessional. American churches were much slower to place their official blessing on contraceptive practice than were their British counterparts. It was only in 1946 that the General Convention of the Protestant Episcopal Church followed the lead of the Lambeth Conference resolution of 1930, while the policy change implemented by the General Conference of the Methodist Church in the United States came seventeen years after that made, in 1939, by British Methodists.

In 1960, Richard Fagley, a leading spokesman on international affairs at the World Council of Churches, lamented the failure of the Protestant churches to come to terms with the problem of responsible parenthood. Roman Catholic scholars, he believed, far surpassed their Protestant peers in the volume and quality of work they had produced on the subject. He suspected that the explanation lay partly in the view that

because husband and wife must finally make in Christian conscience their own decisions regarding responsible parenthood, the church is thereby freed from obligation to provide spiritual and ethical guidance.[2]

The Roman Catholic church had experienced its own difficulties. Ever since the publication of the unequivocal encyclical *Casti Connubii*, many Catholics had been looking for some softening of the stance therein adopted. In 1951, Pius XII not only endorsed the use of the rhythm method but acknowledged the existence of social and economic reasons for avoiding pregnancy. Catholic clergy and laity protested against the prohibition by the same pontiff of the use of the newly marketed contraceptive pill, in 1958. With many, Catholic and non-Catholic, looking to Rome for some liberalization of dogma, the publication of the encyclical *Humanae Vitae*, in 1968, came as a considerable disappointment, reasserting, as it did, the traditional view, which has been reaffirmed in recent pontificates.

Recognition of the international problem of a rapidly growing world population attempting to survive on limited resources certainly encouraged church leaders to support strict regulation of family size. On the individual level, the socio-economic aspirations of Christians in general, and Protestants in particular, enhanced their commitment

73

to family planning. Among western Christians, the battle to gain relief from the physical and economic burdens imposed by too large a family was won. It gave way, however, to another problem of more threatening proportions, namely, how to protect the family from complete disintegration. In the realm of the ethics of fertility control, attention shifted to the moral acceptability of abortion, sterilization, artificial insemination, and surrogacy.

Modern Adventist philosophy and practice: 1915–1985

The Home Physician and Guide to Health

In 1928, the Pacific Press published the first of five volumes about human development through the life-cycle. The first volume, *Makers of the Home*, treated the subject of contraception with great suspicion. The author, A. W. Spalding, feared that the use of contraceptive methods would bring sterility and other unforeseen physiological hazards. Tampering with the laws of nature in order to evade fundamental responsibilities, he thought, would also produce spiritual and mental problems. However, the need to limit family size was recognized, and the rhythm method recommended as a supplement to continence. Indeed, Spalding even conceded fleetingly that, in certain circumstances, the use of contraceptives might be necessary:

When it becomes clearly apparent that the birth of more children could only be detrimental to parents and children alike, it can scarcely be maintained that the greater fault is committed by using contraceptive means. (p. 178)

Grudging concession was to be turned into positive approval in a separate publication which appeared three years later.

In 1923, the staff at the church's College of Medical Evangelists at Loma Linda, California, first published a compendium called *The Home Physician and Guide to Health*. A second edition, published in 1931, included a new chapter entitled 'The Divine Purpose of Sex'. While this was not an official statement of the church's position on contraception, it nevertheless provides a useful barometer of changes in denominational thinking. The chapter defended the view that sex was not intrinsically evil, and that to provide a child with a proper understanding of his sexual nature was one of the most sacred responsibilities of parenthood. Great self-control was required in marriage, particularly by the husband, to protect his wife from the nervous exhaustion induced by frequent coitus and excessive child-bearing. Concerning the procreative intention in coitus it stated:

The sexual act is ... primarily a manifestation of love, and not solely the effort to conceive children. That it should be restricted to the intent of procreation is, in the light of physiological facts and of human experience, an untenable position. (p. 676)

The authors believed that it was the wife's prerogative to decide how many children were to be born and when. This, however, was not an absolute right since the husband normally had the right to expect that his wife would bear him children. The virtue of contraception lay in the fact that it made possible 'the graduation of the number of children in any family to the circumstances and resources of the parents' and helped 'to insure a properly balanced and successful home' (p. 678). If brought into the world intentionally, the child would be 'not an unwelcome accident, but the creation of a pure, deep, sincere love' (p. 680).

The book was careful to insist that its views should not be regarded as an evasion of civic responsibility: 'Birth control should not be misconstrued as birth prevention ... the term connotes, not race suicide but race betterment' (p. 677). The chapter went to some lengths to insist that birth control be kept under strict controls:

All medical and surgical science may be misdirected and criminally applied, and so it is with contraception. Possession and application of its means should be wholly within the hands of the medical profession, whose ethical sense should permit them to apply it only in legitimate cases. The distribution of contraceptive agencies to the general public through drug stores and other agents, though common, is against the law in most of the United States, and properly so; for in some cases the agencies used are inimical to health, and, whether deleterious or innocuous, whether efficient or nonefficient, they should not be obtainable for purposes of facilitating delinquency and crime. But the law should sanction the use and direction of contraceptive means by the physician according to his judgment. (p. 677)

The basic convictions underlying the chapter, however, can be judged from the crusading tone adopted in places:

With all its possibilities of abuse, the science of contraception may be justified by its possibility of assuring the number and the conditions of births to the physical, social, and economic status of the family. When, instead of prejudice and unreasoning opposition, it receives the enlightened support and regulation of law to confine it within competent and ethical control, it may take its place as one of the scientific agencies for the relief of suffering womanhood and the betterment of the race.   (p. 678)

While the chapter contained no information on techniques, it can be seen as an important watershed in Adventist thinking, for it was the first time that recognized authorities had endorsed in print the use of contraceptive methods.

General Conference census

In 1949, the General Conference undertook a census in co-operation with the Bureau of Census of the United States.[3] Although great caution must be exercised in interpreting the data, they may permit the formation of certain tentative conclusions. The statistics no doubt conceal many variables, but seem to indicate a trend towards depressed fertility among American Adventists relative to the general population. The statistics in table 6.1 may permit the following specific conclusions to be drawn:

1 that the post-war 'baby-boom' was less pronounced among Adventists than among Americans generally. One can only speculate on the effect which Adventist attitudes to military service may have had on fertility patterns.

2 that the outbreak of hostilities, and the entry of the United States into the war seem not to have depressed Adventist fertility in the way that one might have expected of a group which believed in some sort of Armageddon, a devastating and ultimate conflagration. This was possibly because Adventists believed that the end was to be initiated by divine rather than human instrumentality.

3 that Adventists do seem to have responded to the economic stringencies of the depression years by reducing the size of their families more than others.

Table 6.1 Age distribution in the population of the USA and in the SDA population expressed as a percentage (statistics from 1949)

Years of age	Distribution		SDA differential
	USA	SDA	
1	3.09	1.88	− 1.21
2	1.67	1.31	− 0.36
3	1.61	1.15	− 0.46
4	1.63	1.47	− 0.16
5	1.63	1.46	− 0.17
6	1.56	1.51	− 0.05
7	1.59	1.31	− 0.28
8	1.67	1.23	− 0.44
9	1.66	1.48	− 0.18
10	1.75	1.26	− 0.49
11	1.68	1.36	− 0.32
12	1.84	1.41	− 0.43
13	1.81	1.45	− 0.36
14	1.83	1.42	− 0.41
15	1.84	1.26	− 0.58
16	1.89	1.41	− 0.48
17	1.83	1.42	− 0.41
18	1.96	1.50	− 0.46
19	1.85	1.51	− 0,34
20	1.80	1.59	− 0.21
21	1.80	1.55	− 0.25
22	1.74	1.46	− 0.28
23	1.73	1.56	− 0.17
24	1.73	1.60	− 0.13
25	1.70	1.75	+ 0.05
26−30	8.43	8.95	+ 0.52
31−35	7.58	9.40	+ 1.82
36−40	7.29	9.28	+ 1.99
41−45	6.42	7.91	+ 1.49
46−50	6.24	6.80	+ 0.56
51−55	5.14	5.19	+ 0.05
56−60	4.35	4.27	− 0.08
61−65	3.45	3.31	− 0.14
Above 65	6.21	8.55	+ 2.34

Source: 'Population Sampling Report of the Seventh-day Adventists in the United States', pp. 3−4.

4 that Adventist fertility first became depressed relative to the general population about 1924; it is tempting to speculate that it was about this time that Adventists in large numbers began to use contraceptives to regulate family size. On the other hand it could be argued that the change in the Adventist differential which occurs in the age group of 25 and over, reflects, not relatively high fertility, but rather certain demographic changes caused by the loss of young American servicemen in the Second World War. Adventists, being non-combatant, would not have suffered such losses.

5 that, if it is assumed that children accompanied their parents to church regularly until the age of 15 or so, and thus were included in 'the Adventist population', then there is evidence to suggest strongly that Adventists recently have had smaller families than average. Since, after that age, apostasy becomes an important variable factor in the equation, in addition to births and deaths, statistics for the age groups of 15 and over must be treated with particular caution. Against this must be set the marked general reluctance of Adventists to withdraw membership even from those who have virtually ceased to participate in church life.

6 that the relatively high proportion of people aged 65 and over in the Adventist population reflected a tendency towards longevity which was a consequence of habits of healthful living. Conversely, it may be that Adventism attracted a disproportionately high number of older people.

Table 6.2 is useful only in so far as it suggests that Adventists were marginally less likely to remain childless, to have only children, or to raise large families. The tendency for Adventists to have relatively small families is also demonstrated by Robin Theobald's study of Adventists in Great Britain,[4] and confirmed by the research of Adventist sociologists Charles Crider and Robert Kistler among American church members (see table 6.3).

Published opinion

The Home Physician and Guide to Health failed to stimulate significant published reaction on the matter of human sexuality from any Adventist writer for two decades. The vacuum was eventually filled

Table 6.2   Size of American and Adventist older-generation families
(expressed as percentage)

No. children in family under 21	Older-generation families with children under 21	
	USA	SDA
0	44.3	42.0
1	21.8	20.6
2	15.7	19.9
3	8.3	10.0
4	4.5	4.3
5	2.5	1.7
6 +	2.9	1.5
	100.0	100.0

Source: Statistics taken from 'Population Sampling Report of the Seventh-day Adventists in the United States', pp. 23–4.

Table 6.3   Family size of SDAs

No. children in family	%
0	15.3
1	12.4
2–4	59.5
5–6	5.5
6 +	1.9
No response, or answer obscure	5.4

Source: Statistics taken from *The Seventh-day Adventist Family*, p. 58.

by the work of Harold Shryock, a senior physician at the College of Medical Evangelists at Loma Linda. His major books, *Happiness for Husbands and Wives* (1949), *On Becoming a Man* (1951), and *On Becoming a Woman* (1951), provided the sexual education of a whole generation of young people, married and single. Significantly, the books, which discuss sexual functioning, are entirely without illustration, and chapter headings like 'Secrets about Girls' seem to announce a prudish approach to the subject. However, the author largely succeeded in his aim of approaching the subject with 'a healthy openmindedness' and 'a sanctified frankness that removes superstition and avoids mystery'.[5] Each volume contained detailed information about sexual functions. While these books insisted that young people should not seek 'premature privileges', they also extolled the 'thrills and priceless experiences to which a bride and bridegroom are entitled'.[6] The author chastised mothers who, with the best of intentions, emphasized the vulgar aspects of sex to their daughters, and he dealt sympathetically with the question of masturbation. He was even prepared to record that average American couples had intercourse between three and twelve times a month. The principle of birth control was fleetingly endorsed, on the basis of Ellen White's pronouncements, although no details of techniques were provided.[7] Most readers of *The Adventist Home*, a compilation of Ellen White's counsels on family life first published in 1952, would have inferred that the use of contraceptive methods was legitimate for Adventists. A study guide to that volume, published in 1965, made that explicit.[8]

Stimulated perhaps by the publication of *Humanae Vitae* in July 1968, a number of Adventist writers went into print on the subject of marital intimacy. The consensus appears to have been that since biblical and prophetic counsel seemed to be compatible with contraceptive practice, Adventist couples should act according to the dictates of conscience.[9] One writer asserted more vigorously that 'every child should have the right to be wanted', and that parents were not to be 'mere victims of periodic fate'.[10] Adventist family magazines soon began to carry medical information about various types of contraceptives; the principal cautionary note concerned the possible long-term threat to health posed by the pill.[11]

It was not until the 1970s that Adventist opinion on contraceptive methods was available in more permanent form. In his popular and outspoken *God Invented Sex*, Charles Wittschiebe, doyen of the denomination's counsellors, asserted that intercourse was not solely, nor even primarily, for procreation. He concluded that, since no fundamental questions of morality were at stake, the church left each couple to make its own decision, and observed that his wide counselling experience had led him to believe that almost all Adventists regularly employed family-planning techniques. He further endorsed sterilization as a permanent method of birth control, and artificial insemination (husband and donor) as a legitimate means of dealing with sterility (pp. 121–36).

R. H. Woolsey in his *Christian Sex and Family Planning*, also published in 1974, echoed many of the same themes, and showed a similar awareness of developments in the debate beyond Adventism. He was one of the first Adventists to attempt to refute the Roman Catholic use of Onan's experience, recorded in Genesis 38, as an objection to contraceptive practice, and to advance rapid population growth as a justification for family limitation. His main concern, however, was that Adventist parents should be able to care adequately for the needs of their children, notably in providing a good education. In one of the fullest discussions of contraceptive methods published by Adventists until then, he dismissed the rhythm, withdrawal, and douche methods as unreliable. Other methods, including the pill and the intra-uterine device, were approved, as was sterilization.

In the last decade or so, Adventist publications on sex have displayed certain common characteristics. They have provided much more explicit discussion of the subject, not least in the realm of sexual dysfunction.[12] There has been a developing tendency to celebrate the sexual experience as a central feature of a happy marriage.[13] Contraceptive practice has been universally approved on the grounds that it contributed significantly to marital happiness and economic stability. Particular methods have been recommended on the basis of reliability and emotional appropriateness.[14] Some authors, in an attempt to maintain standards, may perhaps have been perceived as over-moralizing and judgemental, and tending to encourage guilt in sexual matters.[15] Others adopted an extremely open posture, discussing, for example, contraceptive practice for unmarried couples.[16]

An Adventist therapist of long experience, Alberta Mazat, identified a number of areas of sexual anxiety among church members. The notion that sex is only for procreative purposes had, she observed, largely been buried. It is worth noting in passing, however, that a recent official church decision seemed to correlate increasing marital breakdown with a growing emphasis on the relational function of sex at the expense of the procreative.[17] Mazat further affirmed that the acceptance of sexual activity as something intrinsically valuable and beautiful had been a very gradual process. Similarly, only recent

81

generations of Adventists had felt sufficiently uninhibited morally to engage in acts of oral-genital sex. Adventist ambivalence over sexual functioning, she claimed, was typified in the often-expressed concern as to the moral rightness of love-making during the hours of the Sabbath, and the frequency with which sex might be legitimately enjoyed.[18] However, on the basis of recent Adventist publications about sex, it seems safe to infer that the sexual habits of Adventist couples married in the last decade or so differ only marginally from those of their non-Adventist peers. The emphasis in such publications seems to be more on a couple achieving satisfactory adjustment than conformity to some set of externally imposed norms.

In this connection, it is very significant that the first substantial attempt by an Adventist to produce a theology of sex occurred only in 1980, with Sakae Kubo's *Theology and Ethics of Sex*, in which he held that the primary function of intercourse was to serve 'the mutuality of communion between man and woman' (p. 20). Drawing on a wide spectrum of non-Adventist scholarship, he argued that the rational control of nature was legitimate in so far as it prevented the birth of unwanted children, a worsening in the world's population problem, and damage to the health of women arising from excessive child-bearing. He found the Roman Catholic position inconsistent in that the permitted rhythm method, like other contraceptive practices, basically involved the use of human intelligence to prevent conception. He saw it as an Adventist responsibility not merely to permit but to promote the use of contraceptives, particularly to minimize the human suffering arising from over-population. Sterilization also seemed to him a legitimate option. Kubo's book was a new departure in Adventist thought in that it went beyond the essential pragmatism of previous publications and attempted to work from first principles. Furthermore, it provided a coherent rationalization for what Adventists had long accepted as normal practice.

Recent Adventist practice

Home and Family Service

The General Conference established its Home and Family Service in 1975, in response to the growing pressure under which the nuclear family found itself. The purpose of this agency was to improve the quality of life of Adventist families by providing information about various aspects of personal relationships, and forums in which to discuss this. It sought to co-ordinate similar activities in North America which previously had been somewhat random,[19] and to promote them in other parts of the world. The materials produced by the Service have followed the trend already noted in other recent denominational publications, in that they have urged the need for mutually satisfying sexual adjustment and contained a clear celebration of the sexual experience. They further contained an unequivocal commitment to family planning. This policy was justified on the following grounds:

1 it allowed a couple to mature as partners before they became parents,
2 it permitted a couple to achieve that measure of economic security essential to responsible parenthood,
3 it gave time for the preparation of an environment in which a child could safely mature on a physical, mental, spiritual, emotional, and intellectual level.

One of the Service's principal publications, *Marriage Education*, contained a survey of contraceptive methods, assessing them solely on the basis of reliability, while embodying a clear presumption in favour of child-bearing.[20]

Adventist hospitals

Adventist hospitals in the United States normally provide a service to the wider community and thus function as any general hospital would. In most cases, many of the staff are not Adventists, and it may thus prove difficult to maintain a distinctive denominational ethos.[21] The kinds of services available in such institutions may therefore differ very little from those in non-denominational facilities. For example, the Tel-Health service, a system of taped medical information available on the telephone from Adventist hospitals, has provided counsel on contraception and sterilization which closely resembles that available via its secular counterparts. Individual physicians decide what types of contraceptives to recommend, and whether to prescribe contraceptives for those patients who are unmarried.

The commitment of Adventist institutions to the principle of family planning is very evident also in the Third World. Detailed evidence from Adventist institutions and agencies in the Far East indicates that the church both advises members to regulate carefully increases in their families, and provides a local family-planning service. Most methods are used, but the pill and the IUD seem to be favoured; sterilizations are also quite widely performed.[22] This reflects practice in Adventist hospitals around the world generally, although institutions in Asia seem to promote family planning more vigorously than in other parts of the world.[23] The American-based Adventist Development and Relief Agency sometimes serves as an agency for family-planning organizations, although this is not one of its principal functions. Rather, ADRA has tended to avoid involvement in government family-planning projects, first, because of the political dimension, and, secondly, because the agency would be obliged to cater for all-comers irrespective of marital status.[24]

It is clear that Adventists, both on an institutional and a personal level, are strongly committed to the careful practice of contraceptive methods.

A sociological perspective

Socio-economic factors

While only a little sociological investigation has been conducted specifically on Adventists, certain general conclusions can be drawn from it with some confidence if care is taken to set it in the wider context of research into the relationship between religion and fertility generally. Fertility studies completed in the USA have generally indicated a perceptible, if declining, correlation between religious denomination and family size. Most studies have contrasted Protestant and Roman Catholic fertility, but research carried out among

Protestants has demonstrated that liberals are more efficient planners than fundamentalists, and tend to have smaller families (see table 6.4).

Table 6.4   The relationship of religion and fertility in the USA

	Average number of births	
Denomination of wife	By 1965	Most likely expected
All Protestants	2.3	3.0
Fundamentalist sects	2.8	3.4
Baptists	2.3	2.9
Lutherans	2.5	3.2
Episcopalians	2.1	2.9
Methodists	2.2	2.9
Presbyterians	2.2	2.9
Congregationalists	2.2	2.9
Evangelicals	2.2	2.8
Other Protestants	2.4	3.2

Source: 1965 National Fertility Study, cited in R. Andorka, *Determinants of Fertility in Advanced Societies*, p. 305.

Adventism, however, is somewhat difficult to locate on the liberal–fundamentalist continuum, as Theobald observed when he accurately described it as 'a curious blend of intellectually disciplined ascetic protestantism' and 'populist adventist fundamentalism'.[25] Fertility rates among those sectarian groups with which Adventism is often associated vary quite markedly, sometimes for doctrinal reasons; fertility levels are relatively high among Mormons and relatively low among Jehovah's Witnesses.[26]

However, the relationship between fertility and religious affiliation is far from unambiguous, and a more adequate explanation must be sought in another direction, as Petersen has argued:

The effect of religion *per se* on the reproductive behaviour of most persons in the West is now probably close to nil. What may seem to be a religious influence often reflects the fact that the members of any denomination are typically concentrated in a very few places in the social structure as defined by occupation, education, income, or any other of the usual indices.[27]

There is a good deal of evidence to confirm the view that Adventists value material success, are upwardly mobile, and are disproportionately highly represented in the professional and skilled occupations. Schwartz's research among Adventists in Chicago led him to conclude that

Seventh-day Adventists have experienced a small but significant measure of both inter- and intra-generational mobility and expect that they or their children or both will continue to prosper in the occupational realm.[28]

He further observed that Adventist men seek jobs where they can work hard, and which offer them a measure of independence, particularly so that they can avoid difficulties with Sabbath observance. Theobald's more recent work among Adventists in Great Britain substantiated this position.[29]

Adventist sources confirm this assessment, and suggest that it has applied for the last three decades at least. A study completed in 1949 showed clearly the relative occupational success of Adventists (table 6.5):

Table 6.5 Patterns of employment among Adventists compared with national occupational trends

Occupation	National distribution in USA	Distribution of SDA employed
Professional	7.4	31.44
Farming – farm management	11.4	11.71
Proprietorial – managerial	8.3	4.00
Clerical – sales	16.6	14.71
Craftsmen – foremen	11.2	19.07
Factory operatives	18.3	4.00
Domestic service	4.7	4.70
Service other than domestic	7.7	3.33
Farm labourers and foremen	6.9	1.26
Labour other than farm	6.8	5.78
Not reported	0.7	

Source: 'Population Sampling Report of the Seventh-day Adventists in the United States', p. 27.

The same study also showed the marked tendency for Adventists to be engaged in higher-status occupations than their parents. A more recent study showed Adventists to be disproportionately highly represented in high-status occupations (table 6.6).

Table 6.6   Occupational Status of SDAs (%)

Professionals	42.6
Skilled workers	13.9
White-collar	12.5
Semi-skilled workers	10.8
Housewives	9.8
Unskilled workers	3.6
Social security/disabled	1.9
Students	1.2
No response	3.7

Source: C. C. Crider and R. C. Kistler, The Seventh-day Adventist Family, p. 55.

It would seem that Adventists are firmly established in the middle of the social hierarchy, where fertility rates are at their lowest. Recent demographic data seem to suggest a U-shaped relationship between fertility and socio-economic status, with the higher and lower status groups having highest fertility rates.[30]

The matter of socio-economic status is, of course, inextricably bound up with education. The mid-century study of Adventist young people showed that they spent relatively longer in the educational system and that they were much more likely to receive an education at a tertiary level (see table 6.7).

More recently, both Adventist and non-Adventist commentators have judged this to be the case.[31] Adventists do, of course, need a reservoir of highly qualified workers to operate their medical, educational and publishing institutions.

Many demographers have inclined to the view that there is a negative correlation between level of education and fertility, perhaps because the educated seek fulfilment in roles outside parenthood, and perhaps because they have greater access to contraceptive information, and are more efficient planners.[32] The hypothesis that

Table 6.7   School attendance of SDA and non-SDA youth

Age	Percentage attending school	
	National	SDA
15	87.6	97.5
16	76.2	91.8
17	60.9	79.4
18	36.4	54.0
19	20.9	53.0
20	12.5	48.0
21	8.5	38.0
22	5.5	30.0

Source: Statistics taken from 'Population Sampling Report of the Seventh-day Adventists in the United States', p. 18.

Adventist fertility is depressed by the relatively high educational aspirations of young members is an attractive one. Furthermore, the concept of responsible parenthood, as understood by many Adventists, includes the idea that they should have children only if they can give them a denominational education. This is a costly undertaking, possible only with a small family. Moreover, to finance this, wives have to become wage-earners, and so the period available for child-bearing is restricted. There is, then, a strong weight of evidence to indicate that educational aspirations, and related socio-economic motivations, are principal factors in depressing Adventist fertility.

Socio-psychological factors

The emerging discipline of 'population psychology' which analyses the mood predominating in a social group at a given time, may prove helpful here. Just as, for example, the unsettled political situation existing in Hungary in the early 1950s led to a temporary decline in the birth rate, so there may be something in the ethos of Adventism which has inclined its adherents to have small families. The most obvious candidate is the belief in an imminent second advent. As Andorka observed, 'To bear and educate children means a certain confidence in the continuity of life and in the security of future conditions.'[33] This factor plainly featured in the thinking of James White in 1845, although it did not long deter him from marrying and becoming a parent. It might be suggested that it is not so much the advent but the social turmoil and persecution which Adventists believe will precede it which influences members considering parenthood. The evidence is insufficient to allow an irrefutable judgement, but it seems likely that belief in an imminent advent *per se* has influenced procreative patterns among Adventists only very marginally. Schwartz observed that the life-style of middle-class Adventists was such that he 'could not easily gauge the strength of their conviction about the imminence of the Second Advent of Christ'.[34]

Schwartz further asserted that Adventists tended to associate righteousness with socially acceptable middle-class life-styles. According to him, church members emphasized strongly refinement of character, and growth in respectability as part of the spiritual process of sanctification. Moreover, he found that Adventists placed great weight on the role of the will and individual responsibility. To some extent, therefore, personal circumstances were seen as an indication of the moral effort exerted in life by an individual. Self-control was highly regarded as a virtue at the expense of spontaneity. The concept of stewardship, the proper husbanding of all the resources entrusted by God to his people was, he found, a further prominent motivating factor.[35] In Seventh-day Adventism, therefore, theological principles and socio-economic aspirations fuse to produce a powerful motivation to limit family size.

Conclusion

The general bounds of Adventist debate on matters of faith and practice are still very much those established by Ellen White. In sexual matters, one critic, Ronald Numbers, has found her extremely puritanical:

Throughout her long life Ellen White remained generally antipathetic toward sex, though unlike Ann Lee and Jemima Wilkinson she always stopped short of advocating celibacy. In her waning years she looked forward expectantly to an idyllic existence in the new earth free from such unpleasant activities.[36]

The judgement is, however, a superficial one supported by rather unconvincing evidence, specifically a letter written in 1904 regarding E. J. Waggoner, a notable minister in the church, who promoted the view that there would be sexual activity in heaven.[37] First, it is not surprising that a woman of advanced years should not wax lyrical about such a prospect. Secondly, and more importantly, Ellen White had on a number of occasions witnessed the damage done to the church in various locations by particular preoccupations with sex, and no doubt lamented the possibility of further strife created by Waggoner's ideas.

Even if the charge is pressed on the basis of more general evidence, it seems an exaggerated one. The views stated by Ellen White are of the sort which one would expect from a female religious leader writing in a much more restrained age than our own. Her condemnation of excessive sexual indulgence arose out of a practical concern for the spiritual, emotional, and financial well-being of individuals and of the church. Her avoidance of puritanical extremes can be attributed to her awareness of the moral problems which followed in the wake of exhortations to abstinence. It is possible to discern in her writing a cautious approval of the sexual experience, as the following intimates:

[Your wife] is not demonstrative. It is not natural for her to make advances and manifest affection. She looks upon the manifestation of affection between husband and wife as weak and childish ... Your wife should make strong efforts to come out of her retired, dignified reserve ...[38]

On another occasion, it is reported, Ellen White's response to one who was urging the case for celibacy in marriage was: 'Go home and be a man.'[39]

It may very well be the case, then, that Adventists have at times inadequately understood Ellen White's ideas, and generated views about sex which were unduly puritanical. The observations of Charles Wittschiebe seem to confirm this, although there always exists the danger of generalizing on the basis of clinical experience. Wittschiebe found that many Adventists

still feel guilty about what is really a normal, happy expression of sex. Many Adventists feel this because of their upbringing ... they were taught to believe that sex was dirty, and nice people indulge in it only in a dark room, partly clothed, and then with reluctance and regret and apologies.[40]

Impressionistic evidence suggests that modern generations of Adventist couples are much less prone to this kind of guilt. Indeed, living as they do in a sexually uninhibited culture, Adventist young people may well experiment sexually before they marry.[41] Within marriage, there has developed among Adventists a greater willingness to recognize sexual experience as an important part of marital happiness, as pressure upon the nuclear family has grown, as the importance of sexual fulfilment has been acknowledged, and as divorce rates have soared.

The following sort of judgement is disappearing only slowly among Adventists: 'A couple having fewer children than it can afford is considered selfish, ill or neurotically weak, while one having more than it can afford is considered as having poor judgement and lacking discipline'.[42] Socio-economic factors, in tandem with theological principles to some extent, have determined Adventist fertility. The need to ensure the well-being of the individual family unit has, however, had to be balanced against the fact that a large proportion of growth in membership is derived directly from Adventist families. Thus, although Adventism embodies a presumption in favour of child-bearing, families tend to be small. Like other Protestant denominations, however, Adventists have been reluctant to pronounce on such matters, being content to leave fertility to individual judgement and to economic forces.

7 · Adventists and abortion: early hostility

Abortion in the United States

In the first half of the nineteenth century, American women encountered relatively few legal and practical obstacles to obtaining an abortion, partly owing to the fact, no doubt, that theirs was a young and rapidly expanding nation where moral ideas retained a certain fluidity. Abortion legislation was slow in coming also because of the significance attached to the notion of quickening. Many ordinary people, and indeed professionals, felt that there was no moral principle involved until such time as the mother felt the child move within her. As a consequence, publishers of medical dictionaries could list methods designed to produce a self-induced abortion without attracting criticism. In 1821, Connecticut became the first state to enact law dealing with abortion, although its primary concern was to control the distribution of poisonous substances by apothecaries to women 'quick with child', who were not themselves indictable. Other states, for example Iowa in 1832, Missouri in 1835, and Ohio in 1841, also adopted similar measures, but only as minor insertions in omnibus legislation, and these remained largely unenforced.

It is possible to discern a significant change in the pattern of abortions after the middle of the century. There is evidence to suggest that the practice of abortion had become so widespread that as many as 20 per cent of pregnancies were being terminated,[1] with practitioners like the infamous Madame de Restell running highly lucrative businesses. Furthermore, there was a change in the type of woman seeking abortion. Whereas it had once primarily been the resort of young unmarried women attempting to conceal an indiscretion, now, likely candidates were women 'whose moral character is, in other respects, without reproach; mothers who are devoted, with an ardent and self-denying affection, to the children who already constitute their family ...'.[2] Such women were 'perfectly indifferent respecting the foetus in utero'.[3]

Such a development is perhaps not too difficult to explain. As the twin processes of industrialization and urbanization gathered momentum, the need to control fertility increased. Women who had begun to use artificial methods to control the size of their families, resorted to abortion in the event of contraceptive failure. In the social conditions prevailing, many parents, no doubt, anticipated a bleak future for a family in which growth went unchecked.

More states and territories passed abortion legislation, for example, Minnesota in 1851, Oregon, Texas, and Washington in 1854, but still only in the context of the introduction of a coherent legal system. The principal intent of these statutes was to curb flagrant commercialization and to protect women from incompetent practitioners. The need to prove a woman pregnant, to show that quickening had taken place, and that the intention to abort was present made most abortion law virtually unenforceable. No reliable methods existed for confirming a pregnancy before quickening, and menstrual irregularities were often attributed to the 'blocking of tubes', investigation of which invariably induced an abortion. By 1860, almost half of the thirty-three states still had no abortion legislation, and only three had removed the immunity to prosecution which existed for women seeking abortion. Although in some places some stigma did attach to those procuring an abortion, it was generally not sufficient to damage a woman's reputation seriously.

As the century progressed, however, concern over the growth of the practice grew. Open advertising of abortion services aroused the public conscience. The furtiveness which had once characterized the trade in abortion increasingly disappeared. Furthermore, it gradually became clear that the great majority of those seeking terminations were native-born Protestants of British or north European origin, a fact which provoked concern over the preservation of Puritan stock, and fears regarding the growth in the size of the Catholic population.

However, the medical profession was probably the principal agent in effecting a change in public opinion and legislation. The American Medical Association, formed in 1847, provided support for a campaign against abortion instigated by Horatio R. Storer. Mohr has argued that the success of the crusade stemmed largely from the fact that it was the point of confluence for a number of vested interests. First, most physicians had, by then, concluded that abortion was no more ethically defensible before quickening than after. Furthermore, members of the AMA wished to establish their vocation in the public esteem, and so sought to regulate the activities and standards of physicians. 'Regular' doctors wanted also to strengthen their position against their competitors, the 'irregulars', practitioners of alternative medicine, who had succeeded in attracting their clients in large numbers. The medical profession was conservative regarding the evolving role of women, as their suspicion of female doctors testified. Any change in the primary domestic role of women they regarded as a threat to the fabric of society. Religious and nativistic motivations were not without significance; the doctors were encouraged to oppose abortion by the fact that most of the women who sought abortions were, like themselves, Protestants.

The campaign, designed to overthrow 'the grim Moloch to whom our children are being sacrificed yearly in numbers that would seem incredible to one not familiar with the statistics of the horrible rite',[4] attracted the support of the national press, notably *The New York Times*. Home medical encyclopedias, which households throughout the country commonly possessed, were, by the 1880s, virtually unanimous in condemning the use of abortifacients. The forty or so abortion laws passed by states and territories between 1860 and 1880 indicate the success of the campaign. Although legislative detail varied from state to state, the following position was widely established: the interruption of a pregnancy at any time was deemed a criminal offence; the immunity to prosecution traditionally granted to women was lost; the state assumed responsibility for restricting abortion, some jurisdictions making it a felony, others manslaughter, yet others murder; a curb was placed on the advertising of abortion services. Connecticut was again the first to establish a restrictive code, in 1860, followed by Michigan, where many Seventh-day Adventists were now resident, in 1869. While the federal government did not involve itself directly in the abortion issue, it exercised an influence through its agents, who were conducting a campaign against obscenity generally. Most notable among these, Anthony Comstock, was responsible for the arrest of the most infamous of abortionists, Madame de Restell, whose suicide immediately before her trial may well have had some symbolical significance in the campaign against abortion.

By 1900, every jurisdiction had anti-abortion provisions, with the exception of Kentucky, where case law effectively prohibited the practice. Courts showed a greater willingness to move against abortionists than hitherto. This appears to have brought a relative decline in the number of abortions performed, with typical candidates tending to be poor, unmarried young women, and married women of poor immigrant stock. Women higher in the social scale increasingly employed contraceptive techniques with greater efficiency. The anti-abortion statutes in place by 1900 were to remain untouched for more than half a century.

It is not entirely surprising that the churches in the United States were reluctant to confront this issue, given the social context just described. In the nineteenth century, religious journals, both Protestant and Catholic, maintained almost total silence until after the Civil War. Designed to be read by all members of a family, they long displayed a reticence to deal with human sexuality in anything but the most oblique fashion. Most Protestant clergy, adhering as they did to the doctrine of quickening, may have considered abortion an unpleasant affair but not a major moral issue. If, as has been suggested, it was Protestant women who most often sought abortions, many clergy might have thought it judicious to leave the matter to conscience. Some, no doubt, believed that the problem did not impinge on the lives of the chaste ladies in their congregations.

Whatever the case, the medical profession plainly resented the silence observed by clergymen:

The clergymen who minister to the native population for the most part, exert no influence in this respect over the majority of their parishioners, and but a feeble one with their most devout adherents. The discipline of the Church is seldom or never brought to bear against the crime, although its frequency among professors of religion is notorious.[5]

When the church did occasionally raise its voice, it was quick to identify the root of the problem:

Fashion, inexorable, tyrannical, with its whirl of amusements and frivolous enjoyments, has come to demand of religion not only, but of nature herself, that they bend to her despotism, and sacrifice upon her bloody altar.[6]

Although the Presbyterian church offered a public condemnation of abortion in 1869, no other Protestant group seemed ready to enter the debate.

The Roman Catholic church renewed medieval censures on abortion with the publication of the encyclical *Apostolicae Sedis* in 1869, but the churches in general, it seems, thought it unwise or simply unnecessary to act in the matter.

Ellen White

Not once in the whole of her vast literary output did Ellen White approach the matter of abortion directly. This is not entirely surprising in view of the general reticence of churchmen of this period to pronounce on the subject. It is almost certain that she would have been aware of the problem since her protégé, John H. Kellogg, had much to say on the matter, as will be shown below. Adventists perhaps had more reason than most to maintain silence. In the first decades of its existence, the fledgling Adventist church had to resolve too many theological and organizational matters vital to its survival to allow it to confront such social problems. Furthermore, any religious group which believed it had the responsibility of sounding the 'last warning' to earth's inhabitants concerning the impending judgement and advent would surely have seen preoccupation with such issues as a deflection from its main task. However, one might have expected to see an increasing abortion rate adduced as 'a sign of the times'; no such reference is to be found in the Adventist leader's writings. As has been suggested in the preceding chapter, it may well be that Ellen White felt that to condemn a type of behaviour was in some way to publicize it, and that she therefore chose to remain silent.

There is considerable evidence to suggest that abortion would have been morally repugnant to her. She clearly believed that partners should carefully consider the prospect of a pregnancy before every act of intercourse. She advocated a highly responsible approach to sexual life. It is just conceivable that she might have defended abortion where the sexual irresponsibility of a man placed a woman's life or health in jeopardy. However, this suggestion becomes less plausible when it is considered that abortion too was a hazardous procedure.

A more general look at Ellen White's writings confirms these suspicions. She affirmed that, 'Human life, which God alone could give, must be sacredly guarded'.[7] She furthermore believed that

Life is mysterious and sacred. It is the manifestation of God Himself, the source of all life. Precious are its opportunities, and earnestly should they be improved. Once lost, they are gone forever ... God looks into the tiny seed that He Himself has formed, and sees wrapped within it the beautiful flower, the shrub, or the lofty, wide-spreading tree. So does He see the possibilities in every human being.[8]

The idea that a foetus had value and identity seems to be further confirmed by her counsel that mothers 'consecrate their offspring to God, both before and after its birth'.[9] Those who shortened their own lives by neglect were, in her opinion, 'guilty of robbery toward God'.[10]

Ellen White laid great stress on the importance of pre-natal influences. A mother's attitudes during pregnancy were, she believed, reflected in the disposition of the child.[11] Thus, a husband should ensure that his wife did not engage in excessive labour, and that she had a good supply of nutritious food, for it 'was necessary to nourish two lives instead of one'.[12]

Ellen White, like some other religious leaders of the time, connected the loss of foetal life with a love of fashion: 'A large proportion of the alarming number of miscarriages in respectable society is directly due to tight dressing.'[13] She seems, in one place, even to come close to connecting abortion with the love of fashion:

Hoops, I saw, should be discarded from the ranks of Sabbath-keepers. Their influence and practice should be a rebuke to this ridiculous fashion which has been a screen to iniquity. Its first rise was from a house of ill-fame in Paris. Never was such iniquity practised as since this hoop invention; never were there so many murders of infants and never were virtue and modesty so rare.[14]

The comment is ambiguous inasmuch as the precise relationship between the wearing of the hoop dress and the 'murder of infants' is not explained. Four interpretations seem possible. A proper understanding of the use of relevant vocabulary at the time is essential to the first three: 'The destruction of the child after the mother has felt its movements, is termed infanticide; before that time it is commonly known as abortion.'[15] Ellen White's use of the term 'screen to iniquity' may suggest that hoop dresses were used to conceal pregnancies until such time as they could be terminated. The 'practising of iniquity' and the reference to prostitution may support this view.

Alternatively, the wearing of this fasion might have been thought to result in infanticide because the fashion produced a miscarriage. This was possible either if the corset was unduly restrictive, or if the sheer weight of the dress imposed a strain on the woman's body. It may be that Ellen White believed that hoop dresses could produce a miscarriage in winter by exposing the lower parts of the woman's body to cold air, thus placing a strain on all the major organs. The deliberate attempt to precipitate a miscarriage by wearing fashionable dress would, of course, have called forth greater condemnation from Ellen White. Another possible explanation of the accusation of 'murder of infants' is a post-natal one, that is that young girls died as a result of being dressed in the fashions worn by their mothers.[16]

Other similar serious accusations can also be found in her work. She believed that a father was 'guilty of almost murdering his children' by imposing too many burdens on his wife while she was pregnant; the consequence was the birth of weak specimens unable to fight disease.[17] Again, she condemned mothers who abdicated their maternal role in favour of 'fashion's murderous folly'.[18] Those women who employed wet-nurses to suckle their children so that they could continue to attend fashionable social gatherings failed to see the damage they were doing. Moral characteristics were, she believed, imbibed along with the milk.

She believed that physicians shouldered an enormous responsibility in their endeavour to preserve life.[19] It was, she said, 'a great responsibility to take the life of a human being in hand. And to have that precious life sacrificed through mismanagement is dreadful.'[20] She would probably have advised those who saw termination as a solution to an otherwise unacceptable predicament, to 'Let God untangle the snarled-up threads for you. He is wise enough to manage the complications of our lives.'[21]

Ellen White condemned the 'brutal, fiendish destruction of human life'.[22] She predicted that at the time of the end 'human lives will be sacrificed by millions'.[23] She was, however, referring to the loss of life through disasters and warfare. Given the high abortion rates existing during her lifetime, it is perhaps surprising that she did not inveigh against the practice.

Ellen White always insisted in her writings on the high value God placed on 'every human soul'.[24] She used this expression, however, as synonymous with 'human being' since she, along with Adventists generally, always rejected the idea of an immortal soul infused into a foetus at conception.[25] She omitted to comment in any way helpful to the present issue on those texts which are frequently cited by Christians seeking support for their positions on abortion, namely Genesis 2:7; Exodus 20:13; Exodus 21:22; Psalm 139:15, 16; Ecclesiastes 11:5; Jeremiah 1:5; Luke 1:40−1. She did strike a discordant note in one place. Speaking of married couples who were over-indulgent sexually, she said 'Children born to parents who are controlled by corrupt passions are worthless.'[26] She went on to suggest that little of value could be expected from children born in such circumstances, but probably did not intend her readers to make any inference to abortion.

Such circumstantial evidence as that cited above strongly suggests that Ellen White would have opposed the practice of abortion very firmly. 'Children are not to be treated as though they were our own personal property', she said.[27] She was very critical of behaviour which would seem to modern minds far less reprehensible than abortion. All of this evidence, however, may be regarded as less than compelling. There is no final demonstration that she believed foetal life to be fully human. There is no reference to quickening, no use of the term 'foetus'. It is necessary therefore to try to account for her silence on the matter.

It is improbable that she was unaware of the issue, particularly since her protégé, John H. Kellogg, was not reticent about voicing his own deep objections to abortion. It may well be, as argued above, that experience had taught her the wisdom of keeping silence on matters concerning human sexuality. It may be that, since the state where she was resident passed abortion legislation fairly early, she felt no need to enter the campaign, although Kellogg certainly did not agree. She may have felt it to be in bad taste to include discussion of such an issue in literature provided for the edification of the whole family. This, however, would not explain her silence in personal correspondence. Many Adventists would simply hold that she did not receive divine guidance on the subject. The most likely naturalistic explanation is that she did not perceive the problem to be greatly affecting Adventists or potential members, and so concentrated on proclaiming a gospel of salvation largely to the exclusion of social issues. As will be shown later, she felt that the social gospel concealed many snares.

A Solemn Appeal

The above attempt to reconstruct Ellen White's attitude to abortion may be quite sound if indeed the views expressed in *A Solemn Appeal* accurately represented those of the Whites, an issue which has already been discussed (see above, p. 62). The volume contained a brief extract from *The Cause of Exhausted Vitality*, by Dr E. P. Miller, a non-Adventist, which devoted two short pages to 'this worse than devilish business' (pp. 100–1). Miller's condemnation of 'this terrible sin' (p. 101) bore specifically on the use of devices to procure abortions. He alleged that, when an abortion attempt failed, the consequences were normally disastrous. The child was frequently born with a physical or mental handicap, or 'with murder in its heart', which yielded 'untold degradation' (p. 101). He asserted that, when the evil act attained its purpose, it was not unusual for the woman to die, or to be left sterile and in constant pain. There is censure of both partents for seeking to induce an abortion, and additional censure of the husband for compelling the woman to submit to his amorous advances.

The evidence is admittedly slender, and in places tangential, but it seems sufficient to allow us to conclude that Ellen White would have abhorred any attempt to terminate a pregnancy, although it does not resolve the related problem concerning the omission of the subject from her writing.

The *Health Reformer*

The denomination's health magazine, the *Health Reformer*, first published in August 1866, carried occasional articles on the subject of abortion. The first warned that

Quack-medicine vendors ... Foeticides, and Infanticides, should be classed together and regarded with shuddering terror by the whole human race. And yet in every large city, they hold more control over the public health and public morals, than all the regular medical schools and the pulpit combined ... Child murder, both before and after birth, is a regular and (terrible to tell) vastly extensive business.[28]

One writer was concerned about the commercialization of the practice and its spread in the large cities:

According to the highest medical authority, criminal abortion not only prevails to an enormous extent in New York, but is steadily and rapidly increasing, and the worst statistics of that city are surpassed by those of Boston. One woman, in Boston, testified verbally and by her ledger, to having procured over twenty thousand abortions by instruments alone, in seventeen years, among both married and single women of all grades of society.[29]

Another article claimed that abortion was not a problem confined to large cities but existed in the very state where many Adventists lived:

The number of detestable creatures, both lay and professional, who practice this horrible art, is increasing to a frightful extent, not only in New York and Boston, but here in our midst.[30]

A number of writers identified the pursuit of fashion as a major contributory factor to the problem. One spoke of the 'human sacrifices of the unborn thousands annually immolated in the city of New York before the blood-worshipped Moloch of fashion'.[31] Another castigated women for their desire to rid themselves of 'these little obstacles to convenience or pleasure'.[32] Those who sought abortions for economic reasons were accused of 'arrant laziness' and 'sheer, craven, culpable cowardice'.[33] While the same writer evinced some sympathy for the young girl who had been seduced, he accused the married woman who sought terminations of 'dastardly shirking ... the duty of life appointed you by the Creator'.[34] Another writer perceived a connection between the campaign for women's rights and the increase in abortion.[35] On another occasion the periodical carried a rejection of the quickening doctrine:

There is, in fact, no moment after conception when it can be said that the child has not life, and the crime of destroying human life is as heinous and as sure before the period of 'quickening' has been attained as afterward.[36]

Two major concerns were expressed from time to time in the pages of the magazine. Fears were voiced for the mother's health, not least her mental state; the guilt induced by abortion frequently led women to suicide, according to one writer.[37] Others were distressed by the demographic changes effected by abortion: 'The statistics of the last census show that in the older states, particularly in New England and New York, native Americans are dying out.'[38]

Several writers took the churches to task for condoning abortion. Religious newspapers regularly carried discreet advertisements for various abortion services.[39] Still worse, churchgoers were actually involved in the destruction of life:

The press should speak and the pulpit thunder against this unnatural crime. Especially should the clergy deal with it searchingly and truthfully, for the churches are today filled with 'whited sepulchers' ... who wink at, defend − nay, more − practice, this greatest abomination of the age.[40]

When the *Health Reformer* became *Good Health* in January 1879, it carried only one further article on the subject,[41] tending to devote more space to temperance and physiology.

It is clear that the *Health Reformer* purveyed conservative views characteristic of the period. All of the familiar themes emerged: hostility to alternative medicine, fears regarding a declining birth rate among native Americans, the importance of the pursuit of fashion in the issue, and so on. It is significant that all the major articles on abortion appearing in the *Health Reformer* were reprints from other periodicals and newspapers. Adventists, it seems, took their lead from others, perhaps because they lacked a spokesman able to articulate the problem from a distinctive denominational perspective. That changed in July 1874 when John Harvey Kellogg, aged only 22, succeeded James White as editor of the magazine. It seems likely that Kellogg had influenced the content of the magazine while he was still a medical student.

It should not be assumed that the inclusion of such articles in the *Health Reformer* suggests the existence of a problem among Adventists. More probably, Kellogg wished to increase public awareness of the problem through the pages of the *Health Reformer*, which had quite a large non-Adventist readership. The church's main mouthpiece, the *Advent Review and Sabbath Herald*, generally kept silence on the matter, although one does find the occasional disapproving comment.[42]

ADVENTISTS AND ABORTION

John Harvey Kellogg

Kellogg's books echoed the sentiments about abortion which had already been expressed in the *Health Reformer*. Having found contraception morally unacceptable, inevitably he regarded abortion as 'the same crime postponed till a later period'.[43] In his first major work, *Plain Facts about Sexual Life*, published in 1877, he condemned the United States as 'a nation of murderers' (p. 186). He directed his main criticism at husbands for forcing themselves on their wives when they felt least able to cope with the demands of maternity (pp. 189–91). He utterly rejected the notion of quickening, and reckoned the threat posed by abortion to the mother's life and health many times greater than that represented by childbirth.

Kellogg's subsequent works reiterated many of the themes already mentioned, sometimes maintaining the exact wording. His *Plain Facts for Old and Young*, first published in 1886, fell into this category, although it did contain perhaps his clearest and most concise rejection of the quickening doctrine:

The instant they (the ovum and spermatozoon) come in contact fecundation takes place, and the individual life begins. From that moment until maturity is reached, years subsequently, the whole process is only one of development. Nothing absolutely new is added at any subsequent moment ... It is just as much an individual, a distinct human being possessed of soul and body, as it ever is, though in a very immature form. (p. 498)

Furthermore, he dismissed handicap of any sort as being a ground for abortion and treated with contempt the related business of baby-farming. Again he urged the church to wage a vigorous anti-abortion campaign from the pulpit.

Another of Kellogg's volumes, *Man the Masterpiece*, published in 1885, was rather more general in its scope, and so passed quickly over this 'most revolting of all crimes against human life' (p. 425). His assertion that 'A woman is sovereign over her own body, married or unmarried' (p. 426), was a defence of a woman's right to refuse the sexual advances of her husband, rather than of her right to terminate the life growing within her. At conception, he insisted, a human being was

possessed of its own individuality, with its own future, its possibilities of joy, grief, success, failure, fame and ignominy! From this moment, it acquires the right to life, a right so sacred that in every land to violate it is to incur the penalty of death ... in the day of final reckoning, what will the verdict be? Murder? MURDER ... (p. 425)

His passion for the subject does not seem to have abated with the spread of abortion legislation. His *Ladies' Guide in Health and Disease*, published in 1882, urged that

every pulpit in the land ought to send out in stirring and unmistakable tones, warnings against the gross immorality of this practice, drawing vivid pictures of its cruelty and unnaturalness and pronouncing anathemas upon its perpetrators. (pp. 365–6)

Coming himself from a family of sixteen children, he bemoaned the fact that families in New England now averaged only three children rather than the customary eight or nine. He feared the threat posed to a declining native American population. He recorded the fact that he had tried, unsuccessfully, to bring some court actions against abortionists.

The Home Handbook of Domestic Hygiene and Rational Medicine, published in 1880, was the other of his publications to carry severe condemnation of abortion, even in editions published much later. Like all the others, it showed an awareness of the main literature on the subject. He certainly attempted to bring this important social issue to the notice of fellow Adventists as nobody else had done. Yet, it seems fair to conclude that his professional loyalties as much as his religious convictions led him to oppose abortion so vehemently. He was a proud member of his profession, and lost no opportunity to condemn quackery in medicine. The church's health magazine was made, to some extent, a vehicle for championing the cause of the professionalization of medicine, and the adoption of rational procedures.[44]

As the century drew to a close, Kellogg became an increasingly controversial figure in the church. Many Adventists became indifferent towards his numerous enthusiasms, which were often perceived to threaten to divert the church from its main task. Thus it became less likely that his repeated condemnations of abortion would influence Adventist thinking on the matter. However, he continued to condemn abortion even though he had entered the campaign somewhat late. He was not a person to be content with the multiplication of abortion statutes; he would not rest until the practice was eliminated.

It is impossible to conclude with any certainty whether Seventh-day Adventists figured among that group which sought abortions in nineteenth-century America. The behaviour of those seeking abortion is normally furtive, and evidence would therefore be difficult to locate. In the absence of written chastisements specifically directed at Adventist members, from the pen of Ellen White, or Kellogg for that matter, it seems reasonable to conclude that abortion was not a problem of significant proportions among Adventists. Discussion of abortion in Adventist publications was probably designed to inform, or to warn, rather than to correct; it must also be remembered that Kellogg was writing for a large non-Adventist readership. Despite all his rhetoric, it seems that he was unable to rouse the enthusiasm of his fellow church members for the anti-abortion campaign. Pragmatists that they were, they probably gave their attention only to that which directly touched their own lives or the mission of the Church.

8 · Abortion: tensions in the institutionalized church

The dilemma – a cameo

In the early 1980s, the refugee camp at Sangkhla in southern Thailand received large numbers of Vietnamese fleeing intolerable political conditions in their own country. They crossed the Gulf of Thailand in vessels which were often attacked by marauding Thai fishermen, who subjected the Vietnamese women to repeated and violent rape. On arrival at Sangkhla, a significant number were found to be pregnant, and suffering from venereal disease. Catholic physicians in the camp refused to perform abortions. Adventist doctors there were faced with requests to terminate such pregnancies, which, after some deliberation, they agreed to do.

That is one example of Adventist practice with regard to abortion in exceptional and horrifying circumstances.[1] The contrast between Adventist and Catholic responses in less extreme situations would, however, be less marked. Many Adventists in the United States would be sympathetic to the sort of peaceful 'pro-life' campaigns waged by Catholics. The case illustrates the dilemma in which Adventists find themselves over abortion. One the one hand, their theology will incline them towards a conservative view of the matter. On the other, they operate an extensive network of hospitals, both in the United States and around the world, to which many women have turned at a time of deep personal crisis. Moreover, Adventists have to operate at a personal and institutional level in a world which is very tolerant of abortion as a means of controlling fertility. Consequently, Adventists have experienced real difficulty in resolving the dilemma.

ABORTION

Developments in the United States

The campaign to regulate abortion practice had yielded legislation which was to remain in place until well into the second half of the century. In the intervening period the issue seems to have occasioned little debate. In the inter-war years, studies like Frederick J. Taussig's *Abortion, Spontaneous and Induced: Medical and Social Aspects*, published in 1936, estimated that, despite restrictive legislation, as many as 25 per cent of all pregnancies ended in abortion annually in the United States, although this figure has since been seriously challenged.[2] In 1946, the Bombrest case established that the foetus was a separate biological entity, and thus had the right to claim liability against any who, by their negligence, were responsible for inflicting injury upon it.

It was only in the 1960s, however, that abortion again became the focus of attention. By this time the search for efficient means of family limitation had become urgent. Families were eager to maintain high standards of living, and policy-makers were alarmed by projected increases in birth-rates both nationally and internationally. The approval of the contraceptive pill by the Food and Drug Administration in 1960 was evidence of a strong commitment to family planning. Threats to the quality of life from inefficient fertility control increasingly encouraged Americans to favour abortions as an additional and ultimate means of regulating family size.

The cause of those who argued that quality of life was just as important a factor in the equation as sanctity of life was spectacularly highlighted in the case of Sheri Finkbine. An American citizen, she sought to terminate her pregnancy on the grounds that she had taken the drug thalidomide. Failure to achieve that legal right in her own country led her to Sweden where she had an abortion. In addition, the years 1962–4 saw a high incidence of rubella in the Unites States, and the large numbers of children handicapped as a consequence were adduced as further evidence of the moral rightness of reforming the law.

In 1962, the prestigious American Law Institute produced a model penal code, a major reassessment of criminal law as it then stood. In the area of abortion legislation, it recommended the legalization of termination on three grounds: where continuation of pregnancy

107

would impair the physical or mental health of the mother; where the child would have grave physical or mental defects; where the pregnancy was the result of felonious intercourse. The ALI recommendations were to provide a valuable model to all parties interested in reform. In 1967 the AMA authorized its first revision of abortion policy for over a century, in line with the ALI recommendations. These also constituted the core of the liberalized laws introduced in the same year in Colorado, North Carolina, and California. Other states soon followed suit.

However, the mosaic development of abortion-law reform characteristic of the nineteenth century was not to be repeated in the twentieth; actions brought in the Supreme Court ensured that. An unmarried pregnant woman there contested a ruling that termination could be permitted only where the mother's life was threatened. Supporting actions claimed that the abortion statute violated the citizen's constitutional right to privacy. After protracted litigation, the Court upheld these claims, ruling that the Ninth Amendment gave a woman the right to terminate a pregnancy, and that, under the Fourteenth Amendment, the foetus was not a person. This decision, reached in 1973, effectively struck down all state laws which opposed this position.

The Court tempered its decision, however, by affirming the state's responsibility to guarantee the health of the mother and the unborn child. It allowed a woman, in consultation with her physician, to terminate a pregnancy in the first three months without interference from state authorities. Thereafter the state could establish certain criteria which had to be met before an abortion could be performed.

The Supreme Court ruling was, generally speaking, favourably received by the public. In the first year of legalized abortion the Center for Disease Control reported three-quarters of a million terminations. Now over 1.5 million abortions are performed annually in the United States, some 25 per cent of all pregnancies. Since the Supreme Court ruling of 1973 approximately 15 million abortions have taken place. Such statistics have shocked large sections of the American public, who now seem willing to acknowledge that liberalization was undertaken precipitately. Recent innovations in medical technology have raised further doubts about the adequacy of the 1973 ruling. The more conservative mood of the American public during the years of the

Reagan administration has made legislative reform seem more likely. The frequent aggressive demonstrations by 'pro-choice' and 'pro-life' groups and the spate of bombings of abortion clinics indicated that abortion had once more become a highly contentious issue in the United States.

The attitudes of the churches

While attitudes to abortion remained relatively static in the wider society, the churches showed little inclination to do anything other than re-affirm their traditional views. Successive pronouncements from Rome hardened the Catholic position until the new Code of Canon Law of 1917 made women who sought abortion liable to excommunication. Lay resistance to this ruling ultimately provoked the clearest rejection of all possibility of abortion, even in exceptional cases, in the encyclical *Casti Connubii*, in 1930. In the same year, the Lambeth Conference, the proceedings of which were, of course, of significance for the Episcopal church in the United States, concluded that abortion was contrary to the law of God, even though it liberalized its position on contraception somewhat.

The churches were obliged to give greater consideration to the question of abortion when it became the subject of fierce public debate in the 1960s. The posture of the Roman Catholic church was entirely predictable. In 1961, the encyclical *Mater et Magistra*, promulgated by John XXIII, exhibited little inclination to reform. Any hopes which may have been raised, particularly among the laity, by the Second Vatican Council, were dashed in 1968 by *Humanae Vitae* which re-affirmed the traditional position.

The Protestant churches responded rather differently. The earliest substantial discussion of the issue came from the Board for Social Responsibility of the Church of England under the title *Abortion: An Ethical Discussion*, in 1965. Basically a response to a bill then before parliament, it exerted a strong influence on the discussions of many religious groups on both sides of the Atlantic. The document regarded the inviolability of the foetus as the first principle, and laid the burden of proof on those who wished to terminate a pregnancy. It contested the view that the suspected existence of a foetal imperfection was, in itself, a justification for abortion. Similarly, it opposed termination simply on the grounds that pregnancy followed a sexual offence. On the other hand, it rejected the Catholic absolutist position by arguing that the mother should enjoy a certain protection under any new legislation. It conceded that rape or congenital deformity might form a part of a cluster of considerations relating to maternal health, which, taken together, might provide grounds for abortion. The report declined to enter the debate on when the product of conception became human, suggesting that any such definition was always based on a prior commitment to protect or dispose of the foetus. The report was generally conservative in tone but did include the clause in the bill which acknowledged the relevance to the decision of the pregnant woman's 'actual or reasonably foreseeable environment'.

Evangelical views on abortion were most clearly expressed in an influential symposium on the wider topic of the control of human reproduction, held in 1968.[3] Contributions contained a great deal of agonizing but there emerged a strong presumption in favour of preserving foetal life, while retaining a recognition that a foetus might have to be sacrificed to safeguard greater values. Much attention was focused on the life and health of the mother, with the Mosaic provision on miscarriage in Exodus 21:22–23, being frequently adduced as supporting evidence. Family welfare and social responsibility were further cited as relevant considerations, although these were to be interpreted strictly.

Opinions varied between and within denominations in such a way as permits no easy classification, except in so far as fundamentalists tended to reject abortion on any indication while members of mainline groupings were more liberal.

The churches became heavily involved in the anti-abortion campaign of the early 1980s, particularly the so-called 'Moral Majority' under the leadership of the Rev. Gerry Falwell. Many of the mainline Protestant churches, long identified with a 'pro-choice' stand, began to reassess their policies, with the United Methodist church, the Lutheran World Federation, and the Church of the Brethren being the first to adjust their positions. The Presbyterian church and the Episcopal church were under strong pressure to do the same in 1985.

Those groups with which Seventh-day Adventism is often identified have displayed varying attitudes. The Church of Jesus Christ of

Latter-day Saints has consistently opposed abortion. In 1885, a Mormon president had written: 'And we again take this opportunity of warning the Latter-day Saints against those ... practices of foeticide and infanticide'.[4] Nowadays Mormons make exceptions only in the case of rape, incest, and, on rare occasions, where a serious threat to maternal health exists. Suspected deformity of the foetus is not considered a sufficient justification for termination. A Mormon would normally proceed with an abortion only after consulting a priesthood leader. However, 'a person may repent and be forgiven for the sin of abortion'.[5] Mormons do tend, of course, to raise large families.

The Watch Tower Society has adopted no formal resolution on abortion but its publications reflect an unrelenting opposition to the procedure. Christian Scientists do not publish official statements on social, political, and personal issues. Members are free to act according to the dictates of conscience, but, because of their reliance on spiritual healing, are less likely than others to resort to abortion. *The Christian Science Monitor* has periodically carried objective reports on the abortion issue which have tended to oppose resort to abortion while applauding the individual freedom promoted by the Supreme Court decision. The Salvation Army, with its vast experience of working with social problems, is convinced of the need for long-term solutions to such complex matters.

Published Adventist reaction

With abortion creating relatively little controversy in the first half of the twentieth century, Adventist literature maintained an almost total silence on the matter. An exceptional case was Evans, Magan and Thomason (eds.), *The Home Physician and Guide to Health*, which found abortion to be 'a sin in the sight of Heaven', as well as being a violation of the laws of the country, and a dangerous procedure. It suggested that women unwillingly pregnant, who, it assumed, would be young and unmarried, should continue their pregnancy, preferably in the safety of an agency established for the purpose (p. 645).

The Adventist church did not again enter the debate for nearly half a century. The controversy begun by the thalidomide and rubella tragedies drew no reaction from Adventist writers. In 1971, with crucial cases pending in the Supreme Court, and numerous requests for guidance being received from Adventist hospitals, the General Conference published its first response.

'General Conference Guidelines on Abortion'

This statement, available to Adventist hospitals since May 1970 but first published in *Ministry* magazine, in March 1971, merits close attention since it was the first formal pronouncement on abortion to be made in the history of the church. It did not attempt to wrestle with any of the profound questions concerning the beginning of life in the womb. Rather it sought to outline a policy for the performance of therapeutic abortions in Adventist hospitals. As such it was designed to inform Adventist medical personnel who might be called upon to provide the service, rather than Adventist members who might wish to avail themselves of it. Moreover, the guidelines applied only within the United States; elsewhere, standards and regulations had to be established with reference to the local context.

The church wanted to make it clear that it opposed a 'lowering of moral standards of society' (p. 10). It insisted that the procedure be performed only by qualified physicians, in accredited hospitals where practice was controlled by standing committees, and in harmony with the laws of the state. Terminations should be performed only with the informed written consent of both parents, the woman if she was unmarried, or of the nearest responsible relative if she was under the age of consent. The opinions of two physicians other than the one who was to perform the operation were to be sought, except in the case of rape or incest. One of these consultants should be an obstetrician-gynaecologist, the other should have special competence in the medical area in which the indications for the procedure resided. A conscience clause was included for staff who did not wish to participate in terminations. Therapeutic abortions could be performed when any of the following indications were established:

1 When the continuation of the pregnancy may threaten the life of the woman or seriously impair her health.
2 When continuation of the pregnancy is likely to result in the birth of a child with grave physical deformities or mental retardation.

3 When conception has occurred as a result of rape or incest.

When indicated therapeutic abortions are done, they should be performed during the first trimester of pregnancy. (p. 11)

In June of the same year, the same body of administrators produced another report[6] which was sent to denominational hospitals although it was not generally available. It amplified the former statement while differing from it in several respects. The report began by acknowledging that 'no set of moral generalizations can substitute for individual conscience' (p. 231). It then proceeded to address the question of the soul:

According to the Bible, man's soul is a functional, rather than an objective reality. Man does not have a soul; man is a soul. The soul is not infused in a 'thing' at a specific moment in life such as at the time of conception. It is rather a human capacity to function rationally and morally, achieved fully through growth and development and an increasing investment of human life so that at the time of fetal viability (... approximately 20 weeks) and thereafter, only another human life could balance the scale. (p. 231)

The report then broke more new ground:

The Adventist position does not measure a human being's right to live primarily in terms of happiness, utility, functional viability, or the desires of the mother, the family, or the society, but rather in terms of a human being's uniqueness as a child of the Creator. Humanity is first a God-given endowment, then an achievement. (p. 231)

There followed an acknowledgement that the biblical evidence did not settle the issue, although the Mosaic code did not apply the *lex talionis* to the loss of foetal life. There then appeared a statement which needs to be cited in spite of, or perhaps, because of its opaqueness:

The Adventist position must be conditioned by the Bible's exalted sensitivity for life in general and for human life in particular. This includes a protective regard for what is 'not yet' or 'no longer' functionally human but 'means' (symbolizes) human, as well as for those social institutions such as the family that serve to nurture and preserve 'humanness'. Any act that immediately or potentially threatens such symbolic values, or institutions, must never be carried out lightly. Even when for some reason the requirements of functional human life demand the lesser, real or symbolic human values, this must never be done for trivial or self-serving

reasons or carried out in such a manner as to diminish respect for them lest reverence for the prior human values to which they point be also sacrificed.
(pp. 231–2)

The theoretical preamble concluded by asserting that the church had the responsibility to resist all dehumanizing agencies in society.

There then appeared certain procedural stipulations which were substantially the same as those contained in the previous document, except that the need for consultation with two other licensed physicians was not specified. A list of established indications was provided, which was significant in that it differed from the original statement:

1 When continuation of the pregnancy may threaten the life of the woman or impair her health.
2 When continuation of the pregnancy is likely to result in the birth of a child with physical deformities or mental retardation.
3 When conception has occurred as a result of rape or incest.
4 When the case involves an unwed child under 15 years of age.
5 When for some reason the requirements of functional human life demand the sacrifice of the lesser potential human value.

When indicated interruptions of pregnancy are done, they should be performed as early as possible, preferably during the first trimester of pregnancy.
(pp. 232–3)

The statement is interesting principally in that it provided some kind of rationale for the policy which had been adopted. However, that rationale seemed somewhat at odds with the list of indications which followed. Impairment of the woman's health no longer had to be regarded as 'serious', nor did the physical deformities of the foetus have to be judged 'grave'. Moreover, the statement seemed to allow termination after the first trimester. The official position now also included a provision for statutory rape, and a concluding indication, ambiguously worded, which, if divorced from the confused introductory theoretical statement, might very well have seemed to be a social clause. The internal consistency of the statement might also be challenged with regard to the imperfectly formed foetus. The second indication does not appear immediately compatible with the assertion that an individual's humanity should be defined in terms of its divine origin rather than its function.

Further consultations, following on the Supreme Court decision of 1973, failed to produce any amendment to the original statement.[7] As the controversy subsided after 1973, Adventists occupied a position which was in line with the law but which was more liberal than might have been expected.

When these guidelines first appeared in print, they were accompanied by articles by two senior administrators of the church.[8] Walter Beach acknowledged that the issue was difficult to resolve inasmuch as the scriptural evidence was ambiguous. He was disturbed by the fact that a large proportion of abortions in the United States were being sought by mature married women as an ultimate form of birth control. The Adventist church, he insisted, must assert reverence for human life in an age of dehumanization. Furthermore, it must protect women from the pain of remorse following an abortion sought without reflection. He also asserted that it must reconcile abortion with its view on military service; Adventists should always oppose the wilful destruction of human life.

He was, however, ready to acknowledge that 'extreme circumstances' might justify termination, although he did not specify them. In addition, he believed, the church must always stand ready to forgive a woman who had abused her creative powers, and help to make provision for the care of unwanted babies.

In the second article, Ralph Waddell, then secretary of the church's health department, recognized the problem as a pressing one for Adventist employees and members. His article affirmed the mother's right to an abortion if the pregnancy threatened her life or health. More surprisingly, he argued that, since man was made in God's image, those concerned should ensure that the foetus was perfect, and able to become a 'normal individual'. The presence of some abnormality, he considered, indicated the need for an abortion. Furthermore, he believed that children should be born as the result of the true marriage of two persons; anything short of this arrangement was sinful, and thus pregnancies arising from rape or incest could be justifiably terminated. The implications for pre-marital pregnancies were not explored. Waddell invoked the authority of Ellen White to support his views on the sanctity of life. Some would have found his view that abortions be performed in the first three months before the embryo could 'be considered to possess life in itself', and before it had an identity of its own, difficult to reconcile with his views on the sanctity of life. The title of Waddell's article, 'Abortion Is Not the Answer', in some measure belied its contents.

The 'Spectrum' Debate

Immediately following publication of these guidelines, a complete issue of *Spectrum* was devoted to abortion (vol. 3, no. 2), with contributions from the staff of Loma Linda University, which possessed the denomination's largest medical school. The dominant theme of the discussion was struck by Jack Provonsha, professor of Christian ethics at the University.[9] After rejecting all those points which had at one time or another been taken to demarcate the potentially human from that which was actually so, he insisted on the need to celebrate life, to regard the foetus as a gift from God. The foetus, as a symbol of life, must be protected, he believed, and sacrificed only when it threatened that of which it was a symbol. However, in Provonsha's view an abortion was morally defensible not only when the mother's life was at risk but when her physical, emotional, or social health was endangered. He insisted, then, that an abortion might be performed not simply when continuation threatened life, but when it threatened that which made life human. He viewed the period during which an abortion might be legitimately carried out as a basically technical question, although it should generally be done as early as possible since the symbolic value of the foetus grew daily. He also emphasized the responsibility of the community to assist the woman in coming to a decision, to help her to cope psychologically with termination, or to provide practical support should she decide to continue her pregnancy.

Like Provonsha, Harrison Evans, chairman of the department of psychiatry, maintained an essentially conservative position, arguing that abortion was 'not an innocuous act'.[10] It was the psychiatrist's job, he felt, to help a patient deal with the unwanted pregnancy in a mature and farsighted manner. Learning to cope with such a crisis, he argued, often increased a person's self-esteem; having an abortion tended to produce feelings of remorse. It was, he concluded, frequently in the best interests of the patient to continue the pregnancy, although she would often resist this option initially.

Harold Ziprick, chairman of the department of gynaecology and obstetrics, confirmed that Loma Linda University medical school accepted the General Conference guidelines, and had begun to implement them. He acknowledged both that the medical staff were not unanimous on the issue (which was not surprising since it included many non-Adventists), and that the institution was under some pressure from its constituency to maintain a conservative position, partly to protect the reputation of the Adventist church. However, he was able to confirm that

Relatively few abortions have been performed at the University Medical Center because the obstetrical staff is united in believing that restraint must be exercised, and a fetal life should be taken only to preserve greater values.[11]

He wondered whether the Seventh-day Adventist church should not establish some kind of agency for the adoption of unwanted babies born to Adventist mothers, who could satisfy themselves that their children would be raised in a manner acceptable to them. Furthermore, he suggested that it would be worthwhile to establish a home for single Adventist women who were bearing, or had borne, a child unwillingly. He suspected that opposition to such projects would come from those Adventists who did not wish to acknowledge the existence of such a problem in their ranks. Ziprick's conjecture might help to explain the late entry of Adventists into the field of abortion ethics.

The main dissenting voice in the debate was that of Betty Stirling, then professor of sociology at the University.[12] She argued that the child-bearing practices of any society were ultimately determined by the needs of that society. Religion had traditionally been enlisted to support a society's perception of its needs. The problem which now faced our society was one of culture lag; patterns of behaviour appropriate in an agrarian society were now being followed in contemporary technological society. Many social arrangements, for example in the field of taxation, sustained the presumption in favour of fertility. It must be recognized, she argued, that conventions found in scripture concerning child-bearing were social rather than sacred in origin. She concluded that ultimately the woman must be left to choose abortion if she so wished. The state should both facilitate access to abortion services, and provide sex education so as ultimately to render them unnecessary.

The *Spectrum* debate raised many questions and provided fewer answers. Although opinion was mainly conservative, there was a clear consensus in favour of granting abortions in circumstances which remained somewhat ill-defined.

Seminar on genetic engineering

The most serious official attempt to resolve the problem facing the church in the realm of bioethics since the Supreme Court decision of 1973, was a Seminar on Genetic Engineering, convened in Washington, DC, in February 1979 in response to numerous requests for guidance from Adventist institutions and individuals around the world. Most of the contributors simply elaborated on opinions already expressed in the *Spectrum* debate.

Provonsha argued that a moribund person was still symbolically human, although perhaps not functionally so, and it was thus very important for the moral life of the community that all the treatment reasonably required to keep the patient comfortable should be provided. Similarly, the foetus, another locus of important symbolic value, could be legitimately sacrificed only when it posed a serious threat to that of which it was a symbol.[13]

Ziprick noted his staff's great relief that the final decision was no longer theirs following the Supreme Court ruling. Individual practitioners were, he felt, morally justified in referring a patient to another facility offering abortion services when they wanted to avoid involvement in the procedure themselves. It is clear that at this time the University personnel were still agonizing over the issue.[14]

Gerald Winslow, an Adventist scholar from outside the Loma Linda community at that time, introduced some new dimensions to the discussion. He alluded to the futility of trying to discover the point at which human life begins, since it began in fact on the sixth day of creation, and thereafter had merely been transmitted. It was, therefore, otiose to search for a period in which life could be discontinued without profound regret. The heavy burden of proof for the need for abortion, he said, must be squarely placed on the one seeking it. On the other hand, one must maintain respect for personal autonomy, and honour a decision freely made. The widespread availability of prostaglandins at some time in the future, he felt, would ensure that the decision was a personal one anyway. Winslow took exception to the provision in the General Conference guidelines for aborting abnormal foetuses. It would inevitably involve the sacrifice of normal foetuses, and the erection of criteria of normality, which he found morally distasteful. He lamented the dearth of Adventist scholarship on the matter, and urged those concerned to engage in a continuing debate.[15]

Stirling maintained her liberal stance, arguing that an unwanted pregnancy placed enormous strains not only on the family concerned, but on the wider society which had to provide various services. Furthermore, the enormous problem of overpopulation in the world argued for maintaining abortion in our contraceptive armoury, even though other methods were greatly preferable. She welcomed the development of 'morning-after pills' and self-administered abortifacients as means of solving the practical problem of unwanted pregnancies, although she recognized that these would not necessarily dissolve the moral difficulties. She observed that the General Conference guidelines had failed to solve major difficulties at an institutional level. First, they were more concerned with the legality of the procedure than its morality, she felt. Secondly, many Adventist hospitals appeared to be unaware of their existence. In those institutions electing not to perform abortions, some personnel found themselves compromised when confronted by a legitimate request for termination. Elsewhere a more open abortion policy proved distasteful to some staff, and made the business of employing Adventist personnel extremely difficult. Stirling's observation was important as it related to those denominational hospitals which provided a town with its sole medical facility; there was then considerable pressure on it to provide an abortion service regulated only by the terms of the Supreme Court ruling.

The seminar extended Adventist discussion of the subject without producing any recommendations. The General Conference clearly felt that in this controversial matter wisdom lay in granting to individuals and institutions a high degree of autonomy.[16]

Other published opinion

In the years since the General Conference statement appeared, Adventist literature has regularly carried opinion on the abortion question. The *Review* was quick to print a view which implicitly opposed the General Conference guidelines.[17] Subsequent *Review* articles tended to support an anti-abortion position; for example, one writer was persuaded by the distressing evidence provided by ultrasound technology of the behaviour of a foetus about to be aborted.[18] A more recent editorial attempted to do justice to what was perceived to be a wide spectrum of opinion within Adventism, and speculated that most Adventists actually would agree with the guidelines produced by the General Conference. It further observed that

Our church leaders have noted that neither the Bible nor Ellen White say anything definite about elective abortion. They have felt that where Inspiration is silent, we should not legislate. Because of this silence in the inspired writings, there is a broad spectrum of opinion on the subject in the Adventist Church.[19]

Ellen White's authority was invoked, however, to emphasize a major principle in the debate: 'In matters of conscience the soul must be left untrammeled. No one is to ... judge for another, or to prescribe his duty. God gives every soul freedom to think, and to follow his own convictions'.[20] The editorial attracted considerable criticism for maintaining an open stance on the question.

The most eloquent rejoinder, from Richard Müller, a European Adventist scholar, appeared in *Ministry*, a magazine for clergy. He produced an impressive array of evidence, particularly from the Old Testament, to show that personhood begins at conception. It included a careful reinterpretation of the passage in Exodus 21:22–23, often used to demonstrate the lesser value of foetal life. He cited Ellen White's comment that 'All acts of injustice that tend to shorten life ... are, to a greater or lesser degree, violations of the sixth commandment.'[21] His article concluded with a call to the church community to help to solve the abortion problem:

The church has often desperately failed to help people in need. If the church says No to abortion, then I hope that every member of this church may live up to the caring, loving and serving spirit of the Lord. Then we will be willing to help in the various situations that bring suffering, inconvenience and hardship to individuals and families.[22]

A similar insistence on the fact that abortion was a community problem came from Provonsha, also in *Ministry*.[23] The community, he argued, should be prepared to pay the cost, financial, emotional, and social, of providing a viable alternative to abortion. His case centred on the need to care for the marginal members of society in order to prevent society itself from becoming dehumanized. *Ministry* has maintained a conservative position on the abortion question, apart from those articles which formally opened the debate in Adventism in 1971. Daniel Augsburger, an Adventist church historian, cited biblical and clinical evidence to show that the foetus had its own identity.[24] He opposed abortions in the case of pre-marital pregnancies since he believed that men and women should learn sexual responsibility. He hesitated to recommend, however, that a woman bear a child conceived as a result of a sexual offence or likely to be born handicapped. He insisted that the role of the clergy was to clarify issues rather than to usurp the authority of individual conscience.[25]

Most contributors to the magazine for young Adventists, *Insight*, have tended to oppose abortion. By reference to the developmental stages of the embryo, several writers pointed out that a distinct human identity was unfolding often before the woman discovered that she was pregnant, and thus abortion was not an option.[26] Several saw adoption as an alternative preferable to abortion, particularly through an Adventist adoption agency.[27] One writer, more open to the possibility of abortion, reckoned that in the case of an unwanted pregnancy there existed only a choice between evils; he quoted Thielicke approvingly, 'Whatever we do, we incur guilt.'[28] It might be argued that anti-abortion articles published in *Insight* were as much an attempt to discourage pre-marital sex as a condemnation of abortion.

Other Adventist magazines adopted a generally conservative position, while failing to achieve unanimity on the definition of exceptional cases and the desirability of adoption. It is undoubtedly true that Adventists with more liberal views on abortion would feel less inclination to publicize them, and that editors would be reluctant to publish them. *Liberty* has reported several times on the political dimensions of abortion.[29] Attention focused on legislative attempts to restrict public funding of abortion services, thus enshrining one religious view of abortion in civil law. In an important article in *Spectrum*, Winslow considered the influence of the principles of respect for human life, human autonomy, and justice on the question of abortion.[30] He concluded that there was a strong moral presumption against abortion, and that a heavy burden of proof lay on those who wished to terminate pre-natal life. Adequate grounds did exist, in his opinion, notably in the cases of rape and serious threat to the mother's life or health, but he was unhappy with the disposal of defective foetuses. The proper solution to the problem seemed to him to involve the cultivation of sensitive consciences in the context of the prevailing open legislation. He insisted that his article was not a call for legislation on the part of the church administration, although he did find it odd that Adventists had established a position on trivial matters like card-playing while leaving weightier matters unresolved. He again exhorted Adventist scholars to engage in serious discourse on the matter.

Several books written by Adventists have included consideration of abortion. Charles Wittschiebe was inclined to inform rather than advise in his *God Invented Sex*, published in 1974. Similarly, John Knight, in *What a Married Couple Should Know about Sex* (1979), was content to restrict his comments to the medical aspects of the procedure. It was, he said, a safe procedure but one which could increase the likelihood of miscarriage in a subsequent pregnancy. Most women, he thought, experienced relief rather than guilt after an abortion. He averred that availability of abortion increased sexual irresponsibility but offered no further comment on the moral aspects of the issue.

Kubo, in his influential *Theology and Ethics of Sex* (1980), argued against the adoption of any extreme attitudes. Neither those who ascribed absolute value to the foetus from the time of conception nor those who refused to recognize any problems until a specified time in gestation involved themselves in the agonizing which was an ineradicable part of questions of life and death. Although there must be a presumption in favour of preserving foetal life, he acknowledged that social and emotional factors were just as relevant to the decision to abort as physical ones. He further argued that views on the status of the foetus should be informed by notions concerning death. Just as death was widely defined in terms of the cessation of electrical activity in the brain, though breathing continued, so it might be argued that a foetus had human life without its being classified as a human being. Whatever the ethical strategies adopted, he concluded, abortion was at best a necessary evil.

A similar conclusion was reached by James Londis, a prominent pastor, in his slim volume *Abortion: Mercy or Murder?* (1980). It also resembled Kubo's work in that it drew on a wide range of Protestant and Catholic thought. Londis' purpose was not to persuade the reader of the rightness of a particular course of action, but to inform the enquirer of the complexity of the issue. He believed that, although there must be weighty reasons to justify the destruction of a foetus, it was naive to assume that carrying a pregnancy to term was in all circumstances morally preferable to abortion. The dominant principle was, he believed, that, after all consultation, the mother's right to make the final decision was absolute.

There are certainly those Adventists who feel that the 'pro-life' position has not had a fair hearing among Adventists. Carsten Johnsen, a European academic, in his self-published *God – the Situation Ethicist*, which appeared in the late 1970s, criticized the guidelines produced by the General Conference. He asserted that we could not in good conscience perform abortions in cases of suspected abnormality because that would inevitably involve the sacrifice of normal foetuses. Moreover, handicapped children often brought fulfilment to parents despite their early fears. Hardship and sacrifice were in his opinion an inescapable part of life. He believed that abortion on the ground of rape was morally unacceptable because even a child conceived in this fashion had the right to a chance at life. Similarly, where the life of the mother was jeopardized by continued pregnancy, abortion was not justified. Ultimately it was God's prerogative to dispose of life. Johnsen's work was neither widely circulated nor influential, but it did represent the view of a minority who feared that their co-religionists adopted too cavalier an approach to the problem.[31]

Although Johnsen's view was an extreme one, opinion published in Adventist literature had been markedly more conservative than the thinking represented in the General Conference guidelines.

The reasons for this can perhaps be found in an analysis of actual practice among Adventists.

Practice among Adventists

Institutional practice

A survey, conducted for the purpose of this research, of practice in the fifty-six hospitals run by Adventists in the United States, had a response rate of 36 per cent. Those responses gave the impression of a marked reluctance to divulge statistical information on abortion procedures. There are no particular grounds, however, for concluding that institutions were withholding information to conceal a level of abortions unacceptably high to members. The risk of being involved in costly litigation makes most American physicians extremely cautious about disclosing information about their professional conduct.

The survey did show it to be common practice for Adventist hospitals to employ obstetricians and gynaecologists who were not church members, and that these were not infrequently appointed to lead their departments. Such a state of affairs would tend to dilute the Adventist ethos of denominational hospitals. Karel Dobbelaere has shown this to be the case in Roman Catholic hospitals in Belgium.[32] The fact that many physicians run their private practices from offices in Adventist hospitals further increases the risk of dilution. So too did the rapid expansion of the Adventist medical empire in the United States. Adventist hospitals have now been brought under the umbrella of Adventist Health Systems Inc., currently one of the largest health-care corporations in the United States. A significant number of new facilities have been taken over recently by that organization. No doubt the distinctive Adventist character of some of the church's hospitals has come under threat as the enterprise has grown larger, but in the area of abortion practice there are some safeguards. Hospital boards require physicians to follow codes of practice, which often stipulate that opinions of colleagues must be sought where abortion is contemplated. Those policies tended to be more liberal the further west the hospitals were situated, although attitudes do not simply reflect geographical location. Some hospitals in the east and south provided no abortion service whatever; some recorded only a couple of terminations in a calendar year, while one facility performed three abortions in a total of 5,205 admissions to the obstetric-gynaecological department. Further west, some hospitals stipulated only that individual physicians should not terminate pregnancies after the first three months;[33] one Adventist institution in the western United States had a rate of one abortion to every nine admissions to the obstetric facility.[34]

Before the abortion debate in the United States grew in intensity, Adventist policy-makers were relieved of the burden of resolving such difficult moral questions, by state laws. The Supreme Court decision of 1973 changed all that. The fact that the General Conference guidelines appeared before 1973 indicated that some Adventist hospitals were encountering difficulties because of their location in states which introduced legislative reform independently. Those guidelines conformed quite closely to the model code produced by the American Law Institute, and showed the church responding promptly, and some would say precipitately and uncritically, to the climate of opinion. The public expectation that physicians provide abortion on demand no doubt placed Adventist personnel under pressure, which was in time felt by non-medical administrators at the General Conference.

Public opinion has of course changed considerably in the intervening years, and it seems likely that relatively fewer abortions are now being performed in Adventist hospitals than a decade ago. If this is so, it may reflect political and prudential considerations rather than a change in moral posture. Given the strength of feeling against abortion currently in the United States, there would be wisdom in the church's scaling down its services to those seeking termination. One Adventist medical administration unit narrowly escaped damage when a non-Adventist abortion clinic housed in the same building was bombed by 'pro-life' campaigners.

A survey of abortion practice carried out, for the purposes of this research, among Adventist hospitals beyond the United States offered an instructive comparison.[35] Most of these hospitals were situated in the Third World and operated stricter policies. Some of the hospitals were in countries where abortion was still illegal. Even where abortion was permitted by law, abortions were performed generally only where there were pressing medical indications, particularly where the life of the mother was threatened. By no means all of these hospitals had the equipment to allow early detection of foetal defects. Some hospitals simply refused to perform abortions on the grounds that it was an immoral act. A probable explanation of this difference in practice was that western physicians who were attracted to mission service were generally more conservative in their views. Further, it seems clear that Adventists in the Third World perceived behavioural and doctrinal matters in more clear-cut terms than their western co-religionists.

However, Winslow's suspicion that abortions still took place in Adventist hospitals for 'trivial reasons'[36] was confirmed in confidential correspondence with medical administrators. The apparent discrepancy between the generally conservative recommendations for personal behaviour, which have appeared in Adventist publications, and the somewhat more open stance of Adventist institutions, needs further investigation.

Personal practice

Ryder and Westoff noted in the 1965 National Fertility Survey that questions on attitudes to abortion yielded reliable data, but that many women were reluctant to admit having had an abortion. This would probably apply to a group like Adventists where the morality of the practice was still in doubt, and where, therefore, considerable guilt attached to interrupting a pregnancy. There can be no doubt that Adventist women do seek abortions. One survey of Adventist counsellors showed that church members figured among those seeking advice on abortion.[37] Charles Wittschiebe's counselling experience led him to conclude that 'a disquieting number of our young women' were resorting to abortion.[38] Another Adventist college professor testified to the existence of the problem among young Adventist women.[39]

The survey of abortion practice in Adventist hospitals provided no useful insights into the actual numbers of church members seeking terminations. Indeed, an Adventist woman seeking an abortion might use a non-denominational facility in order to conceal her action.

A recent survey of the attitudes of a representative sample of 712

Adventists, on a range of social issues, revealed considerable diversity of opinion on the subject of abortion. The proposition 'Abortion is never an option for terminating a pregnancy' drew the responses indicated in table 8.1.

Table 8.1 Responses to proposition that abortion should never be an option (%)

	Disagree	Agree	Undecided
Youth	38	35	27
Mothers	43	41	16
Fathers	50	35	15

Source: R. L. Dudley and M. G. Dudley, 'Adventist Values: Flying High?', *Ministry*, April 1985, p. 7.

Each grouping contained a majority in favour of retaining abortion as an option, and at the same time a proportion of undecided respondents sufficient to cancel out that majority. Although the proposition contained an extreme sentiment, it did reveal the ambivalence of Adventists on the subject.

In the absence of reliable information on the actual practice of Adventist women, the major option available is to examine those various factors which would influence church members in the abortion decision.

The general institutional context

Socio-economic factors

It has already been demonstrated that Adventists as a group are occupationally ambitious, and that the attainment of a good education has a high priority among them. An unplanned pregnancy might very well seriously disrupt the plans of a young couple who both had high vocational aspirations. Similarly, an Adventist couple in a higher age category, who wished to provide a denominational education for their children, might find that goal jeopardized by an unplanned pregnancy. An unmarried Adventist woman might incline towards an abortion if she felt it to be in the interests of children legitimately conceived in the future.

There is considerable evidence to show that those who use birth-control techniques efficiently are more likely to resort to abortion in the case of contraception failure, than those who do not.[40] Ryder and Westoff have demonstrated a positive correlation between the use of the pill and sterilization, and favourable attitudes towards abortion.[41] Impressionistic evidence suggests that Adventists employ both contraceptive methods widely. An uncritical attitude towards the intra-uterine device, which some would regard as an abortifacient, might also indicate a willingness to consider the option of abortion seriously in a family crisis.

American sociologist, Kristin Luker, has produced profiles of activists in the abortion campaign; the average 'pro-choice' campaigner was aged 44, married to a professional, herself had a college degree, was employed outside the home, had two children, and a family income of $50,000. The average 'pro-life' activist was married with three or more children, had only a high-school education, was not employed outside the home and had a family income of $30,000.[42] Purely according to the criterion of socio-economic status, Adventist women would certainly seem to figure as candidates for abortion in the event of an unwanted pregnancy. However, the important criterion of religious affiliation must also figure in the assessment.

Religion

There is a division of opinion about the precise relationship between religious affiliation and readiness to terminate an unwanted pregnancy. Potts, Diggory and Peel have observed that, in an emergency, individuals seek abortions regardless of their own religious convictions or the official position of their church.[43] Steinhoff confirmed that matters of expediency would overrule matters of principle.[44] Potts and his colleagues concluded that the main effect of religion was not to stop abortion but to create problems of conscience.

Callahan, however, has argued that the more devout and informed a woman is, the more likely she is to reject an abortion.[45] Similarly, Ryder and Westoff's research led them to believe that 'In general, the more actively a woman participates in religious services, the more opposed she is to abortion.'[46] It seems likely that Adventist women would rate relatively highly on scales of religious devotion based on church attendance, and therefore that their set of religious commitments would encourage them to continue an unwanted pregnancy. It is important to consider whether there is anything in the nature of Adventism which would discourage a member from seeking an abortion.

Seventh-day Adventist theology

The Adventist doctrine of conditional immortality is clearly relevant to the abortion debate, although surprisingly few writers have alluded to it. Adventists believe that God only is immortal; there is no conscious entity which survives an individual's death. They believe that at death a believer 'goes down into the grave there to lie unconscious until the resurrection day'.[47] The resurrection of the dead involves some sort of reconstitution of the individual, and conferral of immortality on believers at the second advent. In Catholic theology, a soul is infused into the embryo at conception, and it, as an inheritor of original sin, must not be allowed to perish without baptism. In contrast, Adventists believe neither that there exists a separate entity called a soul, nor that baptism is essential to salvation.[48] They prefer to say that man 'becomes a soul' rather than that he 'possesses a soul'. Soul is therefore understood to mean both life and individuality.[49] This, then, allows them to say that 'A new soul comes into existence every time a child is born',[50] which might seem to make abortion morally permissible.

At the same time, however, this holistic view of man, which is an important part of Adventist theology, means that a soul cannot exist independently of a body; possessing a body is part of what it means to be a soul. Thus, it could be argued that since a body with a unique genetic inheritance begins to form at conception, so a soul exists from that point albeit in elemental form, and thus absolute value should be attached to it.[51] For our purposes, it is important simply to note that the Adventist doctrine of the soul is not sufficiently elaborated to settle the abortion issue in the minds of its members, nor has it figured significantly in denominational discussions of the issue.

Adventist doctrine overlaps with the abortion issue at several other points. Strong belief in an imminent second advent might, for example, lead some to ignore the justification for abortion on the ground of spiralling world population, which for others is compelling. The strong Adventist emphasis on law might encourage some members to avoid abortion for fear of transgressing the sixth commandment. A common argument in favour of termination is that in the evolutionary process the body has developed a mechanism for aborting abnormal foetuses spontaneously. It is then asserted that induced abortion is only an extension of that process. As creationists, Adventists are unlikely to find that argument convincing. They are more likely to believe that it is the prerogative of God to dispose of human life. It is certain that many members would identify widespread abortion as evidence of the evils attending the climactic 'last days' of human history.

Potts, Diggory, and Peel have noted that members of fundamentalist groups are inclined to reject abortion except on strictly therapeutic grounds.[52] As has already been suggested, the epithet 'fundamentalist' applies only in certain respects to Adventism. And so it becomes clear that Adventist theology, although certainly conservative in nature, is by no means sufficiently clearly defined to preclude the election of abortion in a crisis. Indeed, the experience of the Roman Catholic church is that, even where doctrine is abundantly clear, large numbers of the faithful choose to ignore it when in great personal difficulty.[53]

The ethos of Adventism

Apart from the specific doctrines of Adventism, the general tone of the movement is likely to have an influence on members' reactions to an unwanted pregnancy. Adventism does encourage its members to cultivate great moral sensitivity, which seems likely to produce below-average abortion rates among members. Many would undoubtedly regard abortion as a sinful act. Thus for many Adventists a dominant reaction after abortion is likely to be guilt rather than relief. The anticipation of post-abortal guilt might well be sufficient to encourage some to carry the pregnancy to term. The strong emphasis in Adventism on the maintenance of good physical health as a religious duty might incline a woman to pursue the natural, if onerous, path of an unwanted pregnancy rather than undergo an unnatural procedure with possible unforeseen complications. Moreover, some Adventists would be inclined to regard an unwanted pregnancy as God's will. This perhaps would be particularly true of unmarried women who might see a pregnancy as a punishment, or at least a discipline, sent by God. Potts, Diggory and Peel also noted a correlation between a willingness to terminate a pregnancy and a propensity to take risks.[54] While Adventists not uncommonly take risks or 'act in faith', as they would see it, this tendency is unlikely to extend to the moral side of life, where they would incline to caution.

Bernard Häring, the eminent Catholic moral theologian, has observed that, in the United States, legality is often taken to confer moral rightness on a particular piece of behaviour.[55] Adventists, particularly in the United States, have generally been very careful in performing their civic responsibilities and in maintaining solidarity with the surrounding society. There is the possibility therefore that the legalization of abortion has shaped Adventists' perception of the morality of the procedure.

The influence of Adventist publications

Although opinion expressed in the *Review*, *Ministry*, and *Insight* will have been read by large numbers, perhaps a majority, of American Adventists, many have remained unaware that the church has addressed the issue of abortion. It was therefore highly significant that the subject should have been treated in the *Sabbath School Lessons* for 1–7 August 1982. This publication, the basis for Bible study held weekly in Adventist churches the world over, usually confines itself to matters theological and devotional. From July to August 1982, Adventists were encouraged to reflect on a wide range of social and moral issues in a way which was quite unprecedented. The content of the section on abortion was therefore likely to exert considerable influence on the thinking of rank-and-file Adventists. While acknowledging that the Adventist church had not yet taken any official position, and that the Bible offered no direct counsel, it struck a decidedly conservative note. Observing that the early Christians regarded abortion as homicide, it continued:

Children are a gift from the Lord (Ps 127:3). He gives to every new person life and all of its necessities (Acts 17:25) from the moment of conception. Life is a divine gift. The Bible often speaks of the conception of a child as a revelation of God's power and grace . (See Gen 15:1 – 4; 25:21; 1 Sam 1:11) God said to Jeremiah, 'Before I formed thee in the belly I knew thee; and before thou camest forth out of the womb I sanctified thee, and I ordained thee a prophet unto the nations' (Jer. 1:5). Very powerfully is this expressed also in the biblical story of the conception of John the Baptist (Luke 1:13–17). One should not look upon these examples of pre-natal dignity and calling as exceptions. They teach us that God Himself is the Giver of life and of human personhood, which should therefore be held sacred and treated with awe and respect.[56]

In so far as members at all apprehend the church to be recommending a position on abortion at a personal level, they probably perceive it to be a conservative position. The General Conference guidelines would, however, certainly create a dissonance in the minds of those who are aware of them. Whether or not the Adventist woman who is unwillingly pregnant heeds the generally conservative counsel given is another matter.

Winslow believed that

a significant proportion of the Adventist membership holds views somewhat more conservative than the mainstream of published statements, while much of Adventist practice could be characterized as more liberal than the published statements.[57]

Many American denominations have recently undertaken to provide support for women unwillingly pregnant as part of their anti-abortion positions. Pregnant women anywhere in the country can have the benefit of free medical care, room and board for the duration of their pregnancy, and adoption services. Such help was available in a centre run by an independent group of Adventists in Washington State, which has received funding from the church organization but is separate from it. It provides a place where unmarried women, mostly Adventists, can spend the latter part of their pregnancy, face up to life as a single parent, or consider the matter of adoption. They can ensure, if they wish, that church members adopt their child. The centre is in itself an acknowledgement that the matter of illegitimacy must be taken seriously in the church.

Conclusion

Abortion is one of the most commonly performed medical operations in many parts of the world today, particularly in the west, and it is unlikely that some Adventists will not avail themselves of this simple solution to a profound personal crisis. It also seems probable that some Adventist hospitals have performed considerable numbers of elective abortions in the past fifteen years or so.

The following extract from a letter from a senior church administrator provides an explanation for the church's official silence on the matter:

The issues involved and the differences of opinion are so great that it was thought best not to endeavor to establish an official position. There is also the current volatile political situation surrounding this question and the church does not wish to become embroiled ...[58]

The church, it seems, feared the debilitating effects of a dispute within its own ranks, and of involvement in a wider highly politicized moral argument. It has deemed the maintenance of an official silence the best way of pursuing its main task of proclamation of the Christian gospel. Moreover, it has wished to protect the integrity of individual conscience. In these respects Adventism has differed little from many other Protestant churches. It does, however, seem to be more liberal than some other sectarian groups. The activism of right-wing Christian groups recently has marked a departure from the general tendency of the churches to allow the issue to be resolved in the wider social debate.

With the authorities to which they normally look, silent on the matter, Adventists must consult their own consciences. It seems likely that church members will, in practice, adopt today yesterday's secular norms. That may embarrass the church somewhat when, as in the present case, there is a conservative reaction in public opinion.

The sort of pragmatic approach adopted by Adventists over the abortion question provides a flexibility which allows them to respond quickly to situations like that involving gang rape of Vietnamese refugees. It will also satisfy those Adventists, particularly in the west, who value highly the freedom to choose which Adventism confers on them. It will be less to the liking of a not inconsiderable number of church members who wish to be catechized in a sanctified way of life, which will eventuate in eternal salvation.

9 · Early Adventist women: in the shadow of the prophetess

Introduction

Both members and observers of the Seventh-day Adventist church acknowledge the profound influence exerted on the movement by its charismatic leader, Ellen G. White. Robin Theobald rightly judged that

> there are good grounds for doubting whether, in the absence of Mrs White, this particular remnant of the Millerite movement could have overcome the pronounced fissiparous tendencies which typically attend an apparent disconfirmation of prophecy ...[1]

Ellen White's voluminous writings have continued to shape Adventist faith and practice to a considerable extent to the present day. The fact that a woman has had such an enormous impact on the development of Adventism raises some important questions. Did her presence as a church leader help to dissolve prejudice against women assuming positions of responsibility? To what extent was her role restricted by the social constraints of the times? Did her presence as leader have a feminizing effect on doctrine, behaviour, and organization? Some awareness of the social context in which Ellen White lived is vital to the resolution of such questions.

The role of women in the United States

Americans in the nineteenth century shared the view that women should be unassertive and devoted to the moral welfare of their families. Theirs was to cultivate piety and master 'the housewifely arts'. Women were, however, encouraged by popular magazines of the day to exercise an 'influence ... paramount to authority' by employing a 'decorous deviousness'.[2] Exaltation of the maternal role characterized the whole century, and began to waver only as it came to a close. For example, the education of a small minority of wealthy young ladies took place in colleges committed to the formation of better wives and mothers. Only much later in the century were institutions founded with the goal of cultivating in their female pupils an awareness of contemporary society.

A significant number of middle-class women involved themselves in the movement for the abolition of slavery as early as the 1830s, the most celebrated being the Grimké sisters. The denial of admission to duly elected American women delegates at the World Anti-Slavery Convention in London, in 1840, alerted many women to this more subtle form of oppression. The principal outcome was the Seneca Falls Convention of 1848, often regarded as the birth of the American feminist movement, where strong demands were voiced for an expansion of women's rights in many areas. In the *ante bellum* period, feminists were divided on whether priority should be given to the emancipation of the slaves: radicals believed that the campaigns to liberate women and slaves should proceed contemporaneously. Experience in the abolitionist movement certainly taught women important organizational and political skills which were to be immensely valuable when the struggle for women's rights began in earnest.

The ideological division discernible in the feminist movement before the Civil War became more pronounced afterwards. In May 1869, the more radical element in the feminist movement, led by Mrs Elizabeth Stanton and Miss Susan Anthony, formed the National Woman Suffrage Association. In addition to the vote, it sought, among other things, liberalization of the divorce laws. Moderates responded by establishing the American Woman Suffrage Association in the same year. It confined itself to obtaining votes for women, and that by less aggressive means than those employed by the 'National'. Both succeeded in raising public awareness of the matter in different ways, and ultimately they merged to form the National American Woman Suffrage Association in 1890, by which time much of the stridency had gone out of the campaign. In the meantime, many women devoted their energies to the temperance movement, which flourished in the last quarter of the century.

The struggle by American women to secure their rights was somewhat in advance of that of their British sisters. Western states, like California in 1911, were the first to grant women a vote at a time when the suffragist cause was emerging from a period in the doldrums. Female suffrage became a prominent political issue but one which was soon to be overshadowed by American involvement in the war.

The role of women in the churches

It is difficult to escape the view that in nineteenth-century America, piety was regarded as part of women's nature in a way that it was not for men; for a woman to be irreligious was somehow for her to lose her sexual identity.[3] Certainly, the evangelistic campaigns of the Second Great Awakening, which lasted from approximately 1795 to 1830, seem to have attracted a majority of women. Membership of revivalist and millennialist groups created certain tensions, however, for female members. It was widely believed that, if the promise of the Republic were to be fulfilled, then it was important to pursue virtue. The role of women in fostering puritan ideals in the home therefore became of paramount importance. On the other hand, membership of new religious groupings offered women a partial escape from male authority. Faced with what they took to be divine imperatives, some women found the confidence, on occasion, to defy the expectations of their husbands. Furthermore, women gained an opportunity to exercise their gifts in a public context, notably in the weekly prayer meetings.

Perhaps the best example of this came in the Holiness Movement, which had its roots in Methodism in the 1830s, and culminated in the widespread revival of 1857–8. Many women – like Phoebe Palmer, who emerged as the leading light of the movement – enjoyed the freedom to speak to mixed groups on devotional themes. Hardesty, Dayton, and Dayton have suggested that the attraction of the movement to women lay partly in its emphasis on experience, and the view that the Holy Spirit bestowed spiritual gifts on persons regardless of formal qualification.[4] As the century progressed, it grew increasingly acceptable for women to address mixed audiences, and it became inevitable that the mainline religious organizations would, sooner or later, have to face the issue of the participation of women in their formal services. In most communions it was later rather than sooner, although both Methodists and Episcopalians made some small concessions before the turn of the century.

By this time, however, many women in the churches had channelled their energies in another direction. From the 1860s onwards, groups of women in many communions organized themselves to sponsor, quite independently, missionary activity of many kinds. Brereton and Klein have recorded that, by 1882, the sixteen major women's missionary societies had raised 6 million dollars, mostly via small contributions, and sent out 694 single women missionaries, and that by 1900 these societies were supporting 856 single women missionaries, 389 missionaries' wives, 96 doctors, and numerous medical, educational, and welfare institutions the world over.[5] Not only did these women foster missionary activity abroad, but they devoted themselves to the task of christianizing and Americanizing the immigrants who flooded into the nation's cities in the last part of the century.

Barbara Welter characterized the years 1800–60 as the period of 'the feminization of American religion'.[6] She averred that as women, for various socio-economic reasons, made up an increasingly large majority in congregations, religion became 'more domesticated, more emotional, more soft and accommodating – in a word, more "feminine"'.[7] She observed that the harshness of Calvinistic teaching was mitigated by an emphasis on Jesus Christ as the exemplar of meekness, and the sacrificial victim, a model with which the subjugated woman could readily identify. Be that as it may, men remained firmly in control of church hierarchies.

Ellen White on the role of women

The maternal role

In conformity with the spirit of nineteenth-century America, Ellen White laid heavy emphasis on the importance of the mother's role. Hundreds of references in the published works of Ellen White describe, in Talmudic detail, the role of the devoted mother;[8] the role of the father attracts much less attention.[9] Her writings are replete with references to the sacredness of the task:

The mother is queen of her household. She has in her power the molding of her children's characters, that they may be fitted for the higher, immortal life. An angel could not ask for a higher mission; for in doing this work she is doing service for God.[10]

Not only was the mother to care for the religious and moral training of her children, she was responsible for their practical and social education.[11] Moreover, the mother was to make the home a place where the father delighted to be, a place from which he could draw personal resources. The profile of the devoted wife was also drawn in considerable detail by Ellen White.[12] In short, the Adventist woman was to be a model of domestic piety.

While Ellen White regarded motherhood as a privilege and set extremely high ideals for it, she did not have a highly romanticized view of the role. She was well aware of its frustrations:

Her days are occupied with a round of little duties, all calling for patient effort, for self-control, for tact, wisdom and self-sacrificing love; yet she cannot boast of what she has done as any great achievement. She has only kept things in the home running smoothly; often weary and perplexed, she has tried to speak kindly to the children, to keep them busy and happy, and to guide the little feet in the right path. She feels that she has accomplished nothing. But it is not so.[13]

She found that the mother's lot was often rendered more difficult by the uncomprehending attitude of the father, who believed that, since she had not 'acted the merchant' nor tilled the soil, she had 'done nothing to make her weary'.[14] Ellen White believed that the role of the mother even exceeded that of the minister in importance.[15] 'We may safely say', she concluded, 'that the distinctive duties of woman are more sacred, more holy, than those of man'.[16] Reflections of the contemporary notions of 'influence', and female moral and spiritual superiority are clearly evident in her work.

Ellen White's high estimation of the maternal role may seem difficult to reconcile with her own practice as a mother. She and her husband were sometimes separated from their children for long periods:

We left him [Henry Nichols White] in Brother Howland's family ... We knew that they could take better care of Henry than we could while journeying with him and it was for his good that he should have a steady place ... It was hard parting with my child. His sad little face, as I left him, was before me night and day; yet in the strength of the Lord I put him out of my mind, and sought to do others good. Brother Howland's family had the whole charge of Henry for five years, without any recompense, and provided him all his clothing, except a present I would bring him once a year, as Hannah did Samuel.[17]

The other surviving children, Edson and Willie, had similar experiences, although not for such protracted periods.[18]

It is not without significance that a large proportion of Ellen White's comments about child-rearing in general, and motherhood in particular, were written after 1885, many of them long after.[19] This was over thirty years after the birth of their first son, Henry; the two surviving sons had already reached adulthood, and Ellen White herself was over 50 years old. This might lead us to several conclusions, one being that she had largely forgotten the conflict between her own roles as missionary and mother. Alternatively, it is possible that the profound regret she clearly felt at the childhood experiences of her sons[20] led her to caution other mothers about the dangers of neglecting their offspring. She was obviously very perplexed by the moral lapses of Henry and Edson in later life.

However, a more satisfactory explanation of the dissonance between her theory and practice regarding child-rearing is to be found elsewhere. Her four sons were all born relatively soon after the 'Great Disappointment' of October 1844; even after that date Adventists maintained a lively sense of Christ's imminent return. It is not difficult to understand that, under the influence of such a belief, she gave priority to heralding the advent, rather than to caring for young children, whom, she assumed, would never grow to adulthood. Why, in the light of such a conviction, the Whites should have decided to have a family is another matter, although it has already been shown that celibacy, then the only sure way of avoiding pregnancy, was thought by Ellen White to create numerous domestic problems. Ellen White found the separation from her children enforced by her missionary work both distressing and obligatory:

Again I was called to deny self for the good of souls. We must sacrifice the company of our little Henry, and go forth to give ourselves unreservedly to the work. It was a severe trial, yet I dared not let my child stand in the way of our duty.[21]

Ellen White's experience was by no means unique among women religious leaders in the nineteenth century. Lydia Sexton, the first woman to be licensed as a preacher by the Ohio Quarterly Conference of the United Brethren Church, expressed sentiments identical to Ellen White's when she was severely criticized for being absent on a preaching trip when her son died.[22] It is well known also that the son of Mary Baker Eddy was reared by others.

It seems logical to conclude from the foregoing that Ellen White did not give counsel to parents in the earlier years of her ministry because she was engaged in the urgent evangelization of a non-adventist adult public. With the rise of a generation who had imbibed Adventism with their mothers' milk, it became clear that formal education and general socialization would be important means of adding members to the church. Furthermore, by the 1880s, the sense of urgency, which had characterized the infancy of Adventism, had somewhat diminished; the church was beginning to become institutionalized, and it was to be expected that it should turn its attention to more long-term concerns. Neither must it be forgotten that Ellen White's belief in her divinely appointed role allowed her, in all good conscience, to give counsel which was somewhat at variance with her own experience of motherhood.

Women as ministers

While the sacralization of the maternal role was prominent in Ellen White's writing, she clearly came to believe that women had an important missionary role to play beyond the task of successfully initiating the next generation into the faith. By the late 1870s, articles were coming from her pen exhorting Adventist women to extend their missionary work beyond neighbourhood welfare work to a more public form of ministry:

It was Mary that first preached a risen Jesus ... If there were twenty women where now there is one, who would make this holy mission their cherished work, we should see many more converted to the truth. The refining, softening influence of Christian women is needed in the great work of preaching the truth.[23]

A further article suggested that the gospel work undertaken by women should not differ significantly from that done by men:

Woman, if she wisely improves her time and her faculties, relying upon God for wisdom and strength, may stand on an equality with her husband as adviser, counselor, companion, and co-worker, and yet lose none of her womanly grace or modesty.[24]

In a personal letter she affirmed her view that it was 'not always men who [were] best adapted to the successful management of a church'.[25]

The expression of such sentiments was, however, the exception rather than the rule at this stage of her ministry. It was more common for her to encourage women members to engage in a more domestic form of proselytism. It was not until the last few years of the century that she began to expatiate on the importance of the role which women had to play in public ministry. She regretted the fact that they had been content to leave such matters to their menfolk.[26]

A number of factors probably contributed to this new emphasis in her counsel. It was undoubtedly, in part, a response to the growing participation of women in public affairs. In addition, Ellen White was greatly impressed by the work of evangelization performed by women, because of a lack of manpower, in Australia, where she spent the 1890s.[27] Another undoubted influence was Mrs S. M. I. Henry, who was the national evangelist of the Woman's Christian Temperance Union when she joined the Adventist church in 1896. Their correspondence reveals that Ellen White found the social influence wielded by women through the WCTU very impressive.[28]

Whatever the reasons may be, the evidence that Ellen White came to favour innovation regarding the role of women in the church is undeniable. In 1898, she wrote: 'When a great and decisive work is to be done, God chooses men and women to do this work, and it will feel the loss if the talents of both are not combined.'[29] Her counsel became more explicit: 'There are women who should labor in the gospel ministry. In many respects they would do more good than the ministers who neglect to visit the flock of God.'[30] She encouraged such women to seek the proper educational preparation for their work.[31] Furthermore, she insisted that women be paid a fair wage for their work,[32] a wage which might legitimately be paid from tithe sources, normally reserved for payment of ministry.[33] A measure of the strength of her feeling on the subject was her threat to withhold her own tithe money to pay those women whom she felt were being exploited by male church leaders.[34] She believed that, although the desire to conserve denominational funds may have been laudable, the attempt to make women bear the whole of the financial burden was unjust. Such sentiments were particularly significant coming as they did from one, who, together with her husband, had introduced 'systematic benevolence' (an important part of which was tithing) into Adventism. It perhaps should be added, in passing, that it is not unusual for charismatic leaders to contravene the very norms they have established, and thereby confirm their own authority.

By the turn of the century, Ellen White was clearly advocating that qualified women assume a public ministry:

We believe fully in church organization, but in nothing that is to prescribe the precise way in which we must work; for all minds are not reached by the same methods ... Each person has his own lamp to keep burning ... Teach this, my sister. You have many ways opened before you. Address the crowd whenever you can; hold every jot of influence you can ... Every man and every woman has a work to do for the Master.[35]

She argued until her death that Adventists should entertain greater flexibility concerning the allocation of roles in their church. Women would often find easier access to families with the gospel than men.[36] The presence of women workers would, she believed, forestall the dangers arising when female members confided in ministers.[37] In the remaining years until her death in 1915, Ellen White wrote many things which echoed the general theme: 'Seventh-day Adventists are not in any way to belittle woman's work', and in this respect she seemed to think that money had important symbolic significance.[38] It did, however, have more than that:

If a woman puts her housework in the hands of a faithful, prudent helper, and leaves her children in good care, while she engages in the work, the conference should have wisdom to understand the justice of her receiving wages.[39]

It is a sentiment which seems to echo the sense of urgency which led her to countenance long separations from her own children, and yet it is difficult to reconcile with ideas that she expressed on the importance of the maternal role. Her commitment to the principle of involving women in the church's work, while no doubt in part a reflection of the spirit of the age, stemmed from the view that 'a better understanding of the division of labor' was essential to the more successful prosecution of the gospel commission.[40]

General comments

While the great majority of Ellen White's counsels about women concern their domestic and missionary roles, other occasional comments are instructive. In 1864, Ellen White judged that all women who wished to join the women's rights movement 'might as well sever all connection with the third angel's message',[41] although the comment pertained specifically to dress reform. In 1874, she acknowledged that she had not formed an opinion on the question of female suffrage because all her energies were concentrated in other directions.[42] By the following year, she seems to have concluded that women should be enfranchised except where a devotion to fashion and other trivia disqualified them.[43] She remained, however, deeply suspicious of political activity and warned members against involvement on the grounds that it might import divisions into the church.[44] On the other hand, she encouraged members to vote on particular issues, notably temperance,[45] and even encouraged one to run for political office on that platform.[46] She did regret, however, the tendency of some WCTU members to broaden the aim of their organization to embrace other political causes.[47]

Ellen White seemed to favour the protection of women at work because of the threat to health posed by over-exertion.[48] She further advocated that women train and practise as physicians, although rather from a conviction that it was improper for a doctor to treat a patient of the opposite sex than out of any egalitarian concern.[49]

It becomes clear then that the enlarged role for women envisaged by Ellen White arose not out of a basic sympathy with the feminist cause, but out of a concern to exploit all resources for the proclamation of the gospel. She knew no other cause.

The role of women in early Adventism

Published opinion

While the views of Ellen White strongly influenced Adventist opinion about a public role for women in the church, other voices were heard. The matter of women speaking in religious meetings arose frequently in the pages of the *Review*, attention normally being focused on difficult Pauline statements in 1 Corinthians 11 and 14, and 1 Timothy 2. James White resolved the matter thus:

> It is evident that if Paul meant that women should not speak in religious meetings, his words prove also that the sisters should not attend religious meetings.
>
> But as this view of the subject proves too much for our friends, who do not like to hear the Marys preach a risen or coming Saviour, we suggest a position to take on the text which will harmonize with both revelation and reason. It is this. Paul was probably speaking of meetings of church business. The sisters would be quite out of place in meetings of general church business ... the brethren being generally capable of managing such affairs.[50]

The idea that the texts in question applied specifically to a group of disorderly women in the Corinthian church prone to 'prate about Women's Rights' was also voiced.[51] Much ink was spilt in saving the apostle Paul from self-contradiction. It is difficult to escape the impression, however, that the apostle was not the sole beneficiary of all this literary effort. An undoubted concern of some authors was to defend 'a woman who in these latter days is favored of the Lord above others'.[52] Clearly a number of members were 'still troubled to harmonize 1 Corinthians 14:34 with the public labors of Mrs E. G. White'.[53] Ellen White never sought to interpret the problem texts in such a way as to vindicate her own position; she was content to leave that to others.

It is probably a distortion, however, to see the frequent treatment of the subject in the *Review* as purely an attempt to justify the role of Ellen White. It was, no doubt, born in some measure of a desire to know how Adventists should respond to changing social conditions, as the following suggests:

> The queries concerning woman's position in the church come by post and by word of mouth. Devout people, skeptics, believers, advocates of women's

rights, advocates of men's rights, church people, non-church people, husbands of meek wives, husbands of garrulous women, wives of meek husbands, wives of lordly husbands, people that are neither husbands nor wives – all are interested in the solution of this question.[54]

Women's achievements

Before Ellen White set about the business of mobilizing the women of the church, a few had acted on their own initiative. The best example was a group called the Vigilant Missionary Society, formed in June 1869, in South Lancaster, Massachusetts, all the officials of which were women. Members distributed tracts and magazines, helped the needy in their neighbourhood, and wrote letters in order to share their faith. So successful was the scheme that Adventist leaders encouraged the establishment of a 'tract and missionary society' in every church, and, by 1874, the General Conference Tract and Missionary Society was formed to co-ordinate the activities of local societies. As soon as it became institutionalized, the Society became dominated by men, only one of the five-member committee being female. The Society has existed in one form or another ever since to foster missionary work by the laity but has always been controlled by men. Adventism lacked a counterpart to the women's foreign missionary societies formed in many other denominations in the 1870s, mainly because Adventists began their evangelization outside the United States relatively late.

The history of the Vigilant Missionary Society was a microcosm of developments in the Adventist church with regard to women's work. Women enjoyed greater freedom to serve in all parts of the work of the church in its earlier years. Adelia van Horn was, for example, treasurer of the General Conference from 1871 to 1873, a post Minerva Chapman held from 1877 to 1883. As Adventism became institutionalized and adopted contemporary organizational models, and as the family became an important source of new members, the opportunities for women to make their mark on the denomination became reduced.[55]

Some women made an important contribution to the denominational effort in other ways, outside the church hierarchy. Maud Sisley became the first female Adventist foreign missionary when she went to Switzerland in 1877. In January 1895, Georgia Burrus arrived in Calcutta to become the first Adventist missionary to work on the sub-continent. Dr Katherine Lindsay sought the right to a medical education in the face of considerable opposition, and, when qualified, established the first Adventist nursing school.[56]

Of particular interest is the work of Mrs S. M. I. Henry, a leading figure in the WCTU, and, in 1896, a convert to Adventism. She quickly discovered a marked difference between the part played by women in the two movements:

Mrs Henry had been working with a very consecrated and superior group of women, women of education, means, and Christian character. They were tireless, energetic, enthusiastic, and hard-working. By comparison, it seemed that many of the Seventh-day Adventist women were more or less apathetic, unambitious, and provincial in their outlook. They had received wonderful counsel and instructions, they were earnest and devoted, but actually they knew little of their own mission and possibilities in the church. If she could only lead them on to do a work greater than that of the WCTU![57]

She committed her aspirations for her Adventist sisters to print in *A Woman Ministry* (1898). It was essentially a domestic form of ministry:

A woman ministry – not an organized body of women preachers, but an organized service in which all good women might have a part. She felt that a woman's holiest ministry is in the home, among her neighbors and friends as they come and go about her, and it was her aim that the great truths might be served with the dinner, fitted with a dress pattern, bound in the same bundle with the common things about which women are wont to talk.[58]

An important part of this ministry was the organization of a massive correspondence network wherein she and other Adventist women offered advice on a wide range of problems experienced by other women. The *Review* soon began to devote a page regularly to the 'Women's Gospel Work', which tried to create a sense of sisterhood among Adventist women. Ellen White was plainly delighted by the activities initiated by Mrs Henry.[59] Ellen White's pleasure was short-lived, however, for in January 1900 Mrs Henry died, having recently completed a five-month trip covering 9,000 miles in the United States, the sort of venture never undertaken by any Adventist woman other than herself. The 'Women's Gospel Work' soon collapsed without a woman of her stature to guide it,[60] Ellen White's diminishing energies being devoted to wider issues.

Dr John H. Kellogg believed that women had capacities equal to those of men and should be granted equal opportunities.[61] The disproportionately large number of female medical staff in his organization,[62] however, demonstrates not merely a commitment to that view but a concern that medical staff treat patients of the same sex. There is some evidence that, within the denomination, employment opportunities were being extended to women. By 1900, 188 of the church's 1,244 employees (15 per cent) were women, although few occupied positions of executive responsibility, and none was ordained.

By the turn of the century, the model of acceptable Adventist womanhood was still very conventional. Since women were 'far more religious naturally than men',[63] their principal function was to cultivate the spiritual sensitivities of their families. If particularly devout, or married to church workers, they would industriously engage in missionary work in the community. Unlike the 'masculine female politicians'[64] of the WCTU, they were unlikely to be active in socio-political matters.

Ellen White's hope that the women of the church would assume greater responsibility for its mission seems largely to have been unrealized. There were those who saw contemporary modifications to social roles as doors of opportunity for the church: 'It is one of the things that the providence of God has brought to pass, to prepare the world for the last great day.'[65] Another contributor to the *Review* thought it healthy that women should begin to think independently,[66] while elsewhere the role of career women was cautiously defended.[67] A rare example of this role within the church was L. Flora Plummer who, in 1905, despite a pregnancy, became corresponding secretary of the General Conference Sabbath School Department, a department she was to lead from 1913 onwards.

While the principle of the equality of the sexes may have been acknowledged, it was by no means taken to imply identity of function. The notion of 'separate spheres' was closely adhered to.[68] Women were to master the 'housewifely arts', not simply for their own sakes but as a vehicle for spreading the gospel;[69] the main function of women was reckoned to be leading 'a well-disciplined family' which was 'living out the truth'.[70] It was thought to be essential that she learn to work with her hands,[71] and that she should not cherish intellectual ambitions.[72] One writer lamented the fact that the business of emancipation in general, and increased educational opportunities in particular, encouraged women to forsake the home and seek a place in the public arena; in the process they often lost their modesty.[73] The oft-heard call was for selfless women, willing to discover the 'glory of the commonplace'.[74] In Adventist circles, the Victorian ideal of domestic piety was not easily to be supplanted.

The ordination of women

Ellen White

With attention latterly and, perhaps inevitably, coming to focus on the question of ordaining women to the ministry, it is worthwhile pausing to note what the early Adventists had to say on the matter. Within Adventism, as in other communions, those upon whom hands have been laid have traditionally wielded greatest power. The major exception to this was Ellen White, who never underwent an ordination rite but who claimed that God himself had ordained her to a special ministry.[75] Divine ordination or not, certain administrative problems arose regarding her status. At that time, all Adventist ministers received credentials which were endorsed annually. Ellen White received ministerial credentials, in some instances, for example, 1885, with the word 'ordained' deleted, in some cases, for example, 1887, not. In the church's *Yearbook* she was included under the category of ordained ministers. She conducted neither marriages nor the 'ordinance of communion' (eucharist). She exercised a profound influence on the church without ever having held formal office, although she did receive a ministerial stipend. Interestingly enough, she would never occupy the pulpit during a Saturday morning worship service when her husband was present. It must remain a matter of speculation whether she would have done so had her husband survived until the time when she seems to have modified her views on public ministry by women.

There was no word from the oracle on the subject of the ordination of women in the entire corpus of her published works, or in her correspondence, with one enigmatic exception. In 1895, she wrote:

Women who are willing to consecrate some of their time to the service of the Lord should be appointed to visit the sick, look after the young, and minister to the necessities of the poor. They should be set apart to this work by prayer and laying on of hands.[76]

This recommendation seemed to pertain to the traditional Adventist role of deaconess, and created some confusion when first published;[77] it has never become common practice for deaconesses to undergo this rite as deacons do.

Ellen White's writings have sometimes been cited to exclude women from ministry:

Eve had been perfectly happy by her husband's side in her Eden home; but, like restless modern Eves, she was flattered with the hope of entering a higher sphere than that which God had assigned her ... In their desire for a higher sphere, many have sacrificed true womanly dignity and nobility of character, and have left undone the very work that Heaven appointed them.[78]

It is worth noting, however, that this was written in 1890, before Ellen White began to recommend more forthrightly the greater involvement of women in public ministry.

Resort to Ellen White has failed to resolve the issue among Adventists. It could reasonably have been expected that her own ministry would have opened the way for other women to participate. However, Adventists have concluded that her virtual silence on the subject of women's ordination indicated that it was an unimportant matter. Little account seems to have been taken of the fact that the issue was not current in her lifetime.

Other developments in nineteenth-century Adventism

In 1867, James White, describing an ordination service which he had conducted, wrote:

My views and feelings are that the minister's wife stands in so close a relation to the work of God, a relation which so affects him for better or worse, that she should, in the ordination prayer, be set apart as his helper.[79]

The remainder of his report indicated, however, that only the man in question was ordained by the laying on of hands. It is significant, however, that James White did this and felt it necessary to justify having done it.

An inexplicable outcrop of feminist concern occurred at the General Conference session, on 5 December 1881. The minutes read:

RESOLVED, That females possessing the necessary qualifications to fill that position, may, with perfect propriety, be set apart by ordination to the work of the Christian ministry. This was discussed by J. O. Corliss, A. C. Bourdeau, E. R. Jones, D. H. Lamson, W. H. Littlejohn, A. S. Hutchins, D. M. Canright, and J. N. Loughborough, and referred to the General Conference Committee.[80]

There exists no evidence to show that this committee ever considered the matter; unfortunately, church records nowhere offer any help in understanding this unexpected resolution. It may have been another effort to legitimate Ellen White's position, or it may have arisen from a broader feminist concern. It may be that Ellen White, who was absent from the session, succeeded, away from the conference floor, in killing a resolution of which she disapproved. It may be that the male leadership of the church overturned a resolution which arose from a feminist faction. It is surprising that the matter did not attract attention in any denominational periodicals. Until further evidence comes to light, it can only be observed that the strength of feeling on the matter does not seem to have been sufficiently great for it to be raised again.

In 1898, a General Conference Committee agenda item could conceivably have re-opened the subject:

The Secretary called up the question of ministerial license for Mrs S. M. I. Henry. Several remarked that it was their judgement that she should receive a ministerial license, which would be more in keeping with her line of work. A motion prevailed to grant her such recognition from the General Conference.[81]

This vote followed a request from Mrs Henry that she have some authority invested in her as a representative of the Adventist church in her liaison with the WCTU. Although formally recognized as a minister, she did not receive ordination; indeed, she had earlier, when more closely linked with the WCTU, resisted the promotion of women's ordination by the Union's leader, Frances Willard.

Mrs Henry's position, then, did not become the occasion for any activism on the matter. Indeed, the evidence already considered from Ellen White's pen suggests that Adventist women in general were content to occupy a passive role in the church.

10 · Adventist women in the modern church: the pain of liberation

Women's changing role in American society

Female suffrage became a reality just as the United States was emerging from the First World War. The Equal Rights Amendment was passed in January 1918, although strong opposition from a variety of vested interests delayed the actual enfranchisement of 26 million women until 26 August 1920. Women's contribution to the war effort no doubt strengthened their claim to the vote, but the matter must be seen in a broader economic context. Eleanor Flexner has shown that the number of women gainfully employed rose from 4 million in 1890, to 5.3 million in 1900, to 7.4 million in 1910.[1] Women who were contributing thus to the wealth of the country could not long be denied voting rights. It was, however, conflict in the industrial context that soon produced the fragmentation of the feminist movement. Equal rights feminists opposed the introduction of protective legislation for women at work, which other feminists believed was necessary to safeguard the health and dignity of working women. The years of the Depression saw a downturn in the fortunes of women at work, while Franklin D. Roosevelt's 'New Deal' of 1932 made into a matter of social policy much that the welfare feminists had been seeking, thus depriving them of a cause.

As in Britain, a war-weary population sought meaning and security in the bosom of the nuclear family in the decade following the Second World War. 1957 brought for the first time in the post-war period a decline in the birth-rate, with women soon being absorbed into the work-force in increasingly large numbers. Legislative attempts to end sexual discrimination were found not to be working satisfactorily by a number of disparate feminist groups which coalesced, in 1967, into what has become known as the 'women's liberation movement'.

The aim of the movement was to eliminate the widespread oppression it perceived of one social group by another, maintained by the reproductive mechanism. Perhaps the most influential feminist group of the early 1980s was the National Organization of Women, which voiced clear but basically moderate positions on issues like abortion, property rights, and the image of women in the media.

The role of women in the churches

The generally quiet state of affairs in the church with regard to the role of women, in the first half of the present century, can be traced to several causes beyond the fact that the church, as an essentially conservative force, was unlikely to be in advance of general social developments.

The growing acceptance of higher critical methods of biblical interpretation may have led some scholars to reject some of the traditional grounds for barring women from ordained ministry, but it had little effect on the attitudes of ordinary members and clergy. It became clear in the 1920s that the influence of women in the churches was declining. A Presbyterian report, published in 1927, entitled *Causes of Unrest among the Women of the Church*, identified the absorption of women's missionary societies into the main denominational agencies, in the name of greater efficiency, as a major cause of discontent.[2] The problem was, however, much broader than this. The increased educational standards required of church workers, and, indeed, the growing professionalization of the whole structure of the church served effectively to exclude women from positions of responsibility. The fact that women were progressively inclined to take paid employment outside the home increased this effect. The years of severe economic depression also imposed enormous strains on church finances. Wracked by its involvement in two major conflicts and by economic stringencies, the country could ill afford to have its churches dissipating their energies on internal struggles.

After the Second World War, the emphasis on the domestic role was particularly strong among the churches, as the following suggests: 'America needs young women who will build true homes ... where harassed husbands may find peace ... where children may find the warmth of love.'[3] 'Today's daughters need to think twice before they seek to make a place for themselves by themselves in our world today.'⁴ Gradually, attitudes changed, however; Harvard Divinity School first opened its doors to women in 1955, soon to be followed by others, and in 1956 both Presbyterians and Methodists voted to admit women to ministry by ordination.

This was merely a quiet prelude to what was, at times, to become a bitter conflict, most notably in the Episcopal church. In the late 1960s, arguments raged concerning the ordination of women as deaconesses, and as to whether deaconesses thus ordained were in 'holy orders'. These two issues were settled to the satisfaction of feminists in the early 1970s, and, together with certain other developments, encouraged optimism in them. 1973 saw the foundation of the National Committee for the Ordination of Women to the Priesthood. The anger was immense among feminists when, in the same year, the General Convention of the Episcopal Church rejected the motion recommending admission of women to ordained ministry. Such was the bitterness that one faction decided to tread a radical path; on 29 July 1974, three retired bishops ordained eleven women to the priesthood, a rite quickly declared invalid by the House of Bishops. Controversy continued unabated until, in September 1976, the General Convention reversed its earlier decision. The struggle was a protracted and destructive one which served as an object lesson to other communions. Even after the successful campaign, some feminists had misgivings about the gains made, inasmuch as they had indulged the very adversarial spirit which they had sought to eschew.

It has been in those denominations where preaching roles are not endowed with sacerdotal significance, like the Methodists, Congregationalists, and Unitarians, that it has been easier to admit women to ministry. Greater difficulty has existed in sacramentalist churches and sectarian groups. Mormons, Jehovah's Witnesses, Christadelphians, and both Open and Exclusive Brethren groups deny this role to women for various reasons. Greater opportunity exists among the Salvation Army, Christian Science, and some Pentecostal groups for women to participate in worship services. Even in those communions where women have the right to function as a minister, few have shown an inclination to engage in the struggle for acceptance which is frequently involved. Women in the Roman Catholic church have been able to serve in the various sisterhoods but in the period 1965–75 the number of nuns in the American orders declined by 41,000, 29 per cent of the total membership, a substantial number choosing to end their vows.[5] The *Declaration on the Question of the Admission of Women to the Ministerial Priesthood*, issued by the Vatican in 1977, unequivocally excluding women from priesthood on the grounds that there was an elusive sacramental bond between Christ, priesthood and maleness, was not calculated to staunch the flow of the disenchanted away from the orders. An attempt to repair some of the damage was made in *Mutationes Relationes*, published in 1978, which sought to give women's orders a bigger voice in church government.

With this general background in place, the history of Adventist attitudes on this matter can now be described and assessed.

A profile of acceptable Adventist womanhood

There is evidence that a few women served the church as ministers in the first half of the century, particularly in the years to 1915, but these were rare exceptions.[6] One study has shown that the number of women in administrative positions in the church reached a peak in 1915, steadily declining thereafter until the year 1950 found women to be almost completely unrepresented in such positions.[7] This was undoubtedly a reflection of general socio-economic trends. Normally women who were employed by the denomination simply extended their domestic function beyond the home; two notable examples were Fannie Dickerson and Lora Clement who, consecutively, were editors of the influential *Youth's Instructor* for the entire first half of the century.

Fears that the social dislocation produced by the Second World War would create role changes and a diminished respect for the home and womanhood were not immediately realized.[8] The glorification of motherhood and 'the feminine mystique' was as evident in the Adventist church as anywhere else in the 1950s. The *Review* editor contrasted the great contribution made to the work of the Adventist church by its women, with the growing political activism of some women in the larger society:

Our welfare work is carried on almost exclusively by women. The majority of our church school teachers are women. Most of the nurses in our hospitals are women. The secretaries and stenographers in our offices are women. The majority of workers in the children's divisions of our Sabbath Schools are women ...

Women deserve much credit for the great progress the church has made ...[9]

But if the roles occupied by women remained essentially the same, those filling them clearly did not. Following the general trend, Adventist mothers of young children began to leave the home to work;[10] it was an option which the *Review* sought to discourage its readers from taking.[11]

From the mid 1960s, the type of woman celebrated in *Fascinating Womanhood* by Helen B. Andelin (not an Adventist) was projected as a model for Adventist women to follow. In church-sponsored seminars, they were encouraged to be submissive, dependent, and to find fulfilment vicariously; this was thought to be the key to a successful marriage. The subordination was, however, only apparent, since it seemed that women were encouraged to manipulate their husbands by assuming a kind of mystic authority.[12]

The church could not for long, however, remain untouched by the general ferment of opinion regarding the place of women in society. On 4 January 1968, the *Review* carried the first of a new weekly series, which was to last two years, called 'The Adventist Woman'. This development seemed to signal some recognition of the changing role of women. The opening article, however, belied that promise. The author, a male, regretted that a wife's unwillingness 'to make her desires and interests subordinate to her husband's work', frequently made it 'impossible for him to make a major contribution to the cause of God'.[13] The series adhered to a familiar pattern of articles on the care and discipline of children, the maintenance of good family health, the creation of a vital religious atmosphere in the home, and witness to neighbours. The privileges of motherhood were regularly extolled, interrupted only occasionally by articles on the contributions of women in civic work or commerce. A distinctive feature of the series was the way in which women were encouraged to seek fulfilment through their husbands.[14] While the series undoubtedly contained much wisdom on the maternal role, it fostered a somewhat restricted view of womanhood. This undoubtedly reflected editorial concern over the rapidly mounting threat from divorce, and the domestic dislocation which followed.

Adventism and women's liberation

As the women's liberation movement gained strength in the wider society, Adventist periodicals devoted increasing attention to the major issues, and the views expressed were far from unanimous. Some were unashamedly traditionalist,[15] and the virtues of the traditional domestic role of the woman continued to be extolled frequently. Some authors cautiously endorsed the aims of a moderate feminism, seeing therein an opportunity for the church to mobilize greater resources for gospel work.[16] As yet, few voices were raised in defence of a woman's right to work simply in order to find personal satisfaction. One writer found self-fulfilment a notion alien to Christianity, where the watchword was self-denial. The business of character-formation, she believed, would have eternal consequences, and could not safely be left in the hands of baby-minders.[17]

Behind the maternal ideal lauded in the printed word there lay a number of tensions. The first was between the ideal of the Adventist home and the urgency of the church's mission, which as many as possible must be mobilized to complete. If this was, in part, only a theoretical problem, then it found its practical expression in the need to staff Adventist institutions. Hospitals, for example, needed to employ large numbers of nurses who were mothers, if they were not to lose their distinctive Adventist ethos. Further, many members wishing to give their children an Adventist education found it necessary to have a second wage. Another contributory factor was that the disproportionately high number of young Adventist women who were given a high-school and college education came to find the maternal role intolerably restricting. Unwittingly, perhaps, the church had made a considerable contribution to the liberation of women through its extensive educational system. There can be no doubt that some Adventist women found themselves oppressed by the idealized image of the full-time wife-mother.[18] Lastly, most that was written on careers for women addressed the case of married women, entirely overlooking the needs of unmarried, widowed, or divorced members.

One observer believed that part of the problem lay in the reading matter Adventists provided for their children. In an analysis of *Uncle Arthur's Bedtime Stories*, a set of Adventist books which had exerted a profound influence on the denomination's young for over half a century, Karen Schwartz showed evidence of clear sex-role differentiation. Boys figured more frequently in them, were more actively engaged in life, were more often characterized as attractive, exhibited behaviours more highly valued by society, dressed more casually, and showed greater evidence of possessing wisdom. The implicit teaching of the stories, illustrations, and characterizations, she stated, was that the male was stronger, wiser, and generally superior. In her opinion, a diet of such stories was calculated not only to maintain traditional sexual roles but to produce conflict in young Adventists, maturing in a rapidly changing society.[19] Other observers have identified the existence of the problem in a wide range of publications produced by Adventists for their young members.[20] In 1980, when the church's education department undertook to produce a new range of textbooks, it established a clear set of criteria concerning both text and illustrations, designed to eradicate distortions in sex-role differentiation.[21]

One writer saw some reason for optimism in the fact that 42 per cent of teachers in Adventist elementary schools were now male, although many of these functioned as principals.[22] Another writer feared that conventional models of femininity led Adventist women to under-achieve when young, only to recognize the baleful consequences later in life:

Scholastic achievement is on a par with that of boys in grade school but tends to drop off as social interests take over and girls begin to realize that a well-trained mind and a wide range of interests are not as certain a route to social success and marriage as is average achievement in a typically feminine field coupled with external attractiveness and a sort of domestic docility.[23]

To fashion young women in this mould was to do them a disservice since, it was argued, in reality, whether or not they married or bore children, they were at some stage likely to spend a considerable number of years in the work-force. If they were discouraged from seeking training in some worthwhile occupation, they were destined later to accept low-skill, unsatisfying jobs, and to face a mid-life crisis when their children left home. Another writer claimed that some Adventist secondary schools were discouraging female students from entering the professions.[24]

It is possible to identify several major reasons for suspicion and caution regarding the modification of conventional views about the role of women in the church. Considerable resistance came from women themselves. Those who felt comfortable with the traditional domestic role were moved to speak 'in defense of homemakers'.[25] They clearly felt threatened by this new breed of Adventist women with unfamiliar aspirations. Secondly, many perfectly sincere Adventist men of all ages would simply have been unable to echo, or even perhaps fully comprehend, the following sentiments:

> If the Bible gives notice that we are to 'undo the thongs of the yoke', then it is safe to infer that the liberation of women is a part of the real business of Christianity ... Insofar as stereotyped ideas about 'femininity' really do put women at a disadvantage, insofar as they really do stifle freedom and work to keep women down, those ideas must be abandoned, for they are repugnant to the Christian conscience.[26]

The notion that men's attitudes to women constituted a moral offence would have been quite foreign to many. Thirdly, there were no doubt those who feared the consequences of the introduction of a strident feminism into the church; the pains experienced by other communions were to be avoided at all costs.

A fourth and vital cause for concern was the possibility of damage to the family, and thus to the church. A significant *Review* editorial, drawing on research by Bronfenbrenner, argued that children were receiving less adult attention than formerly, particularly with the decline of the extended family. Statistics were cited to show that, in 1975, for the first time in American history, a majority of mothers with school-age children (6–17) were employed outside the home; 39 per cent of mothers with children under six were employed, and about a third of mothers with children under three. The number of working wives had increased from 6.5 million in 1947 to 19.8 million in 1975, an increase of 205 per cent, while the increase in the number of working husbands was only 27 per cent.[27] The editor exhorted mothers and fathers to a greater effort to cement family relations.

Others, viewing the same scene, saw the failure of 'true womanhood' as the seed yielding a harvest of social deviancy.[28] Inevitably, perhaps, modified views about the traditional roles and rights of women in the wider world penetrated Adventist society. Economic necessity and occupational aspirations led women to seek employment outside the home. The major focus of attention became the treatment of women in denominational employ.

A controversial case

With the leaders of the church cautiously offering encouragement to its women to accept responsibility, there was some reason to hope, in the early 1970s, that the issue could be negotiated without undue difficulty. Robert Pierson, the General Conference president, undertook to increase opportunities for women to serve in the church, and to offer remuneration commensurate with their responsibilities.[29] It was evident, however, that a reservoir of resentment had already been created among those female employees who worked in the same capacities as men.[30] This co-existed with a disappointment that the church, 'the organization welded to the highest ideals', was 'the most sluggish in its conscience toward women'.[31] These women believed that the church was engaging in the rhetoric of equality without taking any serious action.

One such was Merikay Silver, an editorial assistant with the Pacific Press Publishing Association, who, in 1973, filed a suit with the Equal Employment Opportunities Commission against her employers for their failure to offer her remuneration equal to that given to men doing the same work.[32] Although she fought a class action, she did not enjoy the support of all female employees at the publishing house. Some objected on the basis of a biblical injunction against taking a fellow believer to a secular court. Others merely feared that higher salaries would diminish the publisher's competitiveness, and eventuate in redundancies. Judgement initially went against the church institution which, a number of years later, decided to halt the process of appeal because the litigation proved so protracted and costly; settlement was made out of court. The case raised a number of important ecclesiological issues,[33] and was the first of several actions brought against church institutions in California.[34]

While the General Conference, in the wake of such events, voted to grant equal pay for equal work to take effect throughout North America from 1 July 1974, considerable discontent still remained concerning the considerable fringe benefits, for example, the housing allowance, available to 'heads of household', who were usually men. These were paid not so much in proportion to the level of responsibility held by an individual, but to allow a family to live decently. Understandably, it appeared inequitable to women who received a smaller financial reward than their male colleagues for identical work. The policy was justified as an effort to conserve denominational funds for missionary purposes, but it assumed attitudes on the part of the membership which seemed to be fast disappearing.

The following editorial comment in the *Review* probably provided an accurate assessment of the situation:

We do not believe that good men – Christian men who sincerely want to reflect the spirit and wisdom of the Master – deliberately discriminate against women either by linguistic sexisms or by acts of policy. We think they merely have a 'blind spot' in this area, as they once did regarding racism.[35]

The church has since accepted the principle of equal pay for equal work.

A theological perspective

The General Conference, anxious to respond in an informed way to changing attitudes regarding women's role, commissioned some of the denomination's leading scholars to write on various aspects of the issue. The venture was undertaken in two stages; the first, in 1973, brought contributions mostly from prominent Adventist women, while the second, several years later, involved some of the church's leading theologians.

The first study, not surprisingly perhaps, produced a clear consensus: that women were discriminated against in denominational employment, and in church life generally, and that this contradicted the spirit of the gospel. Madelynn Haldeman, a biblical scholar, argued that, where the early Christian church appeared to limit the role of women in the life of the church by conforming to the prevailing social conventions, it was with the primary purpose of spreading the

161

gospel more effectively, especially in Corinth. The church, by adopting an unduly literalistic understanding of the Bible, was perpetuating pagan structures by the continued subordination of women. The equality of women was by creation and redemption; Adventist women should enjoy the full rights and privileges of membership, and bear the responsibilities thereto appertaining.[36] Leona Running, professor of biblical languages at the church's principal seminary, enlarged on the dangers of trying to apply scripture without due attention to historical context. Old Testament notions of the inferiority of women derived directly from the patriarchal nature of the society. Pauline prohibitions about women speaking in church arose from his concern about the behaviour of the hetaerae. The vastly different social conditions in which modern Christians lived demanded a realization of the ideal of sexual harmony.[37] Kit Watts, then an editor at the *Review*, argued that the changing attitudes of God's people over the centuries towards the institutions of slavery and polygamy illustrated precisely the same point.[38] One of the denomination's leading theologians, Raoul Dederen, confirmed these views by suggesting that an enlarged role for women in the ministry of the church had nothing to do with the order of creation, the fall, the ministry instituted by Christ, or the sex of members of the godhead. Scripture proclaimed the priesthood of all believers; the central question was whether, in a particular social milieu, it was appropriate, or efficient, for women to engage in a public ministry. In an open society, the church had the responsibility of mustering every resource.[39]

The same consensus emerged in those papers which dealt with the contemporary social setting. Leona Running outlined the opportunities for service for women in other churches.[40] Other papers catalogued the inequities in financial arrangements, the absence of women on the decision-making bodies of the church at all levels, the rigid sex-role differentiation, the inequalities of educational opportunity, and the oppressive nature of language and attitudes in the church generally.[41] Many contributors, though not all, agreed that the key to the resolution lay in the ordination of women to the ministry, rather in the same way that disparate groups of feminists had held suffrage to be the remedy for their grievances early in the century.

Ordination was prominent in the minds of those theologians who contributed to the second phase of the church's study. Before that issue is considered in the next section, the more general findings of that study must be examined. A leading Adventist theologian, Gerhard Hasel, contributed a paper on woman as depicted in Genesis 1–3, a passage which, surprisingly, had not figured large in the history of the debate. He showed, for example, that the Hebrew word *'ezer*, translated 'helper', was used not only to describe woman's relationship to man but that of Jahweh to Israel, and therefore could not imply a relationship of inferiority. He further argued that the prior creation of the male was merely part of a Hebrew literary device, and could have no significance attached to it. He concluded that the most which could be established was that, in marriage, the husband was *primus inter pares*; the opening chapters of the Bible contained no justification for a general male supremacism. Moreover, the ascription of authority to the husband was a consequence of the fall and not part of creation. Thus, if salvation was concerned with the restoration of the image of God, the function of the church was to restore sexual equality and harmony where it did not now exist. Echoing the familiar refrain that the urgency of the task required the full deployment of the church's resources, Hasel averred that he could see no barrier to the 'full participation of women in ministerial activity'.[42] Coming from one of the denomination's leading scholars, this was a significant judgement.

One of a younger generation of Adventist biblical scholars, Jerry Gladson, in his study of *'issah* (woman) in the Old Testament, produced a complex array of evidence. Most images of God were male, he believed, because they were written in a patriarchal society, yet there were some startling exceptions. He noted a certain equivocation in the use of feminine images generally. The Israelite nation was described both as a harlot, and a desolate woman protected by her husband, Jahweh. The book of Proverbs had wisdom taking a feminine guise. Women were permitted to take part in all the major festivals but were excluded from priesthood, this because of their ritual uncleanness, and the danger of assimilating the immoral practices of the Canaanite cults. He concluded by insisting that, if the Old Testament was to be used in seeking answers to contemporary questions on the role of women, Adventists must abandon the simplistic practice of piecing unrelated texts together; relevant passages must be placed in a broad sociological context.[43]

Walter Specht, from Loma Linda University, in his contribution, claimed that Christ had a radical conception of the status of women. By protecting the rights of women over the divorce issue, he challenged the Pharisees' double standards on sexual morality. By interacting with women as he did, he showed that he was willing to disregard the social proprieties of his time, and to become ritually unclean. By accepting the hospitality and support of many women, he flew in the face of rabbinical custom, while managing to preserve his integrity. The fact that he did not appoint a woman apostle, Specht believed to be merely a concession to the most deeply rooted prejudices of the society in which the gospel had to be proclaimed. The fact that he entrusted the news of the resurrection to a woman was an expression of his wish to restore dignity to women.[44] Guy, in his study of the meaning of womanhood in the works of Barth, Brunner, Thielicke, and Jewett, highlighted the paradox which was to be found in the Bible between the equality of man and woman proclaimed in Galatians 3:28, and the precedence of the male found in Ephesians 5. The resolution, he believed, lay in the renunciation, by man, of the prerogatives bestowed on him by tradition.[45]

It fell to Gordon Hyde, then director of the Biblical Research Institute, to draw together the threads of the debate.[46] He recognized that, in the industrialized nations at least, women were completing their maternal role earlier, and living longer than ever before. They could anticipate some thirty years of working life when their main child-bearing responsibilities had ended. Moreover, the economic structure of modern society was such that they were likely to be obliged to work. Thus increasingly high numbers of Adventist women were appearing on the labour market. In addition, with over 60 per cent of Adventist membership being female, many loyal women members were likely to remain unmarried and available for long-term employment. Many were anxious to use their abilities to aid in the gospel proclamation, and were therefore frustrated at the restrictions placed on them in their careers and voluntary activities. He did not perceive any widespread sympathy with radical feminist sentiments but recognized the women's legitimate frustration at not being involved in the decision-making processes of the church. He acknowledged that confused biblical exegesis had too often been employed to defend traditional male supremacism.

These papers were neither published nor did they receive widespread distribution. Their contents, however, did gradually become known to academics and administrators. In time, they helped to establish the view that there was no specifically theological impediment to women serving in all facets of the church's work. Those contributions devoted particularly to the question of ordination, to be considered in the next section, made the full implications of that abundantly clear.

The ordination of women

The 1976 study

The study commission on the role of women devoted some attention to the matter of the ordination of women. Hasel, it will be recalled, saw no obstacle to the 'full participation of women in ministerial activity' (see above, p. 163). The major contribution, by Sakae Kubo, a New Testament scholar with a reputation which extends far beyond Adventist circles, concluded that there was no biblical barrier to ordination:

In a real sense sex should have nothing to do with this function. It is no more a male function than the ability to sing is a male function. It is only tradition and custom, not our doctrines or deliberate reflections that have kept us from ordaining women to the ministry.[47]

Indeed, he intimated that the church's tentative effort to reform its policy was itself a response to the promptings of God's Spirit.

He did, however, sound a note of caution. He recognized that, in many parts of the world, Adventists were simply not ready to consider such a change, and the Pauline exhortation in 1 Timothy 2:11–15 still needed to be applied literally. He concluded that, while the principle of ordaining women should be affirmed universally, the implementation of the principle should be determined according to local readiness for such innovation.

In his concluding report, Gordon Hyde, head of the Biblical Research Institute, observed that official church policy stood opposed to Kubo's notion of local readiness:

... because the Seventh-day Adventist Church is a world church which includes in its fellowship peoples of all nations and cultures, and because a survey of its world divisions reveals that the time is not ripe nor opportune, therefore, in the interest of the world unity of the church, no move be made in the direction of ordaining women to the gospel ministry.[48]

He recognized that the obstacle was not theological in nature, and doubted whether the unity of the church was really so fragile as to be shattered by the issue. He took the cautious view, however, that the church should proceed gradually, seeking to discern the will of God in the matter. Dederen agreed, while conceding that the church's theology of ordination was anomalous and in need of revision.[49] Specht, however, rejected the view that there were in the Adventist world some universally accepted criteria governing ordination, and thus found the argument from unity to be extremely suspect.[50] Another paper, by LaVonne Neff, an Adventist writer, showed that relatively few women were presenting themselves for ministry in the many denominations which had proceeded less cautiously on the matter.[51]

While some parts of the study commission's work did find their way into print, its findings remained unpublished as a whole.

Surveys of Adventist opinion

In 1974, the General Conference took soundings in the various divisions of the world church on the matter. Some areas, like the Far Eastern Division, were in favour of the move, while others, like the Trans-Africa Division, were utterly opposed. The church in the western world seemed unsure about the matter and counselled caution.[52]

Whereas the above enquiry reflected the opinion of senior administrators around the world, a survey carried out in 1977, as part of a continuing assessment of membership opinion, tested the views of laity, clergy, conference, and institutional administrators and young members (see table 10.1). It was conducted in North America, and yielded 562 usable responses to questions relating to the ordination of women as ministers and elders of local churches. The survey revealed a considerable polarization of ideas on the issue. A majority opposed ordination of women to ministry. Women opposed the move more than men, older age-groups of either sex more than younger; the age-group 36–55 was more hostile than older groups. Conference administrators were openly opposed to any extended role for women, while institutional administrators favoured this rather more. Local pastors opposed ordination of women to ministry but favoured their ordination to eldership. On the whole, clergy were more open to change than lay leaders. The polarization of ideas and the strength of feeling thus discovered was calculated to impress on church leaders the need to proceed with extreme caution.

Table 10.1   Attitudes towards the ordination of women amongst Adventists in the United States, 1977 and 1985

Issue	Oppose		Neutral		Favour	
	1977	1985	1977	1985	1977	1985
Appointment of women to pastoral responsibilities	51	48	17	11	32	41
Ordination of women to SDA ministry	56	57	15	10	29	33
Appointment of a woman to ministry in respondent's own church	58	60	18	11	25	29

Figures in percentages to nearest whole. Sample = 1,048.

Source: Compiled from F. D. Yost, 'An Inquiry into the Role of Women in the SDA Church', unpublished statistical report, September 1977; and from an unpublished survey on the role of women in the church, completed March 1985, both Office of Archives and Statistics, General Conference.

With the pressure mounting for the church to reconsider its position, a further sample of membership opinion was taken in March 1985 (see table 10.1). The survey showed slightly increased support for women serving in ministerial capacities, particularly those not requiring ordination. Similarly, the opposition to such innovation had stiffened marginally. Fewer people declared themselves to be undecided on the matter. The survey showed that opposition to ordination by women had increased marginally while men seemed somewhat more favourable. Support for the move had declined markedly among the age-group 16–25 and grown in the category 36–55. It remained true, however, that the greatest resistance came from those over 35. Such statistics must always be treated with caution but the basic finding of the research was that, while attitudes to women entering ministry were softening gradually, the resistance to such a move in North America remained such as to suggest that this was not a propitious time to open ordination to women. Another survey of Adventist opinion world-wide showed a lack of readiness to ordain women to ministry, especially in the Third World. The church in the West was more receptive to the idea but support was still insufficient to encourage administrators to proceed.[53]

Published reactions

The admission of women to ministry and positions of responsibility in church life has been a subject of debate now for over a decade, with *Spectrum* being the usual forum for the expression of innovative thought. The opening salvo was fired by Leona Running, in 1972, in an article which vigorously criticized the exclusion of women from leadership roles, and the financial inequities they suffered as a consequence of not having access to ordination, even where they performed a pastoral function. Not only were women discriminated against in material terms, she said, but they suffered deep hurts because of the insensitive treatment meted out by their male colleagues. She observed that the General Conference committee, the main decision-making body of the church, counted only four women among its 275 members. She called for a complete revision of attitudes towards women in denominational employ, and warned that women living in an open society could not be much longer expected to keep silence.[54] The article drew a sympathetic response from readers.

In 1975, *Spectrum* devoted a complete issue to the role of women, much of which has already been alluded to. Kubo identified a major hermeneutical dimension to the debate. The argument in favour of women's ordination depended, he felt, on the use of some historical-critical devices to deal with problematical Pauline exhortations. These would constitute no difficulty to Adventist academics trained in secular institutions but would disturb members unfamiliar with such procedures. The whole matter of ordination he considered to be one of custom rather than of biblical principle.[55]

In the same year, one *Spectrum* writer deplored the way in which laity, and therefore women, were excluded from the decision-making processes of the church, particularly the General Conference session. It was argued that all major decisions rested in the hands of ordained personnel.[56] It was a theme taken up again in the same journal in 1982. Janice Daffern, then functioning in a pastoral capacity at an Adventist church, was at a loss to explain how a church which believed in the priesthood of all believers, and the possession of spiritual gifts by each member, could effectively exclude 60 per cent of its membership (i.e. its women) from its administrative structure. The General Conference now included just eight women on its 365-member committee, there being none among the fourteen members of the president's executive body. In local conferences, women were more poorly represented in administrative positions than they had been in 1940. Daffern was one of only eight women serving in a pastoral capacity in the United States; their status as 'associates in pastoral care' did not permit them to baptize or conduct marriages. Furthermore, she observed, the General Conference Office of Human Relations had hitherto devoted itself almost exclusively to representing the interests of blacks and Hispanics. She concluded that it was not surprising that able women were seeking outlets for their professional expertise outside the church.[57]

One *Spectrum* writer noted in 1976 that the rite of ordination had become inextricably bound up with financial considerations since the Internal Revenue Service had ruled that only ordained ministers were eligible for tax relief. This left young ministers, and incidentally a few women, at a distinct financial disadvantage. It had therefore become the custom to ordain young men earlier than they might otherwise have expected. One *Review* correspondent clearly pointed out the confusion that existed regarding the rite of ordination:

Rightly or wrongly, in present church policy, ordination and the preaching ministry are not one and the same thing. Women often stand before congregations without being ordained, and men are ordained even though their primary ministry is outside the pulpit. We ordain doctors, conference treasurers, hospital administrators, Adventist Book Center managers, academy principals, business managers, and presidents, many of whom are entirely without theological training.[58]

The point has been conceded by denominational scholars.[59] Ordination had become bound up with extraneous financial considerations, rather than being a public acknowledgement of an individual's vocation. In 1983, the need for women chaplains in Adventist hospitals again stirred the controversy since chaplaincy required ordination. *Spectrum* reported that a resolution on the subject had not been permitted on the agenda of the annual council of church leaders.[60] The journal consistently sought to alert its readers to developments related to the ordination issue, especially after 1984 when it became one of the major questions facing the church.

Other denominational magazines have been less inclined to treat the subject. A senior administrator in Washington, DC, Bernard Seton, gave expression in a *Review* article to views with which no doubt many sympathized, although they also provoked considerable hostility. He believed that the biblical pattern of a male priesthood could not be adequately explained by reference to social mores. Furthermore, he asserted that in the Bible the masculinity of God was 'irrefutably expressed'. The equality of the sexes in Galatians 3:28 denoted only equal access to salvation, not identity of function. Man's priority in creation, he believed, gave him precedence in authority. Such reasoning would have weighed heavily in the thinking of rank-and-file members.[61] A *Review* article by Hyde, reflecting the conclusions of the church's study commission on the matter, adopted the more open position that the concern for the church's unity was the major obstacle to proceeding with a move which otherwise had much to recommend it. A major practical problem he anticipated was the need for a woman minister's husband to change his employment every time his wife was appointed to a new parish. The speed with which attitudes were changing led him to believe that women's ordination was a possibility in the not-too-distant future.[62] Another writer feared that the financial investment in a woman minister might be a poor one since she was likely to marry, and devote herself to domestic concerns for a long period. However, it was held that this should not obscure the fact that many women had an important role to play as unordained workers, who should be properly remunerated for their efforts.

The importance of the issue in contemporary Adventism can be judged from the fact that both the *Review* and *Ministry* carried lengthy articles on the subject in March 1985 in an attempt to educate the membership.[63] Both sought to be even-handed by inviting supporters of both sides to state their case. The case for ordination in the *Review* was opened by the depiction of a set of situations in which a woman could minister more effectively than a man, for example in counselling divorced or bereaved women. The article proceeded to argue that God's providence had not infrequently taken his church by surprise; for example, Christ chose some unlikely candidates as disciples, Peter was instructed to preach to Gentiles, and there was no precedent for the institution of the diaconate. God took initiatives, and the church cautiously followed. It was implied that the ordination of women was just such a case of a bold divine initiative. The Old Testament provided examples of suitable women being called to fill roles not traditionally open to them, and the New Testament period witnessed an even greater expansion in the roles assigned to women. The author argued that since, according to Adventist theology, ordination conferred no new gifts and merely indicated the church's approval of a person's work, the church could open ordination to women whenever it chose. The doctrine of the priesthood of all believers opened the role to all who felt a vocation to ministry. Opposition to the move was rooted in custom not in scripture whence Adventists have traditionally sought to justify their faith and practice.

The opposing article made much of the complementary nature of sex roles and of the importance of the maternal function. Ellen White's failure to endorse the General Conference resolution of 1881 was also thought to be significant. The writer was suspicious that women would seek the prestige attaching to ministry rather than the work of a Bible instructor. There were thought to be considerable dangers and difficulties involved in a woman's attempting to adapt to a male role. More than that, a single woman minister would have to accept a life of loneliness, while a married woman would face the constant conflict of trying to reconcile domestic and professional priorities. Conferences should certainly adopt policies to promote the employment of women in pastoral capacities but ordination was not necessary.

The *Ministry* articles adopted a more theological approach to the issue. The proponent of ordination saw the root of the conflict in the use of different hermeneutical principles. His opponents tended to focus on isolated biblical statements or specific cases, while it was his concern to discover certain general principles underlying the scriptural record. He believed that the authority ascribed to the male both in Genesis 1–3 and in 1 Corinthians 14 was confined to the marriage relationship, and not of wider application. The work of the church was to proclaim redemption which restored all relationships to their pre-fall configuration. It was, he believed, significant that the Christian church replaced the rite of circumcision, an exclusively male sign of identity, with the rite of baptism, which was sexually indifferent. The apostle Paul did little to elevate the women in the early Christian community for precisely the same reasons that he did not attempt to seek the emancipation of slaves. Cultural conditions were overwhelmingly opposed to it, and he sought only to curb the worst excesses of such a system, as in the case of Philemon and Onesimus. The sanction against women assuming a public role in the Corinthian church arose, he believed, from a local problem, evidenced by the fact that no parallel directive was issued to the church in Galatia. Paul wished to avoid all possibility that Christian women could be seen as counterparts to the priestesses at the temple of Aphrodite. Furthermore, having witnessed the conflicts in the church over circumcision and Jew–Gentile relations, he wished to avoid further fragmentation caused by another controversy. The writer concluded that, where the cultural constraints which informed Paul's judgements no longer existed, the church should proceed to use its full resources in the proclamation of the gospel. As a matter of practice, Adventists had never taken the Pauline exhortations literally since women had long held positions of authority over men in the church, and frequently spoke in church gatherings.

The opposition case relied heavily on the claim that God had established a chain of authority in which the female was subordinate to the male. Furthermore, both the Old Testament and the New upheld an all-male priesthood, a state of affairs which Christ never sought to reverse. It was conceded that the Bible did record the achievements of some notable women but these were isolated, and never was any priestly or apostolic function ascribed to a woman.

Galatians 3:28 was considered to have no relevance to the ordination issue; it concerned the scope of salvation only. The writer did not doubt that women had an enormous contribution to make to the life of the church, not least in the area of public speaking. He believed, however, that there was no scriptural justification for the ordination of women to ministry. The articles have been summarized in some detail because they reached a much larger audience than any others and so assumed a considerable influence, and because they conveyed very much the flavour of the debate as it is carried on in contemporary Adventism.

A companion article in *Ministry* raised a series of practical problems raised by the ordination issue.[64] In the 1970s, very few women had in fact offered themselves for pastoral work, perhaps partly because of the uncertainty regarding future employment, a problem which faced male candidates also as the church faced economic stringencies. Secondly, the church's current position was untenable since it permitted and even encouraged women to receive the same seminary training as men, but denied them the vocational opportunities afforded by ordination. Thirdly, the author was anxious about the disruption which a major controversy might have on the fulfilment of the church's mission.

Recent developments

Certain administrative actions taken by the church leadership in the 1970s served to raise expectations of an expansion in the scope of employment opportunities available to women in pastoral work. In 1973, the church first established an enquiry into the theological propriety of electing women to the local church office of elder, which required ordination. There was also expressed a continued willingness to appoint women to pastoral-evangelistic work. By 1974, the scope of the enquiry had been enlarged to include ordination to gospel ministry. A policy decision of 1975 recognized that women might be ordained to the office of local church elder but recommended that the greatest caution be exercised in implementing the decision. It was also judged at that time that the world church was not ready to open the ordained ministry to women. In 1977, church leaders voted to adopt the term 'associate in pastoral care' to identify those doing pastoral work but not in line for ordination, this in an attempt to upgrade the role of Bible instructor. Two years later, the American church made certain provisions to expand the job opportunities of such workers. By 1984, church leaders had voted to advise divisional administrators that local churches were free to elect and ordain women as elders. It also voted to appoint a special commission to study the ordination of women to ministry.

But by this time events had overtaken policy decisions in several important cases. On 25 February 1984, a woman associate in pastoral care performed a baptism – the first time that this had ever occurred in Adventist history. Within two weeks, a second such baptism took place, with a third following several months later, all in the immediate vicinity of the General Conference headquarters. All three took place with the approval of the local administrations (the Potomac Conference and the Columbia Union Conference) but they incurred the wrath of some General Conference officials. The Potomac Conference, recognizing the encouragement it had given to women to serve as ministers, and the integrity with which these women had performed their work, voted to grant them ministerial licences, and authorized them, in their capacity as locally ordained elders, to baptize any whom they had brought to faith. This contentious decision had been reached on the basis of an ambiguous provision in the *Church Manual*,[65] concerning arrangements to be made for baptism in the absence of an ordained minister. The Potomac Conference initially resisted pressure from its parent body to reverse the decision, claiming that as an entity which enjoyed a certain autonomy in ordering practical arrangements, it was acting within church policy.[66]

These women figured in a further three baptismal services before the General Conference intervened; it refused to separate the question of baptisms by women, and the granting of ministerial licences to them, from the larger question of ordination. The General Conference president argued that the matter had now grown to include the matter of church authority. The local conference finally agreed to rescind its interpretation of church policy in return for an understanding that the General Conference would reconsider its position. The expectation clearly was that church policy would be changed in such a way as to legitimize baptisms by women and the issuing of full ministerial credentials to them.

Following closely on this series of events came the deliberations of a study commission established to produce a set of proposals to be presented to the quinquennial session of the General Conference in New Orleans, in June 1985. To minimize the risk of a debilitating controversy on the floor of the General Conference session, each division of the world church was invited to send a delegate favourable to ordination, and one opposed, accompanied by its president. The North American delegation outnumbered all those gathered from around the world, because, it was alleged, the problem was peculiar to North America. Not surprisingly, a large majority of the delegates were men.

The minutes of the enquiry held in Washington, DC, from 26 to 28 March 1985, suggest that the church there engaged in the fullest and frankest official exchange of views in the history of the denomination. It became clear that the plan to ordain local women elders had been successfully implemented in some parts of the world, and that a large majority of delegates favoured such a plan. However, it was felt that women were discouraged from seeking paid pastoral posts in the church by the disapproving responses of some members. Some delegates felt hesitant about proceeding with ordination because they felt it was an uncritical response to cultural pressures; others felt that a woman's sensitivity ideally suited her to the job. Some delegates from the Third World felt unprepared to judge the issue since it was not yet current in their own societies. The question of the unity of the world church was clearly perceived to be important by many delegates, and there was a common concern to avoid schism over the issue. A poll of delegates showed that twenty-seven opposed the ordination of women to the gospel ministry, twenty-six were in favour but thought it unwise to proceed now, and eight believed that the church should introduce it immediately.

The delegates finally voted to present a set of recommendations to the General Conference session, which were ultimately adopted without great dissension. On the issue of the ordination of women, it was decided to take no action but to maintain the church's present position. Further studies of the issue would be assigned to scholars in preparation for another special enquiry to be held early in 1988. Its findings would be presented to the General Conference committee in the spring of 1988, with an entire review of the situation following in the autumn of 1989, prior to the next General conference session. On the issue of the participation of women in church work generally, four proposals were made. Administrators were encouraged to accord the role of 'Bible instructor' much higher recognition in the life of the church. Secondly, church leaders were urged to introduce a plan of 'affirmative action', language emanating from the civil rights movement, to open to women all aspects of ministry not requiring ordination. Thirdly, it was felt desirable to encourage husband-and-wife teams to work in ministry, with suitable financial and educational provisions being made for this new venture. Lastly, it was recognized that considerable education of the membership was needed to help them to accept a larger role for women in the life of the church; a plan was to be presented to church leaders in the autumn of 1985. Also significant was the vote to reform the church's practices so as to limit ordination 'to those performing direct pastoral, evangelistic, ecclesiastical, and other clearly ministerial duties'.[67]

While those favouring the ordination of women have been disappointed by the recommendations made by the enquiry, and the timetable outlined, it seemed clear that the Adventist church, like many others, was taking the gradualist path towards the full participation of women in ordained ministry. The major threat to such a development seemed to be the possibility that the strength of Third World Adventism would have so grown by the time the issue was next debated that innovative measures would be defeated without difficulty.

The association of Adventist women

Although the first-ever conference of Adventist women took place in 1977, and a newsletter called *The Adventist Woman* did occasionally circulate in the years following, it was not until 13 June 1982 that the Association of Adventist Women was officially organized. Its declared purpose was to foster communication between Adventist women and to generate support amongst them; to acquaint the Adventist community with the achievements of its women; to assist Adventist women in achieving their goals; and to help them to increase their professional options within the church. It was decided to publish *The Adventist Woman* regularly from January 1983 as the official voice of the organization.

This bi-monthly newspaper has carried a variety of material catering mainly for women with professional interests. It has particularly sought to inform its readers of general developments in the area of women's participation in church affairs, rather than focusing specifically on the ordination issue. The AAW has, through its newspaper, maintained a firm pressure on church administration to maximize opportunities for service in the life of the church, without, thus far, becoming strident. Indeed, it has adopted a decidedly conciliatory attitude towards church administration in the belief that the spirit of conciliation is one of the gifts that Adventist women have to offer their church.

The Association held its second annual conference in July 1984. Among the conference's actions were resolutions to request editors of church journals to feature articles on the role of women more frequently; to commission a series of monographs on the subject; to request church leaders to publish widely all job vacancies in the church except those requiring ordination; to request all church organizations and institutions in North America to increase the representation of women on all boards and committees to a minimum of 10 per cent within two years; to request the church leadership to establish a centre for women's studies at an Adventist institution of higher education within five years; to request the General Conference to set up a pilot scheme for granting ministerial licences to qualified women candidates. Indicative of the spirit of the conference were those resolutions expressing gratitude to administrators for their efforts to promote the interests of women members in various ways.[68] It may be that the Association will become an important instrument in resolving the present situation amicably.

Conclusion

There is much about Seventh-day Adventism which might lead one to expect that its women would enjoy considerable freedom to serve. First, because of the prominence of a woman in the establishment of the church: Ellen White might have been expected to serve as a powerful role model for the women of the church. Secondly, the church was never compromised respecting the roles which women might play as were the churches which attached sacramental significance to the rite of ordination. Thirdly, Adventists, who have always seen themselves as unique and separate, have never sought formal unity with other religious bodies, and thus have never had to exercise caution over the sensibilities of potential ecumenical partners. Fourthly, Adventist theologians have argued cogently against supposed impediments to the ordination of women. Yet, despite all these powerful considerations, resistance to the idea remains strong.

It is fair to say that Ellen White has never been perceived as a model for the women of the church to follow, even though her writings have done much to fashion the profile of acceptable Adventist womanhood. She was a woman apart. Her prophetic role in the church led her to violate the principles of child-care which she later urged on other women. She exercised a charismatic authority over strong-minded men in a way which other women could never hope to emulate. She addressed large audiences, had a wide circle of acquaintances, and was widely travelled. She was unique; not a woman with whom other women could readily identify. Her presence as a leader in the church cannot be said to have dislodged the presumption against women holding positions of authority in any dramatic way. It is, however, entirely possible that, without a woman in the prophetic role, the women of the church would have been kept in very subordinate roles, as has been the case in other adventist movements.

The reluctance of the church to make any substantial changes in the division of labour would seem to stem from a number of deep-seated fears. The first concerns the prospect of a division within a church which has succeeded in penetrating a large number of cultures, among which there are widely varying views as to the status of women. The most conservative are found amongst Third World countries, which account for an increasingly large proportion of Adventist members. Generally speaking, in the search for unity Adventists have sought the lowest common denominator on such issues.

Furthermore, the administration is aware that to grant concessions to one group with vested interests is to invite lobbying from others. As has been seen, the last decade has witnessed great turmoil in the ranks of Adventists, and understandably administrators wish to avoid further strife at all costs. The painful experience of the Episcopal church has served as a warning to any religious organization contemplating liberalization in this respect. Any calls for social equality and justice within the church will probably sound both secular and political to Adventist ears: the church is likely to be deeply suspicious about the value of 'consciousness-raising' activities, even though it may recognize the presence of injustice arising from sexual discrimination. The strife within the church over racial matters in the 1960s and 1970s is still fresh in the denominational memory. Many Adventists would regard it as their first responsibility to overlook even legitimate grievances in a search for the unity necessary to proclaim 'the everlasting gospel' successfully.

Any serious attempt to expand the opportunities for service available to the women of the church would probably have to involve ordination since real executive power in the church lies almost exclusively in ministerial hands. Such a move would probably have more far-reaching implications than can now be envisaged, as the following observation made by a Catholic of her own church suggests:

For it is not possible to imagine the admission of women to the Catholic priesthood without, at the same time, modifying certain fundamental notions about hierarchy, theology, Church and authority. This even more than women, may be what the hierarchy fears.[69]

To respond sympathetically to criticisms made by, and on behalf of, women would be to accept that there was something wrong with the structures which churchmen themselves had created and maintained, and would be to invite the possibility of radical change in the nature of the church. If the churches were significantly different from other bureaucracies, then such radical change might be in prospect, but in the churches, as elsewhere, those who exercise power generally wish to retain it. To invite women into Adventist pulpits, or on to church committees in any numbers, would be to admit the possibility of significant change in denominational life. Such a change might appear as a tacit admission that church structure has been defective. Those with a less individualistic interpretation of theology might even use the term 'sinful' to describe such an organizational structure. But these are not the modes of Adventist thinking. There is a powerful belief in the basic integrity of their church among Adventists; sinfulness is perceived to be an individual phenomenon, and not something which inheres in organizational arrangements.

Fears may also exist for the possible effects on Adventist theology.

Adventist theology has traditionally been literalistic in its approach
to the Bible; those basic critical tools which are necessary to an
explication of texts which have been the basis of the subordination
of women in the church clearly threaten traditional Adventist
hermeneutical principles. Quite simply, the Bible, rule of faith for
Adventists, was written in male-dominated societies; without the use
of critical methods, Adventism will inevitably reflect that bias. The
biblical models and symbols of faith are, by and large, masculine;
it is unsurprising, therefore, that male experience of God has been
taken to be normative. This has been mitigated somewhat by the
prominence given in Ellen White's writing to a compassionate
Christ,[70] a reflection of which has been called 'the feminization of
American religion'. Furthermore, any major initiative to remedy
social injustice would be in some way a denial of the imminence of
the second advent. If apocalyptic liberation is upon us, then any other
forms of liberation are a snare and a delusion. Underpinning all this,
perhaps, is the notion that the feminist cause is represented as the
pursuit of something better, while many Adventists believe that
Adventism already embraces, at least potentially, the *summum
bonum*.

As has already been observed, Adventist males who see their
membership of, and position within the Adventist church as a source
of status, are likely to see the opening of opportunities to women as
a threat. It is the fear of those who are well placed in any system of
privilege. Adventist men have a vested interest in perpetuating the
myth that women are somehow incapable of the rational behaviour
necessary to public ministry. They may also fear the heightened
emotionalism which women might bring to the services of the church.

Those who are perhaps most vulnerable are the ministers of the
church, because the admission of women to their ranks might have
the effect of diminishing the status of their role, and would introduce
greater competition into the job market at a time when the church
cannot give employment to all who feel a vocation to ministry. The
matter is part of a larger issue too, that of division between clergy
and laity – the Adventist church being more clericalist than one might
expect for a sectarian group.

The Seventh-day Adventist church has communicated an ambiguous message to its women members. It has welcomed them, provided

that they confined themselves in public and in private to a role of domestic piety; it has rebuked them, in a subtle way, if they strayed far beyond those limits. Only in the last few years have the dissenting voices been heard. Perhaps Adventist women became content to subscribe to the myth of male supremacy to avoid the responsibilities which came with privilege. Perhaps they quite simply came to believe what they had been told about themselves.

11 · Divorce in Adventism: a perennial problem

In the beginning, divorce ...

It could well be argued that an accelerating rate of marital break-down is one of the chief distinguishing characteristics of contemporary western society. Whichever statistical instrument is employed to measure the phenomenon, it is clear that increasingly large numbers of marriages encounter difficulties which prove insurmountable. The church in general, and the Seventh-day Adventist church in particular, has not been immune to the malady. Moreover, it would be a mistake to believe that the problem among Adventists is an entirely modern one; divorce has been a contentious issue in the Seventh-day Adventist church from its very inception. At a business session in October 1862, the Michigan State Conference of Seventh-day Adventists tackled an agenda which included the 'matter of divorced marriages'. Delegates considered whether those who had divorced and remarried prior to seeking member-ship, for reasons considered by Adventists to be unbiblical, should be received into fellowship by the believers.[1] Adventists resolved that matter relatively painlessly in favour of the would-be members, but increases in membership, and changes in social mores and laws, have broadened the range of domestic problems with which the church has had to deal. Divorce remains an issue which absorbs considerable energy of administrators who attempt to formulate workable policies, of pastors who seek to apply them, and of members whose personal crises inevitably weaken the church in various ways. The purpose here is to trace the history of this problem in the life of the church.

182

Divorce in the United States: law and practice

The social exigencies facing the early colonists had demanded a somewhat more flexible attitude towards divorce than existed in their homelands. By the beginning of the nineteenth century, divorce legislation was rather more liberal, with New Hampshire, for example, granting the right of divorce to men and women on the grounds of adultery, extreme cruelty, impotence, or an absence of three years. In an effort to conserve time and finance, state legislatures increasingly surrendered their jurisdiction over divorce. Reforms were often incorporated into new state constitutions, as in the case of Pennsylvania in 1838, and, by 1867, only four of the thirty-seven states retained legislative divorce. By way of generalization, one can say that by the time the nation was plunged into civil war, divorce was easily available and on the increase. Grounds for dissolution were readily extended; progressively shorter residency periods were required; women were increasingly allowed to file petitions; there was considerable latitude in interpreting the law; and collusion between spouses was common. As the frontier expanded westwards, divorce became easier to obtain and, indeed, bigamy more easily concealed. The law passed in Connecticut in 1849 illustrates well the liberal *ante bellum* mood. A divorce was permitted for 'any such misconduct as permanently destroys the happiness of the petitioner and defeats the purpose of the marriage relation'.[2]

The Civil War prompted many Americans to question the assumptions with which they had been operating. In the realm of divorce, it created a strong conservative reaction. Anxiety over the liberal law in Connecticut led to the first collection of divorce statistics to be assembled in the United States, which showed a steady rise in the incidence of divorce.[3] An enquiry into the situation throughout the nation revealed the same basic trend; the number of divorces per 1,000 marriages rose from 1.2 in 1860, to 1.8 in 1866, an increase from 7,380 in 1860, to 11,530 in 1866.[4] Some states tightened their legislation, but conservative fears were confirmed in 1889 when the Commissioner of Labor produced the first set of reliable divorce statistics, showing increases in dissolution rates out of all proportion to population growth, from 9,937 in 1867, to 25,535 in 1886.[5]

Western states, however, were quick to exploit the commercial opportunities created by the crises of conscience on the divorce issue being experienced by states to the east. Idaho and the Dakotas, among others, attracted at different times many clients from the east who were seeking an easy divorce. Such states had short residency requirements for the franchise, or any other purpose, since they sheltered very mobile populations which were on the trail westward. The trade in migratory divorces stimulated interest in federal divorce legislation, but the issue proved too contentious to permit a consensus of opinion to emerge.

The churches deplored rising divorce rates, imposed certain sanctions on divorcees, and expressed fears for the stability of the family, and ultimately of the nation. However, any attempts to extend ecclesiastical prohibitions into the civil sphere engendered fears about the erosion of cherished individual rights. Furthermore, the uncompromising indissolubilist views of some Protestant leaders were too close to the Roman Catholic position for the comfort of many Americans. Thus, while the churches devoted considerable energy to the divorce issue in the latter part of the century, their influence was largely neutralized because of the failure to achieve consensus both between, and within, denominations.

At the beginning of the new century, divorce law varied considerably from state to state, and its application was still more uneven. While statutes frequently reflected the orthodoxy of church doctrine, the courts often interpreted them extremely loosely. Although divorce continued to be regarded as some form of moral lapse, increasing consideration was given to the pathology of divorce. Dissolution rates rose steadily from 55,751 (4.0 per 1,000 marriages) in 1900, to 76,571 (4.5) in 1907.[6] Efforts to promote uniform legislation all failed but most jurisdictions tightened their laws, and by 1908 just four states retained a residency requirement of only six months. Strict though the laws of some states may have appeared, it was possible for any determined person to obtain a divorce by migration, collusion, or fraud.

Ellen White

Ellen White's writings consistently maintained an exalted notion of marriage:

Examine carefully to see if your married life would be happy or inharmonious and wretched. Let the questions be raised, Will this union help me heavenward? Will it increase my love for God? And will it enlarge my sphere of usefulness in this life? If these reflections present no drawback, then in the fear of God move forward.[7]

A symbol of the union between Christ and his church, marriage linked 'the destinies of the two individuals with bonds which nought but the hand of death should sever'.[8] The couple must anticipate as best they could the pressures which life would inevitably place upon them, and absorb them when they came.[9]

The corollary of such a high standard was a severe criticism of any form of marital irregularity. The first such testimony came in 1854, when Ellen White was 27 and had been married for seven years. The product of a visionary experience, it was directed at the churches in New York State:

I saw that the seventh commandment has been violated by some who are now held in fellowship by the church ... This sin is awful in these last days, but the church have brought God's frown and curse upon them by regarding the sin so lightly. I saw it was an enormous sin and there have not been as vigilant efforts made as there should have been to satisfy the displeasure of God and remove His frown by taking a strict, thorough course with the offender ... Those who break the seventh commandment should be suspended from the church and not have its fellowship or the privileges of the house of God ... Never was this sin regarded by God as being so exceedingly sinful as at the present time. Why? Because God is purifying unto Himself a peculiar people, zealous of good works ... they sin with a high hand, give way to all the loose passions of the carnal heart, gratify their animal propensities, disgrace the cause of God, and then confess they have sinned and are sorry: And the church receives them and says 'Amen' to their prayers and exhortations, which are a stink in the nostrils of God and cause His wrath to come upon the camp. He will not dwell in their assemblies ...[10]

The rebuke covered various types of sexual behaviour unacceptable to the Adventist community, including remarriage without scriptural grounds. The prophetess urged purity on the believers, convinced that Christ would soon return to seek his sanctified people.

Ellen White consistently maintained throughout her ministry that adultery was the only ground for divorce. The principle was enunciated quite clearly in 1863:

A woman may be legally divorced from her husband by the laws of the land and yet not divorced in the sight of God and according to the higher law. There is only one sin, which is adultery, which can place the husband or wife in a position where they can be free from the marriage vow in the sight of God.[11]

Twenty-five years later she was still affirming it: 'Nothing but the violation of the marriage bed can either break or annul the marriage vow.'[12]

She clearly excluded other grounds for divorce which were periodically brought before her. She did not judge the habitual drunkenness and cruelty of Victory Jones towards his wife sufficient justification for the divorce which she ultimately obtained.[13] Ellen White's judgement was, however, certainly influenced by the fact that Mrs Jones had rather too energetically enlisted the sympathetic concern of a Brother George Lay, a pillar of the local church. With the complex situation threatening Adventist influence in the local community, Lay and Jones were counselled to behave with the greatest circumspection.

Ellen White saw in incompatibility no ground whatever for dissolution of marriage. To one enquiring couple she said quite plainly: 'If your dispositions are not congenial, would it not be for the glory of God for you to change these dispositions?'[14] Adventists were to stop entertaining thoughts of divorce as an escape route from an unhappy marriage. Rather they were to work at improving their marital situation and tending their own souls.[15] It was along such a path, rather than in escaping from present misery, that contentment lay: 'Husband and wife are to be faithful to each other as long as time shall last, ever revealing the self-sacrifice that brings true happiness.'[16] Childlessness was not to be regarded as a curse and an occasion for divorce; on the contrary, it was to be welcomed as an opportunity for service:

Many of our young women missionaries marry and in a few months' time they have children to care for, and are then taken out of the missionary field. You may rejoice that your daughter will not be thus hindered in her work for the Master. She can accompany her husband in his travels, and be a help to him, and when she is left at home, she can work for the Lord as though she were unmarried.[17]

Above all, Ellen White was most insistent that Adventists did not seek divorces from their unbelieving spouses on religious grounds:

If the wife is an unbeliever and an opposer, the husband can not, in view of the law of God, put her away on this ground alone. In order to be in harmony with the law of Jehovah, he must abide with her, unless she chooses of herself to depart. He may suffer opposition and be oppressed and annoyed in many ways; he will find his comfort and his strength and support from God who is able to give grace for every emergency.[18]

Nor were believers to leave when the attitudes of their spouse prevented them from doing the kind of Christian service which they wished to do; they were to remain and become 'home missionaries', giving themselves to the spiritual welfare of their spouse and children.[19] An exception to this was the case of a leading Adventist worker, M. E. Cornell. Ellen White believed it better that he remain separated from his wife, although he had no reason to believe that she had provided him with grounds for divorce by violating the marriage vow.[20]

In all her writings Ellen White laid emphasis on prevention rather than cure. She recognized church workers as being a group particularly at risk, and constantly warned them against developing a dangerous level of intimacy with those they contacted in the course of their work. Ministers, she warned, were using their privileged position to claim the attentions and affections of female members of their congregation:

Licentiousness, unlawful intimacy, and unholy practices are coming in among us in a large degree and ministers who are handling sacred things are guilty of sin in this respect. They are coveting their neighbours' wives, and the seventh commandment is broken.[21]

Danger lurked particularly when ministers operated as confessors to their women members. The danger was most acute in Adventist health institutions where there always existed a tendency to break down the 'barriers of distinction and restraint erected by God' to preserve the modesty and integrity of individuals and of families.[22] For that reason Ellen White encouraged the employment of trained women personnel.[23]

There were, of course, many occasions when Ellen White had to give counsel in marital situations which were far from the standard she had set. In the most comprehensive of her general statements, published in response to a particular case of marital infidelity, Ellen and James White jointly affirmed that:

1 In cases of the violation of the seventh commandment, where the guilty party does not manifest true repentance, if the injured party can obtain a divorce without making their own cases and that of their children, if they have them, worse by so doing, they should be free.

2 If they would be liable to place themselves and their children in worse condition by a divorce, we know of no scripture that would make the innocent party guilty by remaining.

3 Time, and labor, and prayer, and patience, and faith, and a godly life, might work a reform. To live with one who has broken the marriage vows, and is covered all over with the disgrace and shame of guilty love, and realizes it not, is an eating canker to the soul; and yet, a divorce is a life-long, heart-felt sore. God pity the innocent party. Marriage should be considered well before contracted ...

5 But, if they will not do as they should, and if the innocent have forfeited the legal right to a divorce, by living with the guilty after his guilt is known, we do not see that sin rests upon the innocent in remaining, and her *moral right* in departing seems questionable, if her health and life be not greatly endangered in so remaining.[24]

While, then, Ellen White acknowledged the possibility of divorce, it was a course to be avoided if at all possible:

Her marriage was a deception of the devil. Yet now she should make the best of it, treat her husband with tenderness, and make him as happy as she can without violating her conscience ...[25]

In an extreme case, however, Ellen White counselled the opposite course of action:

His best course with this child-wife, so over-bearing, so unyielding, and so uncontrollable, is to take her home, and leave her with her mother who has made her what she is ... He is under no obligation to keep one by his side who will only torture his soul ...[26]

While the man's religious responsibilities might lead him to separate himself from his wife, he nevertheless was to remain faithful to his wife; Ellen White asserted that the extreme behaviour of his wife did not confer upon him the freedom to remarry.

In another case, Ellen White implied criticism of an Adventist woman who had remarried, by insisting on calling her by the name of her first husband.[27] Ellen White condemned her own secretary, Fannie Bolton, for seeking to marry a man whose wife had divorced him; the condemnation derived from the fact that the two had planned the matter prior to the dissolution of the marriage.[28]

Where a second marriage had already been contracted 'unscripturally', Ellen White took a realistic view of the matter. Of the particularly complicated case of one, Will Wales, she said:

I would say that his case can not be improved by leaving the present wife. It would not better the case to go to the other woman [the first wife] in the question ... I am sorry for the man; for his course is in such a shape that it will not answer to be meddled with, for there are difficulties upon difficulties. I would say that the Lord understands the situation, and if Will Wales will seek him with all his heart, he will be found of him. If he will do his best, God will pardon and receive him.[29]

She openly chastised those who felt the need to dismantle members' second marriages and return spouses to their former partners. Far from ostracizing such defaulters, church members should extend sympathy to them, she said.[30] Most illuminating in this connection was the case of a member of Ellen White's family:

Sr White's next oldest sister, Sarah Harmon, was married to Stephen Belden and became the mother of five children. After her death, in pity for his children, he married a woman who had many years been a faithful servant in his household. Shortly after this, the measles visited the vicinity, and she with others had the measles in a severe form. The measles went to her brain, and she became crazy, and had to be taken to the asylum. Belden struggled along for some time, trying to care for his five children, then for their sake, married a very good, efficient woman by the name of Vina Williams. She helped him make a home and bring up his children and was with him in Norfolk Island when he died. At various times, individuals where the Beldens lived, undertook to secure his exclusion from the church because he had married without separation from his wife on the charge of adultery. When appealed to in regard to this matter, Sr White said, 'Let them alone.'[31]

She clearly believed that a scripturally irregular marriage did not involve a couple in a state of 'continual adultery'.

On only one occasion, apparently in a particularly unpleasant case of incest, did Ellen White advise excluding an individual permanently from fellowship:

It is impossible for E to be fellowshiped by the church of God. He has placed himself where he cannot be helped by the church, where he can have no communion with nor voice in the church ... If he repents ever so heartily, the church must let his case alone. If he goes to heaven, it must be alone, without the fellowship of the church. A standing rebuke from God and the church must ever rest upon him, that the standard of morality be not lowered to the very dust.[32]

Generally, she held that there was a way of return to the church available to those who had been disciplined for irregular behaviour with regard to second marriages:

It is a feature in the cases of most who have been overtaken in sin ... that they have no real sense of their villainy. Some, however, do, and are restored to the church; but not till they have merited the confidence of the people of God by unqualified confessions, and a period of sincere repentance.[33]

Ellen White's reaction to the case of another defaulter demonstrated her view that, after manifesting true contrition, such might not only regain their church membership but also be employed in the work of the church.[34]

Although Ellen White was, in the course of her ministry, called upon to counsel and adjudicate in many cases of unhappy marriages, it is clear that she found such a task by no means congenial. The difficulty of her situation is plainly revealed in the following letter:

I am fearful to sanction sin and I am fearful to let go of the sinner and make no effort to restore him ... I am more pained than I can express to see so little aptitude and skill to save souls that are ensnared by Satan. I see such a cold Pharisaism, holding off at arm's length the one who has been deluded by the adversary of souls ... Is this spirit to grow among us? If so, my brethren must excuse me, I cannot labor with them ... I think of Jesus, what love and tenderness he manifested for erring, fallen man and then I think of the severe judgement one pronounces upon his brother that has fallen under temptation and my heart becomes sick.[35]

Furthermore, she sometimes feared that her own forthright condemnation of behaviour encouraged others to treat the offenders severely: 'If we err, let it be on the side of mercy rather than on the side of condemnation and harsh dealing', she urged.[36] Indeed, to one woman who had committed fornication she wrote:

I could say to you to go to trustworthy persons in the Conference (not men but women), and talk with them, but I am inclined to think that should you do this, you would be giving publicity to those things which would cause all to be removed from you, and they would not encourage you or accept you to engage in any branch of the work, when they should understand the matter as it is. I must now leave this matter between you and your God ... I have no disposition to expose you; but leave you to develop character.[37]

There were occasions when Ellen White felt unable to pronounce on difficult cases. She confessed herself to be too burdened to adjudicate in the case of a leading Adventist minister,[38] and again, concerning the request for counsel from an ordinary member, she said:

You asked me if I thought if your wife left you, that you should marry again ... But I am not fully prepared to give you my judgement, whether in a Bible point of view, you could marry again. My mind is so fully occupied that it is not possible for me to consider this vexed question of marriage and divorces.[39]

As the end of her life approached, Ellen White, apparently sensing the vacuum which would be left by her death, refused to adjudicate on the complexities of the married life of members, and urged church leaders to assume such burdens.[40]

She consistently upheld a high standard for marriage, and, when that ideal was broken, maintained a view of divorce based on a strict understanding of scripture. There may, however, appear to be some unevenness in her approach to the subject. For example, the kinds of calls for greater compassion already cited may appear to lie uncomfortably beside the following:

I was shown that you had been wrong in sympathizing with E ... Your influence encourages a slack state of things in the church ... You have too long wrapped up the sharp testimony, and stood opposed to the severe censure which God lays upon individual wrongs ... Ministers must cry aloud and spare not.[41]

Or again:

Cleanse the camp of this moral corruption, if it takes the highest men in the highest positions. God will not be trifled with. Fornication is within our ranks; I know it, for it has been shown to me to be strengthening and extending its pollutions. There is much we will never know; but that which is revealed makes the church responsible and guilty unless they show a determined effort to eradicate the evil. Cleanse the camp, for there is an accursed thing in it.[42]

It is essential to attempt to provide some overall understanding of Ellen White's views on divorce. The key to the matter was probably provided by her son and secretary, W.C. White, when he said:

It was Sister White's intention that there should not go forth from her pen anything that could be used as a law or a rule in dealing with these questions of marriage, divorce, remarriage, and adultery. She felt that the different cases where the devil had led men into serious entanglement were so varied and so serious, that should she write anything that could be considered as a rule for settling such cases, it would be misunderstood and misused.[43]

It seems clear that, faced with a particular marital situation, the details of which are now often unknown, she sought a practical solution which promoted the interests of the individual concerned while protecting the integrity of the church. Secondly, it is important to distinguish between counsel given in a particular context, and rather more general exhortations to the church. The latter would, of course, tend to be more idealistic. Thirdly, it is possible to draw some distinction between those occasions when she believed herself to be in receipt of divine illumination on a particular case, and those when she did not.

Furthermore, it can be argued fairly convincingly that she mellowed in her views over the years. The more strident of her testimonies were written to a group which was striving 'to imitate the society we expect soon to join; namely, angels of God who have never fallen by sin'.[44] Her pleas for compassion, however, were addressed to a church which was more remote from the advent expectation of 1844, a church which had been organized for some twenty-five years, and which now felt secure enough to seek solidarity in ways other than through unbending discipline. Moreover, not only had the movement evolved somewhat, but Ellen White had changed too in the intervening years. The ebb and flow of her relationship with her own husband had no doubt been both educative and mellowing. Life was sometimes very stressful for Ellen White following the strokes experienced by James from 1865 onwards.[45] No doubt, too, the unending stream of cases demanding counsel, sometimes involving influential men in the denomination, had made her increasingly aware of the complex problems and pain which marital disruption brought in its train. It would have become increasingly clear to her that simple formulae for resolving such situations did not exist.

Published Adventist opinion until 1915

The first reference to divorce in Adventist literature was made in 1862 by *Review* editor Uriah Smith, apparently in response to a reader's enquiry. He observed that Matthew 19:9, which cited adultery as the sole grounds for divorce, was to be regarded as the norm, and denied that Romans 7:1−3 in any way modified it.[46] It was in the same year that the Michigan State Conference of Seventh-day Adventists considered the eligibility for membership of those who had already divorced on unscriptural grounds before coming into contact with the church.[47] Writers expressed concern that standards in society at large were declining:

Divorces are increasing to an alarming extent. An old resident of this county recently observed to me with much feeling, that divorces were becoming so frequent in Ohio, and were obtained on such frivolous pretexts, and the laws were so favorable to this, that it threatened the loss of all public virtue ... Such a state of things has a tendency to let down the standard and to form in the public mind an idea that marriage is only a civil contract, to be dissolved at any time, either by mutual consent or by private whim or pretext ...[48]

The clearest statement by the early Adventists came in a *Review* article in 1879, which insisted that only a person whose spouse had committed the overt act of adultery could divorce and remarry with the church's blessing. Adulterous thoughts were not a sufficient ground.[49]

Adventists clearly thought that permissive legislation was the cause of the worsening situation:

Vermont is the paradise of loose marriage laws. During the last sixteen years there have been in that little state 2,417 divorces, of which 632 were for adultery, 941 for desertion, 683 for personal cruelty, 137 for refusal to support, 11 for confinement in the State prison, and 3 for insanity. In 1865 the proportion of divorces to marriages was as 1 to 21.06, and in 1877 as 1 to 14.94. For the first eight years of the sixteen the average ratio of divorces to marriages was as 1 to 18.18, and for the last eight years it has been as 1 to 16.04 ... This subject is worthy of the thoughtful consideration of the legislature of every State in the Union.[50]

In this respect, Adventists were in agreement with the National Reform Party, an influential Protestant group, although they could not join forces with a party which also advocated legislation to impose stricter Sunday observance.

Uriah Smith saw the growing divorce rate as a refutation of the myth that the world was becoming a better place, a view to which many churches subscribed. He further believed that the social evil of polygamy manifested in Mormonism could hardly be resisted while lax divorce laws permitted a kind of serial polygamy.[51]

George Butler was the first General Conference president to go into print on the subject.[52] He sensed the need to do so for several reasons. The increased facility with which divorce could be obtained had produced strife in some Adventist churches and threatened their well-being. The church, he believed, needed to maintain a clear witness to biblical standards, for 'the purity of society, and the salvation of thousands of our fellow men' depended upon it. The case of newly converted divorcees was a problem which admitted of no general solution; each case, he asserted, must be considered on its own merits, particularly where a second marriage was apparently happy and involved children. The 'crime' of divorce was, in his opinion, subversive of the marriage institution, and posed a serious threat to the life of the church.

In 1887, Adventist thinking took a conservative turn under the influence of *Review* editor Uriah Smith. His firmest statement came in response to the request of a correspondent who had divorced by mutual consent and remarried while his first wife was living. Smith argued that his second marriage was unscriptural unless it was the case that his first wife had committed adultery prior to his obtaining a divorce. Smith concluded that 'his last marriage is unlawful; and of course no church could receive him as a member while living in that condition'.[53] The statement was significant in that it was the first formal expression of the notion of 'continual adultery'.

Smith's editorial clearly caused such a reaction that he quickly felt the need to qualify his position. While affirming that adultery was the only biblical ground for divorce, he acknowledged that there might very well be reasons why one party would refuse to live with the other. He even went so far as to allow that a woman who was ill-treated by her husband, might divorce him on any grounds that the state might allow, so long as she did not remarry. On the cases of those converts who had obtained unscriptural divorces before becoming members he advised, 'Take them as they are found, leaving those things that cannot be undone to the past.'[54] His defence of the central notion of 'continual adultery' was, however, unequivocal. Of the woman who entered a second marriage having failed to provide biblical grounds for terminating the first, he said: 'to the day of her death, should her first husband live so long, she will be an adulteress in the sight of God, if she enters into marriage relations with anyone'.[55]

That the matter continued to be a source of concern in the church is clear from editorial acknowledgement that the *Review* received regular enquiries from anxious readers concerning the status of their relationships.[56] George Tenney, an influential church leader, confirmed Smith's position in these words:

Where this [adultery] does not exist, no court can release the parties who before God have promised to love and cherish each other till death ... The solemn obligations there assumed should not be set aside to favor convenience, selfishness or natural desires.[57]

It is significant that church leaders took a position which appeared more rigorous than that adopted by Ellen White. It is true, of course, that they were promoting ideals in a public forum while she could soften the harshness of an external standard by the expression of compassion in private correspondence. It is clear, however, that she opposed the view that anyone remarrying without biblical grounds lived in a state of 'continual adultery' as long as the second marriage lasted.[58]

Other features of the issue were addressed at various times in the remainder of the century. The permissiveness of the law[59] and the practice of migratory divorce [60] attracted severe criticism, as did the collusion in divorce proceedings between spouses, and between a couple and courts.[61] Tenney evinced surprise that the evil of divorce was penetrating all social classes and was not restricted to 'people of baser pursuits'.[62]

Early in the twentieth century, as the incidence of divorce continued to rise, writers in the *Review* showed themselves aware of developments in the wider society as they continued to affirm the traditional position of the church. The *Review* editor, F. M. Wilcox, commenting on a Senate debate, expressed alarm at the way in which divorce was increasingly accepted as normal behaviour, and urged the churches to reawaken the public conscience. He wrote: 'It is safe to conclude that the great majority of divorces which are recognized by our courts of law are not recognized by the court of heaven.'[63] In another editorial shortly afterwards, Wilcox lamented the fact that as many as one in seven marriages was ending in divorce. Those who found themselves locked in an unhappy marriage should display fortitude, for,

If a mistake is made, better the party who made the mistake should suffer than the institution of marriage be brought into disrepute, and the teaching of Scripture disregarded.[64]

Adventists, then, were to do everything to maintain the edifice of their marriages even though the conditions might be unpromising.

12 · Divorcing and enforcing: problems with principles and procedures

Divorce in the United States: law and practice

Although the Depression stemmed the divorce rate, the general trend to higher levels of marital breakdown was unmistakable in the 1930s; the rate rose from 7.9 per 1,000 marriages in 1929, to 8.7 in 1940.[1] Roman Catholic opposition to divorce was reiterated by Pius XI in the encyclical *Casti Connubii* in 1930. The Protestant churches, showing obvious signs of internal division, failed to take any decisive action in the inter-war period, generally allowing remarriage for innocent parties, although there was growing dissatisfaction with the notion of 'innocence'. It became clear that resort to moral suasion was ineffective, and that reasons for marital breakdown had to be sought in such factors as increasing geographical mobility, the anonymity of the city, and the loss of the coercive control of the primary group.

The enormous social dislocation produced by the Second World War irreparably damaged many marriages, as the statistics in table 12.1 indicate. In the late 1940s and 1950s, the incidence of divorce stabilized, although it never returned to pre-war levels. As has already been observed, the 1950s brought a period of relative marital stability when many Americans made domestic happiness their priority. However, following the lead of the Episcopal church, a number of mainline churches, including the Presbyterians and the United Lutheran church, liberalized their policies by demanding simply that those who wished to remarry show evidence of repentance and undertake to enter a life-long Christian marriage.

In the 1960s, support grew for the reform of divorce legislation in line with current practice. The reasons for this change of mood were complex, but principal among them were the growing feminist

197

Table 12.1   Divorce rates in the USA, 1940–77

Year	Number of divorces	Rate per 1,000 total population	Rate per 1,000 married women 15 years and over
1940	264,000	2.0	8.8
1942	321,000	2.4	10.1
1944	400,000	2.9	12.0
1945	485,000	3.5	14.4
1946	610,000	4.3	17.9
1947	483,000	3.4	13.6
1948	408,000	2.8	11.2
1949	397,000	2.7	10.6
1950	385,144	2.6	10.3
1951	381,000	2.5	9.9
1952	392,000	2.5	10.1
1954	379,000	2.4	9.5
1956	382,000	2.3	9.4
1958	368,000	2.1	8.9
1960	393,000	2.2	9.2
1962	413,000	2.2	9.4
1964	450,000	2.4	10.0
1966	499,000	2.5	10.9
1968	584,000	2.9	12.5
1970	708,000	3.5	14.9
1972	845,000	4.1	17.0
1975	1,036,000	4.9	20.3
1977	1,090,000	5.0	21.3

Source: F. D. Cox, *Human Intimacy*, p.450.

consciousness, the erosion of traditional Christian sexual mores, and certain demographic trends. In 1967, New York State became the first to introduce the notion of 'no-fault' into its legislation, with California following in 1969. In both cases, the therapeutic provisions of the new law (namely, attempts to promote reconciliation, and encouragement of education for remarriage) appeased conservative factions at the time, but proved impracticable. Liberalization has rendered divorce proceedings more straightforward, but has by no means eliminated hostilities, especially where child custody and property settlement are concerned. By 1978, most states had included the notion of 'no-fault' into their divorce law, although many incorporated this into the existing framework of fault grounds. Spouses not infrequently resorted to fault grounds when dissatisfied with the terms of settlement.

The churches have generally only been able to look on at the continuing rise in divorce rates, the liberalization of attitudes, and reform of laws. They have had to acknowledge that a marriage may die in ways other than by the death or infidelity of one of the partners. The churches have tended either officially or in practice to liberalize their positions, and concentrate their efforts on counselling those who are contemplating a change in their marital status. Indeed, it is widely acknowledged in American society that, amid all the stresses of modern urban life, spouses have to make a concerted and intelligent effort to nurture their marriages.

Among those sectarian groups with which Adventism has often been identified, marriage is, without exception, accorded an exalted position. They nevertheless experience problems with marital breakdown, and the process of finding a workable solution which is both principled and compassionate is a continuing one. A typical strategy is that adopted by Jehovah's Witnesses, whereby a person remarrying after a divorce not involving adultery is disfellowshipped and reinstated after a penitential period of about a year.[2]

Other features of the situation arouse anxiety in those concerned about the moral fabric of American society. Cherlin demonstrated that 17 per cent of children born in the period 1968–70 had experienced family disruption by the age of 5, compared with 11 per cent of those born 1956–8. Further, in 1979, 5.3 million American women headed one-parent families, an increase of 81 per cent over the 1970 figure. There has also been a sharp rise in the number of working mothers, so that 43 per cent of women with pre-school children were employed in 1979, compared with 11 per cent in 1949.[3] The future of the family is clearly a matter of great concern to many Americans, and not simply to those who espouse traditional Christian values. They feel that they must promote less cavalier attitudes to marriage and divorce if the fabric of their society is to be protected.

Published Adventist opinion: 1915–1985

It was not until 1925, some sixty years after the formal organization of the church, that the General Conference issued its first official statement. Church leaders resolved

that we greatly deplore the evil of divorce, and place our emphatic disapproval upon any legal action for the separation of those once married, on any ground other than that given in Matthew 5:32.[4]

The article gave open expression for the first time to the fear that Adventists would be drawn into the whirlpool of mounting marital disruption. Conspicuous by its absence was any provision for dealing with offending members. However, the *Manual for Ministers*, published in the same year, did require that any minister who committed adultery be disfellowshipped and never restored to the ministry (p. 8).

In 1932, the first *Church Manual*, or compendium on church order, contained a reference to the problem of divorce. It reaffirmed the 1925 resolution, and underlined the importance of working for the reconciliation of the couple. This pastoral concern was balanced, however, by a recognition of the importance of maintaining standards. The manual directed that sin should be reproved, offenders disfellowshipped, and ministers debarred from conducting a wedding ceremony for any but the innocent party (pp. 175–6). It is evident, however, that considerable confusion over the matter existed, either from ignorance of, or failure to apply, the church's declared position.

The subject was clearly one which increasingly occupied the minds of church leaders. Articles deplored the fact that large numbers of children were the innocent victims of divorce, that the Episcopal church appeared to be ready to liberalize its canons, that certain states were competing for the trade brought by 'divorce tourists'.[5] Various writers saw in the rising incidence of divorce, not least among Adventists, a development of cosmic and eschatological, rather than merely sociological, significance. One believed that Satan was making 'every effort to ruin this primary institution'.[6] Another believed that 'The breakdown of the home is one of the important signs of the end.'[7]

The *Review* carried significant comment in 1942, in response to the deteriorating situation in society at large, and to the fact that divorce was 'making its inroads upon us', especially in large Adventist communities.[8] The author believed that the situation called for an unequivocal statement of the church's position. He argued that it was vital for a church which upheld one Edenic institution, the Sabbath, to defend the other, marriage, with equal vigour. He reaffirmed the traditional view that adultery was the sole grounds for divorce, and concluded that those divorced for unscriptural reasons should not 'be admitted to church membership or retain their membership in the church unless they can find some way to regularize their status'.[9]

Church leaders duly responded with an official pronouncement in the same year; it became the first official declaration in the church's history that the second marriage of an offending party constituted a continuing state of sin. As far as affiliation with the church was concerned, there was little room for misunderstanding: 'Should such a person [a 'guilty' party] marry another, he be not readmitted to church membership so long as the unscriptural relationship continues.'[10] Any claim to the right to remarry should be thoroughly investigated by representatives of the church. These measures were to replace those existing in the *Church Manual*.

In 1948, attitudes hardened further as a *Review* editorial urged that the church resist by all means the erosion of its standards. It reasserted that those seeking the right to remarry must produce evidence of their partner's adultery which could be investigated by the church. It called for vigilance by Adventist churches to prevent offenders from going from congregation to congregation to find acceptance. Even if such an itinerant person, seeking membership through baptism or re-baptism, was successful in her (*sic*) search for acceptance, she should be aware that 'the baptism does not absolve her from her state of adultery. She is continuing in this state as long as she lives with her second so-called husband ...'[11] Moreover, the church was urged to recognize that 'in receiving her and this husband into church member-ship' it was 'condoning her state of adultery'. The editorial rejected incompatibility and mental cruelty as grounds for divorce; in extreme cases there should be resort to separation by mutual agreement with all settlements to be conducted privately. Insanity was clearly stated not to be grounds for divorce; if physical illness gave no cause for dissolution, then there was no reason why mental illness should. There was evidently some fear that such a ground would be open to abuse.

This article marked the full development of the conservative policy on divorce pursued by the editorial board of the *Review*, designed to preserve the integrity of the church, and to remind members that they could not with impunity adopt the changing mores of the wider society. It must be recalled, however, that editorial comment in the *Review* enjoyed nothing more than semi-official status, had no legislative force, and indeed sometimes attracted criticism from both membership and administration. It both reflected and shaped denominational thinking at the same time.

Recognizing the ambiguities of the church's position, senior administrators commissioned a study, the first of its kind, which was submitted in April 1949. The author of the document, A. V. Olson, a prominent church leader, traced the increase in divorce and remarriage in Adventism directly to the failure of the church to operate a consistent policy: 'Our present policy has been so diluted and emasculated that with the best of will on the part of our churches, we cannot hope for a uniform practice.'[12] In dealing with cases of marital breakdown, pastors had very little in the way of an official statement of principles or procedures to consult, apart from *Review* articles. What little there was could be supplemented by consulting Ellen White's counsel, much of which, existing only in letter form, was then not readily accessible. In addition, it was only to be expected that the disparities which existed in legislation and attitudes from state to state, would be reflected in church practice to some extent. There was, Olson said, 'a glaring lack of guidance'; the church needed a policy which was 'comprehensive, clear and positive', if practice was to be uniform (p. 2).

Part of the confusion resulted, he opined, from recent emendations to the *Church Manual*. The original statement had been altered to read:

Resolved, That we recognize adultery as justifiable ground for divorce, with the right of the innocent party to remarry as taught by the Saviour, recorded in Matthew 5:32 and Luke 16:18.   (p. 2)

This modification of official policy had encouraged the view that the church recognized causes other than adultery as legitimate grounds for divorce. Furthermore, the inclusion of 'the remarriage of a divorced person' in the catalogue of 'reasons for which members may be disfellowshipped' seemed to leave such discipline to the discretion of the local church.

The document went on to make certain radical departures from the semi-official *Review* position. It defended the view that the act of adultery itself broke the marriage bond. Unless there existed a mutual will to reforge that bond, the marriage was in fact dead, and there was no longer anything to which to remain faithful. Both parties were free to remarry. It followed then that the notion of 'continual adultery' in the later marriage was false, and in practice the church acknowledged that by retaining so many 'guilty' remarried divorcees in its midst. It rejected the view that only the dissolution of a second marriage was sufficient evidence of the repentance required for restoration to membership. This was impracticable, and out of harmony with counsel found in Deuteronomy 24:1–4, and Ellen White's correspondence. If the church truly espoused more extreme views than these, it must inform its members quite unequivocally for the sake of their salvation. Inequities, he observed, arose sometimes in the treatment of new converts and longstanding members; the only safe course was to accord the same rights to, and impose the same obligations on, all. The only reasonable and compassionate option available to the church was to admit the guilty party who evinced true contrition. The document rejected cruelty and desertion as grounds for remarriage but was less certain about cases of insanity.

In the light of this analysis, the most coherent ever to be offered by an Adventist at that time, Olson made a series of recommendations concerning the admission of 'guilty' parties to membership: that five years elapse after remarriage before any application be considered; that offenders acknowledge their sin as grievous and a disgrace to the church; that they give evidence of genuine repentance; that they be readmitted by rebaptism; that where admission of offenders would produce dissension in the church, they be obliged to wait indefinitely (p. 10).

Olson had provided a bold analysis of the situation, which attempted to accord principle with practice and to provide a clear, workable policy; it would inevitably have been interpreted by some as unduly liberal. His work quickly bore fruit in a new policy statement approved by the General Conference session in 1950.[13] Much of it had a familiar ring. Significantly, however, it stated that those who genuinely repented of their act of adultery were to be placed under censure, 'to express the church's abhorrence of such evil' (p. 228), and those who remained unrepentant were to be disfellowshipped. By introducing the distinction between censure and disfellowshipping, the conference had perhaps unwittingly created a provision which was open to abuse. The rest of the new policy contained a further liberalizing strain. First, in its preamble, it made the significant acknowledgement that 'victory and salvation can as surely be found by those who have transgressed in the matter of divorce and remarriage as by those who failed in any other of God's holy standards' (p. 228). More important still was the provision which stipulated that

in a case where any endeavor by a genuinely repentant offender to bring his marital status into line with the divine ideal presents apparently insuperable problems, his (or her) plea for readmittance shall before final action is taken be brought by the church through the pastor or district leader to the conference committee for counsel and recommendation as to any possible steps that the repentant one, or ones, may take to secure such readmittance.   (p. 229)

Further it was provided that

every care should be exercised to safeguard the unity and harmony of the church by not giving such a person responsibility as a leader; especially in an office which requires the rite of ordination, unless by very careful counsel.
(p. 229)

Church unity would not, however, be easily maintained when the new policy contained an evident ambiguity in a major provision and failed to be explicit about disciplinary procedures. A poll of ministers who had to interpret and enforce the policy showed a majority who found its provision unclear.[14] Whatever the intention of its formulators, the new policy had undoubtedly made it easier for some to contract a second marriage on 'unscriptural' grounds, and to retain, or regain, their church membership.

Not surprisingly, the innovation evoked widely differing reactions. It was welcomed by R. R. Bietz, then president of the Southern California Conference, with possibly the highest concentration of Adventists in the world, and certainly one of the most liberal. The policy would, he felt, aid the church in the 'fulfillment of her divine mission as a rescuer of the lost'.[15] Clearly the policy would ease pastoral and administrative problems raised by irregular second marriages.

There were those who vehemently opposed the provisions of the new policy. Most notable among these were R. O. and M. S. Williams, a lay couple, who, in 1952, began to circulate in printed form their opinion that by adopting its new policy the church had accommodated to contemporary trends, and thereby compromised its integrity. For some thirty years they sustained a campaign to convince their readers of the reality of a continuing state of adultery. Their hermeneutic was simple and not untypical of Adventism: they compiled lists of biblical references, and quotations from Ellen White to support their conservative position. Their concern was clear: 'Could the slow growth in membership in the western world be due to the "sin in the camp" that is hindering the work of the Holy Spirit, which is to finish the work?'[16] Others also feared that compassion could degenerate into indulgence, which would blight the reputation of the church and limit its effectiveness:

If the sins of the people are passed over by those in responsible positions, His frown will be upon them, and the people of God, as a body, will be held responsible for those sins.[17]

The subject of divorce received little attention in Adventist periodicals in the 1950s, a reflection, to some extent, no doubt, of the greater stability of marriage in the United States generally in that period. It was not until the mid 1960s that it became a matter of editorial concern again.[18] Since that time, there have been frequent admissions that the divorce rate amongst Adventists was rising rapidly.[19] Many Adventist periodicals have regularly devoted space to various aspects of the problem. The injurious consequences for the children of a broken marriage have been a principal cause for concern. The changing role of women has been cited as a prime cause of marital unhappiness.[20] Fears have been expressed about the divisive effects of a divorce on the local church community. Some have been disturbed by the uneven and indecisive application of church policy.[21] Others have contended that there always exists a spiritual solution to the problem of marital unhappiness; an experienced Adventist marriage counsellor, however, doubted whether many members could resolve their marital problems on a spiritual level:

Ideally, all Adventists having trouble in their marriages would present their problems to the Lord, and let the Holy Spirit deeply convert and heal them of their psychological disease. In actual life, for one reason or another, such a thing doesn't often happen.[22]

In 1975, there appeared a slim but widely circulated volume, *Considering Divorce?*, by C. J. Oliphant, which reflected sentiments common among Adventists. It maintained that adultery was the only legitimate grounds for divorce. It emphasized the damage to health, children, self-esteem, and the church caused by divorce proceedings. It especially highlighted the fact that love was a principle not a feeling, that a commitment should endure even when the positive emotional accompaniment was lost. It asserted that 'The Bible insists that true believers never need divorce ... God's kind of love, operating in a born-again Christian, overcomes every possible incompatibility' (p. 13). To deny that was to deny the gospel. It did, however, recommend counselling; spiritual efforts to generate good will were not sufficient.

Another writer, addressing himself to the administrative problems of divorce, concluded that the business of attributing responsibility for breakdown was so fraught with difficulty that the church should make no effort to prescribe personal behaviour. The writer's plea that the church withdraw from the very personal issues surrounding divorce, as it had done in the case of abortion, overlooked the more social nature of the former.[23] An Adventist theologian, John Brunt, writing in *Spectrum*, argued the radical view that the church could not obtain a divorce policy from the New Testament since the latter never connected divorce with discipline. He further challenged conventional Adventist thinking by declaring that the diversity of opinions among New Testament writers was such that it was impossible to harmonize them into a single biblically based policy. This, however, was not a rejection of the need for a policy; the church must create one and accept responsibility for so doing, but it could never claim to have identified *the* ultimate truth on the matter. Such a policy, informed by the moral thinking of the New Testament, would witness to the ideal of permanence in relationships, would attempt to mediate God's healing grace, and would treat each case on its merits.[24] That the problem of divorce has recently been perceived by Adventists to be acute within their own ranks is confirmed by the fact that the *Sabbath School Lessons* have made frequent references to it, and to the related matter of prevention.

The policy statement of 1976

Although no precise indication of the extent of the problem has existed until very recently, the devotion of so much attention to the problem of divorce in denominational literature was evidence enough that Adventist families were falling victim to the ills of the wider society in increasingly large numbers. Confirmation came in the early 1970s when administrative leaders of the church established a commission to investigate the problem. Its work came to fruition in 1976 when the annual conference of leading administrators from all parts of the world issued a detailed policy statement.

In an introduction to the new policy, Neal Wilson, a General Conference vice-president, noted the extreme difficulty of ensuring that a world church acted in unison. Uniformity was necessary, he felt, to effect a 'change in the tragic and embarrassing picture that exists in too many lives and in too many churches'.[25] This conviction notwithstanding, the new policy was for use only in the North American Division, although it was to provide a basis for study and practice in other divisions. The most satisfactory solution, he believed, lay in improving the quality of relationships so that the point of breakdown was simply not reached. This was important not only for personal happiness but 'to purify a church so that it will reflect the character of God'. Since this is the most comprehensive policy statement ever produced by the church, it is worth considering its provisions in some detail.[26]

The preamble affirmed marriage as God's ideal established at the creation, and recognized marital disruption as one of the signs of the imminent advent, and part of the satanic strategy to launch the fiercest assaults on the church. Thus members must resist attacks on their marriages and the church must uphold Christ's standards at all costs. The main purpose of the statement was to 'enable the church to deal consistently and helpfully with remarried divorced people who seek admission or readmission to membership in the Seventh-day Adventist church' (p. 14). Those who framed this new statement insisted that it represented no shift in position; its purpose was merely to facilitate the functioning of existing policy.

The statement identified two main problems: the first concerned the emotional trauma which divorce brought in its train, and the possible eternal consequences of such disruption; the second was the administrative problem caused by remarried divorcees who sought to maintain or re-establish their church membership when the church asserted that they were guilty of adultery. An appendix broadened the definition of adultery normally accepted by Adventists and concluded that an individual had legitimate grounds for divorce if a spouse had

1 had sexual intercourse outside of marriage;
2 maintained a persistent and intimate relationship with another even though this fell short of coitus;
3 manifested perversions and deviations which inhibited normal sex life, and which treatment did not alter and for which therapy was not sought;
4 engaged in homosexual practice.

Provisions 2 and 3 of this new definition were clearly capable of being abused. They offered scope to those who wished to be considered the 'innocent party' but who lacked evidence of unfaithfulness by their spouse.

The policy ruled that any person found guilty of adultery might be re-admitted to the church only when he or she had

1 shown sincere repentance for violating the ideal of marriage, for the 'damage done to the fair name of the church', and for the adverse effect on church members and the community at large;
2 confessed his/her wrong-doing to those whom he/she had most harmed and made such retribution as lay within his/her power;
3 shown evidence of genuine repentance by developing a wholesome family life, by renewing his/her Christian experience, and by establishing a praiseworthy reputation both in the church and in the community;
4 attended church services regularly;
5 faithfully carried out those financial and child-care obligations imposed by the court at the time of the divorce.

An applicant for re-admission to the church who fulfilled the above requirements was to be received into fellowship through the rite of baptism. Those who had dissolved a marriage on 'unbiblical grounds' and remarried before becoming Adventists were not required to satisfy the above criteria formally. They were to be treated as 'new creatures' (on the basis of 2 Corinthians 5: 17), and were eligible for membership provided that this present marriage was legitimate.

A detailed procedural model was provided for those ministers who, in the course of their work, had to handle such cases:

1 'A period of years' must elapse between the time of an unbiblical divorce and re-admission to the church where no remarriage had taken place, or between the time of a remarriage and an application for re-admission. This period served several functions: it gave occasion to the individual to show evidence of his/her renewed Christian experience, it allowed deep emotional wounds to be healed, it provided opportunity for the individual to set up a stable new home, and it served as a disciplinary measure.

2 Application for re-admission to the church must be made to the local minister who should assemble all the information relevant to the case which should then be submitted to the local Conference Standing Committee on Divorce and Remarriage.

3 The local church board should then consider the case in the light of the advice given by the Conference Committee.

4 The business meeting, an open forum of all church members, should then consider the case in the light of advice which they had received on the matter from other bodies, and give particular study to whether or not re-admission would cause the community to question Adventist beliefs on the sanctity of marriage.

5 An individual must attain a two-thirds majority of the business meeting before being re-admitted to the church.

6 The successful applicant was to be re-admitted to the church by re-baptism.

7 Any applicant who did not accept the outcome of the above procedure might refer the matter back to the Conference Standing Committee, and, if still dissatisfied, might request a full hearing from the local Conference Executive Committee.

8 Some exceptional cases might involve such flagrant sin that it would be deemed improper to renew the membership of the penitent although he/she might be allowed to enjoy the spiritual and social benefits of fellowship with the believers.

9 Since the damage done was far greater if it was the minister himself who was involved in such a process, it was recommended that such a request for re-admission to membership be treated with great caution.

Such procedures might be judged to favour the one seeking re-admission more than previously existing policy. It is certainly evident that, while uniformity of practice was a major concern of the policy-makers, it was still possible for identical cases to be treated differently in different church communities.

The statement went on to offer guidelines on the counselling strategy to be pursued with those contemplating a divorce:

1 The church should ever seek to protect the ideal, by encouraging a couple to renew their vows.
2 A decision to start legal proceedings must originate from the couple; the minister should never advise this.
3 The couple should be urged to consider the impact a divorce would have on the church and the community, and should consider their responsibility to preserve the fair name of the church.
4 When a divorce did take place the minister should discourage the parties concerned from entering precipitately into a new marital relationship; a time of self-examination was needed.
5 The minister should maintain neutrality in the matter and avoid labelling one party as 'innocent' and the other 'guilty'.
6 While it was thought necessary to ensure that any adultery cited as a ground for divorce had taken place, its occurrence need not be publicized in the proceedings.
7 A divorcee who wished to remarry must be encouraged to recognize that the divorce might indicate certain things about his own personality. Moreover, he should be aided in understanding what effects his remarriage might have on the families involved, the church, and the community, and be encouraged to consult a Christian marriage counsellor. Where an individual chose to marry a second time, 'good taste' would favour a private ceremony.

Some further observations on general church order followed. Gossip should be avoided and the church should recognize its task of encouraging the individuals involved by manifesting a compassion-ate attitude. At the same time those who had erred should be helped to see the need for repentance. In the waiting period between divorce (or remarriage) and re-admission to membership, persons should be encouraged to attend services but should not, even after re-admission, be given positions of leadership, especially those involving ordination, except in rare cases. Where a person was seeking re-admission, the church to which he was formerly affiliated (if different from the present one) should be consulted to investigate the grounds for the original action. Local conference officers should be asked to adjudicate if the two churches involved assessed the case differently.

Laudable though this attempt at producing a clear, comprehensive, and equitable policy was, its provisions demonstrated the extreme difficulty of achieving a consistent approach to the problem. That it should be perceived by some members as a liberalizing, and therefore unacceptable, revision of traditional denominational standards was inevitable. One *Review* correspondent, for example, lamented the fact that it made 'unbiblical divorce and remarriage ... a valid option for Seventh-day Adventist members'.[27]

Experience has shown that the adoption of the policy has done little to settle the issue among Adventists; disciplinary measures continue to be unevenly applied. Subsequent attempts by church administrations to discover new ways of handling the problem have not been fruitful and the subject did not figure on the agenda for the General Conference session in 1985.

Developments at Loma Linda

It was perhaps to be expected that the greatest difficulties in applying policy with regard to divorce, remarriage, and church membership, would be experienced on the West Coast, which has the reputation, inside and outside of Adventism, of being the breeding-ground for innovation and liberalism. Furthermore, a large community, offering its members relative anonymity, was the most likely to become a trouble-spot in this connection. So it proved that Loma Linda, near Los Angeles, location of a large teaching hospital, a university, a food factory, and numerous other Adventist concerns, and thus of a large Adventist population, became the focus of the debate about divorce within Adventism in the late 1970s.

The Nies lectures

In 1978–9, Dr Richard Nies, an Adventist clinical psychologist in private practice, led a series of seminars on divorce in the University Church, probably the most thorough and systematic study ever completed by an Adventist. The printed materials and tape recordings of the seminars were widely disseminated, and thus they came to have a significance far beyond the Loma Linda community.[28] The seminars were not merely of academic interest; within that particular church, and others in the vicinity, the divorce of church members was a continuing problem.

The seminars included a consideration of Israelite culture, particularly of the social arrangements which underlay the Deuteronomic law. They contained a study of the conflicting schools of rabbinic thought led by Shammai and Hillel. Attention was given to the pronouncements made by Christ and Paul relative to the subject. Traditional Adventist responses were analysed, and clinical insights shared. The information provided was extensive but the basic argument can be summarized fairly precisely.

Nies contended that marriage involved commitment by a man and a woman to sexual unity for the purpose of nurturing a love which was both exclusive and permanent. Sex therefore pertained to the total relationship of affection, and not merely to coitus. Thus, Adventists had long been guilty of adopting an understanding of adultery which was far too narrow, limited as it might be to a single illicit, physical act. He understood adultery to be that which rendered spouses incapable of entering into full sexual unity. Thus, some of the worst adulterous acts took place between those who were still joined together in the sight of the law, and the church, but who refused unity by withholding affection, or by exploiting the spouse's body. Divorce was the acceptance of such disunity, and was morally justified only when that unity could not be restored. In other words, divorce became an option only when one of the parties so lacked contrition and the will to rebuild the marital unity that the marriage could be said to be irreparably damaged. This might not necessarily be the case when one spouse had been unfaithful. An illicit sexual encounter gave no automatic justification for a divorce. He concluded that remarriage was morally allowable when it had been demonstrated, over a period of time, that there was no prospect of reconciliation.

He took the Adventist church to task on several counts. First, he charged that emphasis on the physical act of adultery as the sole ground for divorce was at once legalistic and liberal. Secondly, he lamented the failure of the church to study the historical and sociological context of biblical injunctions and exhortations. Thirdly, he criticized the imposition of an 'adulterous' relationship on marriage partners who, though cohabiting and not guilty of sexual infidelity, had no prospect of finding real marital unity.

He concluded, then, that the church must ultimately allow partners to judge whether a unity could be forged, or whether a divorce would be merely a formal acknowledgement of the actual death of their relationship. By this method he sought to preserve the integrity both of the spouses and the church. The couple could never complain that they were under undue pressure from the church, which nevertheless would be setting before them the highest of standards. The church representatives could never be sufficiently cognizant of the progress towards the rupture to apportion blame properly; it was naive to believe, he argued, that one party could be judged 'innocent' and the other 'guilty'. Moreover, it was unseemly for the church to involve itself in the business of gathering evidence of the alleged sexual indiscretions of the so-called 'guilty' party. The church would be relieved of the responsibility of making some very thorny judgements, and could devote itself to ministering to the wounds of those involved. For the spouses, there would be occasion to demonstrate their maturity and sense of responsibility; it was an invitation to serious self-examination. Nies claimed that his solution to the problem was more biblical, more redemptive, easier to administer, and ethically more sound than the current official position.

His system was, of course, not without its opponents, whose principal objection was that, despite his concern to promote a more exalted conception of marriage, he was in effect lowering the standard by allowing 'easy' divorce. He was open to the criticism that his solution owed more to clinical procedures than sound biblical exegesis. It could well be argued that he was offering, albeit unintentionally, a convenient rationalization of the course many were contemplating, and, more, that he was in fact discouraging others from attempting to salvage their marriages. His position seems to have been a genuine attempt to encourage Adventists to act responsibly in their marital affairs, to improve the quality of their marriages, and to allow the church to deal effectively and constructively with a problem which was assuming increasingly large proportions among them. His solution, however, appeared to assume a high level of maturity on the part of the church membership, and a high level of trust on the part of the church leadership. Furthermore, it appeared to allow for a departure from traditional church standards at a time when those standards generally were the subject of considerable conflict between members of varying persuasions.

Loma Linda University Church pilot project

The Loma Linda community still had, in some way, to resolve the frequent instances of marital breakdown. In 1980, the University Church first produced its own policy, which showed something of the influence of Nies but went beyond it in providing a clear structure of disciplinary procedures.[29] While acknowledging the biblical ideal for marriage,[30] it recognized the church's responsibility to heal in a world full of 'alienation and brokenness'. It also accepted that the Seventh-day Adventist church would be judged to a considerable extent by the way in which members dealt with each other. The document found present church policy to be unsatisfactory in a number of respects. First, it did not take any disciplinary action until one of the divorcees remarried; the provision in the *Church Manual* for an official action of censure to be taken was, in fact, rarely invoked. No formal expression of concern was made by the church at the time of separation or when legal proceedings were initiated. To proceed, then, to disfellowship a member at the time of a legally sanctioned remarriage, presented a confusing prospect to observers. The Loma Linda document found current church policy, which required guilt and innocence to be established, unsatisfactory in that church committees had to make judgements on partial evidence. Unfortunately, the church provided a forum in which each partner might damage the reputation of the other, thereby deepening the wounds of divorce. Furthermore, withdrawal of membership took place at local church business meetings, often convened long after a remarriage, and at which a majority vote was required; church discipline therefore frequently seemed 'capricious and inconsistent'. Lastly, the present policy provided no point at which the divorcees could consider this painful chapter in their lives closed. Too often, divorcees lacked the assurance that forgiveness was theirs, and they nurtured the unchristian hope that their former spouse would 'fall into sin'. In fact, the only situation where the policy seemed to function adequately was where one spouse showed no desire for continuing church affiliation.

By the new policy, the University Church staff undertook to marry only those who gave three months' notice of their intentions and who agreed to attend various courses or private sessions for marriage counselling. At such times the staff would clarify the church's understanding of the marriage relation, and the responsibility of the couple to seek help early if difficulties threatened. The next step in the procedure was, without doubt, the most innovative:

As soon as legal action is taken by a married couple signifying that the dissolution of their marriage is a real possibility, they are no longer representing the Church's official commitment to the permanence of the marriage vow. Recognizing this, in consultation with a pastor, the couple will acknowledge the state of their relationship by requesting that they will be designated 'affiliate members', i.e. still members of the visible body of Christ, but not at this time fully representative of the official position adopted by that body. (p. 3)

Such a request for affiliate membership constituted a request to the church to provide professional help to attempt to avert a final breakdown of the marriage.

If such efforts fail and the estrangement should continue, the affiliate membership category would provide a period of time for healing to occur free from the pressure and distractions of involvement in church leadership. During this time such members will be expected to refrain from holding church office.
(p. 3)

The two-tier system of membership, it was argued, permitted the church both to bear witness to the sanctity and permanence of marriage, and to dispense loving concern at a time of personal crisis. It also worked actively for reconciliation.

Any member choosing to remarry while holding affiliate membership status would be disfellowshipped together with the new spouse if he/she was a member in regular standing. An affiliate member was to seek counselling over an unspecified period of time until such time as a member of the pastoral staff considered it appropriate 'to seek closure on the episode of brokenness' (p. 4). A request for change of status would be granted when sufficient time for emotional healing had elapsed. In the intervening time, an affiliate member would be encouraged to participate in all church activities, except those in which to participate would be to represent the church officially. The remarriage of a former spouse would have no bearing on the renewal of full membership. After going through such a procedure, a person would be free to remarry if he so wished and to enjoy the full rights and privileges of membership. In addition to the requirements listed above, the affiliate member would also be expected to meet all the legal requirements of the settlement, to refrain from making new liaisons until the issuing of a divorce decree, to protect the reputation of the former spouse, and generally to live in an exemplary fashion.

In 1982, the University Church received General Conference permission to implement the policy on a two-year experimental basis, although it had been operating for some time. The scheme functioned successfully inasmuch as it minimized the pain of divorce for those thirty-five or so couples who separated in the first four years of operation in this 5,000-member church. It has been less successful in effecting reconciliation between couples. The pastoral staff of the church believed that members generally sought help too late because they did not wish to acknowledge the existence of difficulties. They also believed that pre-marital counselling reduced the number of marriages at risk. Considerable resistance to the term 'affiliate' has been encountered because of the second-class status it seemed to confer; procedures have remained the same even though the term has fallen into disuse. Those occupying this status have, in fact, held offices of responsibility in the church, though not senior positions like that of elder. The average time lapse between the public acknowledgement of marital difficulties and remarriage has been two years. This pilot scheme has continued to operate because the General Conference has had no viable alternative to offer. Significantly, several other large Adventist churches have adopted a similar policy which, it seems, may in time by default become the norm.

Empirical enquiries

A sociological study

As the foregoing part of this chapter has indicated, Adventist leaders have frequently expressed alarm at the rising incidence of divorce among church members. No evidence existed, however, as to the exact extent of the problem, until, in 1979, two Adventist sociologists, Charles Crider and Robert Kistler, published research about the Adventist family unit, called *The Seventh-day Adventist Family.*

The research was carried out in 1974−5 and is thus somewhat dated. However, in so far as it was completed when the process of liberalizing divorce laws was well advanced, and at a time when divorce rates were rising inexorably, it remains a valuable indicator of trends in Adventist family life in the United States. A total of 2,004 members responded to the questionnaire from a distribution of 3,124, a response rate of 64 per cent. While this constituted a good return, the question remains as to whether the non-respondents were predominantly of a particular type. It could well be the case that those who had marriage difficulties were disproportionately highly represented in the group of non-respondents, since they especially might not want to acknowledge, either to others or themselves, their failure in an area of life in which their church placed a high premium on success. A second limitation of the study was that it was introduced to church members from the pulpit on the Sabbath. This would tend to produce a disproportionately low representation in the sample of those who were less than regular in attendance and who, it might be surmised, would be more likely to experience marital difficulties. Thirdly, the sample was predominantly white, and so failed to reflect the family practices of the large number of black Adventists; in the United States blacks generally have higher rates of marital breakdown. All of these factors would tend to depress artificially the rate of family disintegration recorded in the Adventist community. Despite these limitations, the research provided a valuable insight into the state of the American Adventist family.

The study indicated that 12 per cent had experienced divorce, or the functional equivalent thereof. It was clear, however, that some respondents had difficulty in acknowledging that they had acted in opposition to the ideal or, perhaps, feared the discovery of an irregular marriage. The researchers felt that the figure might well be revised to 17 per cent. While it would clearly be a matter of great concern to denominational leaders that as many as one in six Adventist marriages was ending in divorce, that rate was nevertheless considerably below the national average. On the other hand, it seemed clear to Crider and Kistler that rates of divorce were rising among church members, and that annulment was an increasingly attractive option to some (p. 159). The relatively low rate of divorce among Adventists did not, they felt, necessarily imply a correspondingly high rate of marital happiness. It might, particularly among older Adventists, have arisen from an unwillingness to go against traditional denominational values concerning marriage and divorce even in the face of marital unhappiness. At the same time, church members with non-Adventist or ex-Adventist spouses had the powerful motivation of seeking their spouse's salvation by remaining in a marriage which was not congenial.

In other respects, Adventist marriage reflected the patterns prevalent in the wider society. It was those Adventists who were in the early years of their marriage who were most at risk (p. 110). Adventists who lived in urban areas were more vulnerable to marital breakdown than those located in rural settings. Predictably, divorce rates were higher than those in rural areas in those communities clustering around the denomination's medical or educational facilities (pp. 197–8). Adventist patterns also resembled those in the wider society, in that there was an inverse relationship between divorce and occupational status. The divorce rate among professionals and white-collar workers was 7.5 per cent; among skilled manual workers 17.7 per cent; and among the unskilled 18.8 per cent. Divorce was more common among Adventists in the western states, followed by those in the Midwest, then by those in the East and South (p. 198).

According to the respondents, a major source of marital conflict was money. Above and beyond the usual pressures which finance placed upon a marriage, Adventists faced several other areas of potential conflict. Generally speaking, the church paid a lower salary than roughly comparable secular employers, making the careful planning of priorities more important (pp. 149–57). Where church workers wanted to maintain a high standard of living, wives had to work. This was particularly the case where parents wished to educate their children in Adventist institutions. The obligation to pay tithes and give offerings would further drain the family finances. It is not difficult to see that money could easily become a symbol of differing priorities in such a situation. On the other hand, Adventists would ideally make finance a matter of religious trust.

A second area of conflict was child discipline. While this may be a source of stress in most marriages which produce children, it is obvious that within a generally authoritarian ethos, differences about how to command obedience, and the extent to which the young may be granted freedom, are more than usually liable to produce disagreement. Similarly, it is easy to see why 'nagging, fault-finding', was cited as a major area of conflict in a system which had erected such high behavioural standards, and which had encouraged members to see matters of faith and practice in absolute terms. Possibly for the same reasons, difficulties with in-laws figured prominently in the list of areas of conflict; Adventist in-laws could be anticipated to have behavioural expectations of a young married couple which one or neither of them was prepared to fulfil. Given the kinds of conservative attitudes towards sexuality already outlined in this research, it is not surprising that some Adventists, men more than women, saw sex as an area of dissatisfaction in their marriage. For others, work was a source of difficulty; one can imagine this to be the case where one spouse was more committed to the work of the church than the other, or where the perceived inadequacy of the main wage demanded that the family find another source of income (p. 205). As Crider and Kistler observed, many of the above problems had a common root in the high behavioural standards set by the chruch:

Thus Adventists who are very conscious of the high ideals set for them in family life by their church often feel guilty or distressful. Many of them interpret the difference between the ideal and what they are able to attain to be so great that they become discouraged about the quality of their own home and family life. (p. 46)

So much for the forces at work in a marriage of which the spouses were aware. There were, of course, other sociological factors involved which placed couples more or less at risk. The high geographical mobility of Adventist couples seemed not to place intolerable stress upon them; indeed Crider and Kistler found that non-mobile Adventist families had a slightly higher divorce rate. The reason for this, they suggested, lay in the usually highly specific motivation for migration – to live near a church educational institution, or to be near their family. Such motivation would tend to mitigate the stress caused by relocation. While mobility did not seem to play an unusually prominent part in Adventist divorce, it should be repeated that divorce may give rise to some mobility. Some, valuing their church membership but unable to tolerate an unsatisfactory marriage, have sought admission to a church in a distant location without divulging information about previous marital failure (pp. 180–2).

Crider and Kistler found that nearly 70 per cent of Adventist marriages took place in church, and that a further 19.5 per cent were conducted by a minister, though not in church (p. 51);[31] only 9.1 per cent acknowledged being united by a civic official (p. 51). The research also showed that Adventists enjoyed an unusually high level of college education and were disproportionately highly represented in the professions and skilled work. All of these elements would tend to make Adventists relatively less susceptible to marital breakdown. At the socio-economic level, Adventists have, perhaps more than others, a great motivation to keep the family stable. A divorce might very well threaten members' employment if they were in denominational service, and would possibly tarnish their reputation in the community. On the spiritual level, a belief that their marriage was ordained by God would sustain some through times of difficulty, and reinforce more earthly considerations.

The findings of Crider and Kistler sounded anew the alarm about Adventist families:

This research indicates that the Adventist home is under stress in the United States and enough family units are faltering to pose a crisis to the church as a whole. The church needs to respond affirmatively and forcefully to meet the need ... To the extent that any part of the body suffers, the whole body is affected ... family evangelism may be one of the most pressing concerns at the present time.   (p. 247)

Family education has indeed received increased attention in the Adventist church recently. The research of Crider and Kistler itself grew out of a series of human relations workshops and family enrichment seminars conducted in various parts of the United States. Others have conducted similar kinds of programmes to consolidate the marriages of Adventist members.[32] An indicator of official concern was the establishment, in 1975, of the Home and Family Service by the General Conference. It has organized seminars, produced written materials, and functioned as a resource centre for churches seeking to improve the quality of their members' marriages. This is clearly perceived to be a key to the future health of the whole denomination.

Home and Family Service study

The same Home and Family Service recently conducted an enquiry into current levels of divorce in the church. A random sample of 3,076 members in Delaware, District of Columbia, Maryland, Minnesota, New Jersey, Ohio, and Texas displayed trends likely to disturb any Adventist administrator. In the country as a whole there were 10.8 marriages per thousand population in 1982, compared with 5.1 divorces. In the same year, the marriage rate in the Adventist community was 11.05 per thousand members, with a divorce rate of 5.5.[33] However, the fact that the instrument of comparison was, in one case, the undifferentiated population, and, in the case of the church, a largely adult membership, introduced major distortions into the statistics. It must, however, be observed that the churches surveyed contained few black members, and that information on infrequent attenders was often unavailable, both of which factors would have tended to depress artificially the rate of divorce recorded among Adventists. More recent information has suggested that about one in four Adventist marriages ends in divorce, roughly half of the national rate.[34] The very least that could be deduced from these studies was that the difference between Adventist and national divorce rates was being reduced.

An attitudinal survey

The random distribution of 1,200 questionnaires to Adventists all over the United States yielded 712 usable surveys. The proposition 'Divorce is a valid option when marriage is unhappy' elicited

Table 12.2   Responses to proposition 'Divorce is a valid option when marriage is unhappy' (%)

	Disagree	Agree	Uncertain
High-school youth	46	34	20
Mothers	65	21	14
Fathers	60	32	8

Source: R. L. Dudley and M. G. Dudley, 'Adventist Values: Flying High?', *Ministry*, April 1985, p. 7.

the responses indicated in table 12.2. This survey lent further weight to the argument that Adventist standards with regard to divorce were being eroded.

An ideological perspective

The approach which the Adventist church has adopted, and will in the future adopt towards marriage discipline, centres upon the response to certain issues which, while depending on the denomination's theology, are perhaps more properly described as ideological. The major ones are discussed below:

1   The contemporary upward trend in divorce rates owes not a little to the Enlightenment doctrine that the individual has the inalienable right to pursue personal happiness. Thus, if a person's marital arrangements fail to provide satisfaction, then he or she has the right to change them. Adventists have inevitably imbibed the hedonistic ethic of modern society to a certain extent. Yet it is an ethic which may well be judged anathema to a Christian view of marriage. Christian teaching views suffering as an intrinsic part of living, insists that growth comes through struggle, and emphasizes duties rather than rights, sacrifice rather than satisfaction.

A major duty which is often urged upon spouses who are unhappy in their marriage is the welfare of their children. However, there is evidence to support the popular wisdom that the children of divorcees fare better than those who remain in homes where there is a high level of conflict.[35] The protection of the 'fair name of the church' might also be advanced as a cause for maintaining an uncongenial marriage, but it is one which is likely to appeal less to modern generations of believers than it did to their forebears.

2 If an Adventist couple do attempt to salvage their ailing relationship, they face several options. If, as has been argued elsewhere (see below, p. 267), Adventists are generally distrustful of their emotions, they may be inclined to believe that a rational solution to their problem is available. They might well tend to the view that this approach, together with the 'guidance of the Holy Spirit', offers the best chance of reconciliation. However, if the view of the Catholic marriage expert, Jack Dominian, is at all accurate, they would be unlikely to succeed:

It is now widely recognized than [sic] in marital counselling as in every other form of counselling involving inter-personal relationships, feelings and emotions are the principal experiences which need recognition, ventilation and understanding.[36]

There exist in the Adventist mind certain obstacles to the resort to this kind of assistance. There is a real, if diminishing, suspicion of those specialists who treat the mind rather than the body, a suspicion which can be traced back to the writings of Ellen White, or perhaps rather to a misunderstanding of them.[37] There is, for some, an admission of failure, specifically of spiritual failure, attached to any request for such help. Furthermore, some would feel that to acknowledge need of this sort would be to break the 'sacred circle' of the family.[38] There exists, then, resistance to the use of psychiatrists, therapists, and counsellors. Adventist specialists in this area would, of course, not be accessible to most Adventists, and some members would regard it as a betrayal of the church to expose their problem to a non-Adventist. The remaining option would be to consult an Adventist minister. Such a course would have several drawbacks. First, most Adventist ministers are not qualified in counselling techniques, although increasing numbers are seeking training of this type. Secondly, those facing marital difficulties need to communicate with one who is non-judgemental,[39] and the minister is inevitably perceived to be in the business of making judgements.

3 A major reason for extreme caution in regard to therapeutic

techniques is the fear that they have a humanistic foundation. The idea that unstable marriages result from personality defects developed in childhood is a threatening one because it may seriously undermine the concept of sin. On this kind of account, man is born into sickness not sin. Yet the whole Adventist theological and administrative position is built on certain value judgements; 'no-fault' grounds are inadmissible to Adventists. Traditionally, Adventists have sought to attribute blame before permitting the dissolution of a marriage. According to Dominian, some marital difficulties actually result from personality problems relating to low self-esteem, which derives from failure to meet lofty Christian ideals and high expectations.[40] One would expect Adventist couples to be vulnerable in this respect.

4 A larger but related question revolves around the matter of how tolerant the church should be towards those who deviate from certain norms of faith and practice. If the church, in pursuit of its perceived mission, chose to impose more rigorous discipline on dissenters, then it might expect to lose more members with irregular marital arrangements, for, as in the secular context, stricter rules do not appear to reduce the incidence of divorce. If, as seems likely, the church continued to maintain a certain flexibility in its attempt to minister to a secular society, then further accommodations in policy could be expected. Much would depend on whether Adventists were to adopt the kind of simple approach to the biblical evidence employed by the early leaders, or whether, as seems likely, the following sort of attitude would prevail:

The New Testament does not contain definitive rulings on every circumstance of marriage or of breakdown which are so unequivocal and so simple of interpretation that the Church has nothing to do but apply them.[41]

Since a large majority of divorcees remarry, it is likely that most Adventist divorcees will do the same. A strict policy, rigorously applied, would in effect exclude large numbers from membership, since most members would not regard a life of celibacy as an attractive option. The result would be a loss of resources to the church, both human and material. If church policy on remarriage and membership were followed strictly with the assent of divorcees who valued their membership highly, the situation might be little improved. The existence of a significant number of divorcees in the church with no sexual outlet would create a potentially volatile state, of a type which the church has already witnessed in its history (see above, pp. 67–70).

A sociological perspective

1 It has been demonstrated by Udry,[42] among others, that lower divorce rates are directly correlated with high socio-economic and occupational status, higher income, and higher educational attainment. It has already been shown that Adventists are disproportionately highly represented in tertiary education and in the professions. It might therefore be argued that a relatively low divorce rate among Adventists is, to some extent, a function of economics rather than a product of religious discipline. Udry's claim that higher divorce rates are related to lower incomes seems to receive some confirmation in Rheinstein's observation that the incidence of marital breakdown is lower in those countries with a system of family allowances.[43] If this is so, the comparatively low salaries paid by the church may be a cause of stress among denominational workers. Halem has argued that development of 'no-fault' reform in the late 1960s and 1970s was a tacit acknowledgement that divorce had invaded the middle classes; prior to that, she said, divorce-seekers were mainly from the lower classes.[44] If this observation is correct, it would seem that rising divorce rates among Adventists have been in some measure a function of social class.

2 Many scholars share the view that recent progress towards sexual equality is a major factor in rising divorce rates. It is quite evident that the greater educational and occupational opportunities available to women, together with legal reform, have conferred some measure of autonomy on them. A major factor in many breakdowns will be a failure to adjust to gender roles which are not traditional; a husband may particularly feel discomforted by the fact that his wife occupies a role very different from that played by his mother. A wife may become irritated by her husband's inflexibility about domestic responsibilities.

This may be a source of difficulty in many Adventist marriages. Young women are encouraged to seek a college education and have high occupational aspirations. Mothers are often obliged to work so as to provide an Adventist education for their children. Adventist institutions rely heavily on the services provided by married women. Furthermore, Adventists generally wish to share in the nation's prosperity. Yet there exists the expectation that these women will also fulfil a maternal and domestic role. The occasion for marital stress in Adventist communities is thus clear. It is conceivable that one of the reasons for denominational reticence about employing women in ministry is that this might appear to confer some absolute or visible approval on the aspirations of the career-woman.

3 Adventist insistence on the scriptural principle of not being 'unequally yoked' seems to be vindicated by sociological research. Scholars have frequently identified a shared religious faith as a factor in marital cohesiveness.[45] Joint church attendance exposes a couple to a network of connected affiliations and to a range of conventional attitudes which function as powerful external pressures on the marriage. Exogamous marriages increase the possibility of disagreement over basic ideological matters which often finds expression in conflict over everyday practical arrangements.

Being under pressure to contract an endogamous marriage, and being a highly mobile group, young Adventists are perhaps unusually liable to form liaisons with those whose homes are remote from their own. This may be a source of some stress, particularly where marriages are international. Remoteness from an extended family network tends to place added pressure on the nuclear family to provide emotional warmth, and so perhaps increases the likelihood of breakdown. On the other hand, Adventist communities often serve some of the functions of a kinship system. While the presumption in favour of endogamous marriages is obviously important to group stability, it also conceals a danger in a group where singleness is not a favoured option. The inclination to regard similar denominational affiliation as the first qualification to be sought in a spouse, may lead a person to overlook other important factors concerning compatibility.

4 Rheinstein makes the following observation about divorce practice in the United States:

Contrast between paper scheme and actuality is the very characteristic of the entire system of divorce. It has to be. It is the only system that can function in a democratic country where the social climate is as diffuse as it has so far been in the United States ...[46]

It may be that the Adventist church will have to remain content with precisely the same sort of compromise in order to satisfy, on the one hand, the more liberally minded members (particularly in the western states), and rising generations of Adventists generally, and, on the other, the older, more conservative members in the United States, and those in the Third World. A policy which appears traditional but which is capable of some divergence of interpretation may resolve many of the difficulties. The following *Review* editorial comment suggests that the church would live uneasily with such a double standard: '... the church must never be indecisive or flabby in its attitude toward sin. It must speak forthrightly on moral questions'.[47] The Loma Linda experiment may suggest otherwise. The lesson to be learned from American divorce history is that tightening rules does not appear to reduce levels of marital breakdown.

Conclusion

An increasing divorce rate is clearly very debilitating for the church. The financial resources of those involved in divorce are strained, and church funds inevitably suffer. Broken homes are likely both to increase the loss of young people from Adventist ranks, and per-petuate the spiral of divorce.[48] The sympathies of church members are often engaged on behalf of one of the parties, so that the process becomes divisive in the local church. Much administrative energy is devoted to the debate on the rights and wrongs of various positions. Members leaving the church often seek a pretext for so doing, and divorce may be just such a crisis to occasion a severing of church affiliation. It may be tempting for some to lament the passing of some golden age of marital stability in the church. It should be remembered, however, that more divorces are not necessarily indicative of a greater degree of unhappiness; it may be that in the current climate members are simply more ready to acknowledge their discontent and to try to remedy it. Whether the rising number of divorces does indeed indicate a decline in the health of Adventist marriages is impossible to tell.

The problem is clearly one which will have to be contained rather than solved. The most promising road seems to be that of increased and improved family education. The General Conference Home and Family Service is one of a number of denominational agencies devoted to that end. With divorce rates running so high, it may be that counselling should become the norm prior to marriage rather than at the time of crisis. It may be that the church will have to impose more stringent requirements on those seeking to marry for the first time with its blessing, rather than the second.

The failure of a church commission on divorce, established in 1981, to produce a report thus far is a measure of the intractability of the issue. That the church gives close and continuing attention to the problem indicates its acceptance of the task of distinguishing Christian values from social convention. As an Anglican report on this issue has observed, without the effort to achieve this,

> there can be no true conversation between the generations, no mutuality between those who incline to the security of what they have known and those who stretch out for a freedom in which they aspire to live.[49]

In the matter of divorce, as in all other areas of faith and practice, the church has continually to reassess its stance:

> Flight from this task is apostasy, whether the flight be into unconcern with the slow movements or convulsive changes of the world, or into a facile, proud, or comforting identification of the Church of this age with that of an earlier age ...[50]

It is precisely this task which Adventism is urgently confronting at the moment. The matter of divorce is merely one area in which the much larger search for denominational identity is manifested.

13 · Homosexuality: the sin unnamed among Adventists

The unnamed sin

Homosexual practice has traditionally prompted severe condemnation from the Christian church. Indeed, it became known as the sin 'inter christiani non nominandum'. Such thinking has long informed public opinion and the law in many countries including the United States, where legislation, enacted in the seventeenth century, made it punishable by death in some places. Although homosexual practice ceased to be a capital offence in the nineteenth century, only very recent legislation has mitigated the harshness of the law on homosexual behaviour. The reasons why people across such a broad social spectrum and over such a long period of time have had such a deep aversion to homosexual practice are no doubt very complex. Underlying them all perhaps is the sense that anyone who engages in what seem to the majority to be deeply 'unnatural' acts is ultimately capable of betraying any of the foundational values for which their society stands. The very strength of this prejudice makes homosexuality difficult to trace until comparatively recently. Those who recognized homosexual needs within themselves either repressed them for fear of the consequences of expressing them, or were very careful about seeking to satisfy them. Thus, although it is commonly believed that the proportion of homosexuals in the population has remained roughly consistent, evidence concerning actual practice remained sparse until the period of so-called 'gay liberation' after the Second World War.

Homosexuality in the United States

Although the evidence of homosexual behaviour in nineteenth- and early-twentieth-century America is sparse, it is not entirely lacking. Both Havelock Ellis in *Sexual Inversion* (1915 edition), and Dr Magnus Hirschfeld in *Homosexualität des Mannes und des Weibes* (1914) claimed that homosexual practice was rife in the major cities of the United States. According to them, it tended to be organized in a distinct community, and thus was invisible to the casual observer. Nevertheless when homosexuals were discovered to be practising they were subject to various sanctions, mostly fines and imprisonment. The census of 1880 showed that sixty-three people were in jail for committing 'the crime against nature'. Ten years later the number had risen to 224; in both cases, a disproportionately high number were blacks in the South.[1] Hirschfeld believed that Americans tended to regard homosexual behaviour as largely confined to blacks or other minority groups such as Italians.[2]

Among the first to argue seriously that homosexuals had been wrongly criminalized was Dr A. A. Brill, a student of Freud and a psychiatrist at Columbia University. He wrote:

I have met and studied a large number of homosexuals and have been convinced that a great injustice is done to a large class of human beings, most of whom are far from being the degenerates they are commonly believed to be.[3]

He believed it wrong to subject them to penal sanctions or to surgical operations, as was sometimes the case. By psychoanalysis he encouraged homosexuals to come to terms with their 'uranianism', as it was sometimes called, although he advised that they should no longer be sexually active. In the literary field, the work of Walt Whitman encouraged a number of Englishmen including John Symonds, Edward Carpenter and Havelock Ellis to become pioneers of homosexual resistance, although Whitman was ultimately to deny the existence of any erotic homosexual content in his publications.

It must be remembered, of course, that the above is nothing more than a parenthesis in American history. Homosexuals were uniformly execrated and were subject to prosecution, although the letter of the law and its enforcement varied from one jurisdiction to another. The subject was seldom raised publicly.

Ellen White

Nowhere in the vast corpus of Ellen White's published work, or in her extensive correspondence, is there any direct reference to homosexuality.[4] In avoiding the subject, she clearly reflected the spirit of the age. Even the outspoken Dr J. H. Kellogg omitted any extended discussion of the matter.[5] The biblical texts which relate to the matter of homosexual practice, e.g. Judges 19:22, Deuteronomy 23:17, Leviticus 20:13, Romans 1:26–7, 1 Timothy 1:10, etc., elicit no comment from the prophetess. The Sodom and Gomorrah motif does, however, run through her work, and requires analysis.

She believed the inhabitants of the twin cities to be guilty of all manner of sin: disobedience, hypocrisy, oppression of the poor, idleness, inhospitality, idolatry, gluttony, drunkenness, pleasure-seeking, gambling, robbery, crimes of violence, and so on. She did, however, identify licentiousness as a distinguishing feature of life in those cities.[6] There are places where it might be inferred that she, along with virtually all Christian commentators before her, identified homosexual practice as a distinctive feature of life there. She said that the inhabitants had 'defaced the image of God', a phrase which may have been used consciously to evoke the idea, contained in Genesis 1:27, that being made in the image of God was bound up with maleness and femaleness.[7] She described the people as being 'inflamed by the vilest passions',[8] and talked of the 'debasing and abominable iniquity practiced in that 'vile city'.[9] Perhaps more suggestively, she recorded the following:

Sodom and Gomorrah were destroyed through the gratification of unnatural appetite, which benumbed the intellect ... they became so ferocious and bold in their detestable abominations that God would not tolerate them upon the earth.[10]

Although the language might suggest an allusion to homosexuality specifically, the context here, and in similar passages, demands a different conclusion. Her principal observation seems to be that improper habits of eating and drinking excited man's sensual propensities generally. Ellen White was, by this stage in her prophetic career, very much bound up with health reform and believed, for example, that the eating of flesh foods and spices encouraged sensuality. Elsewhere she said of the Sodomites that 'they would have abused

the men that ... were entertained by Lot'.[11] Although all of the
above could bear a homosexual interpretation, on balance it seems
that Sodom and Gomorrah represent, in Ellen White's writing, urban
affluence, idolatry, pleasure-seeking and sensuality generally.

The trustees of her estate seem to be divided on this matter. While
they have claimed that her work contains no reference to
homosexuality,[12] a recent anthology cited a statement under the
heading 'Homosexuality – Sodom's Particular Sin'.[13] However, on
the basis of all that Ellen White said about Sodom and Gomorrah,
it is difficult to defend the view that she held homosexuality to be
the most prominent of the vices of the cities' inhabitants. The most
that can be claimed is that she would have regarded it as one among
the many sins of a thoroughly decadent society. That she did not
specify it among the many other sins which she actually attributed
to the Sodomites was merely a reflection of nineteenth-century taboos,
and, to some extent, a reticence to be specific on sexual matters. But
there can be no doubt that she would have regarded it as one of the
sins contributing to the downfall of the cities. Her moralizing about
sexual relations generally puts that beyond doubt. She regarded the
conditions existing in revolutionary France as resembling those in
Sodom.[14] Her major concern was that the introduction of civil
marriage threatened the whole institution of the family. She would,
no doubt, have seen homosexuality as posing a similar threat.

It is interesting, however, that, while she condemned the licentiousness and other sins of Sodom, she did not regard them as being the
ultimate in godlessness:

The Redeemer of the world declares that there are greater sins than that for
which Sodom and Gomorrah were destroyed. Those who hear the gospel
invitation calling sinners to repentance, and heed it not, are more guilty before
God than were the dwellers in the vale of Siddim. And still greater is theirs
who profess to know God and to keep His commandments, yet who deny
Christ in their character and their daily life.[15]

The issues of masturbation and dress reform, about which Ellen
White did have a good deal to say, bear on the present subject,
if only tangentially. On several occasions she vehemently condemned the practice of masturbation, as indeed did many nineteenth-
century moralists.[16] She claimed divine authority for the view that

masturbation was a 'terrible sin' in the sight of God.[17] It was, she said, responsible for a wide range of physical, mental, emotional, and spiritual problems.[18] She expressed concern about the way in which knowledge of the habit was transmitted, and was clearly perturbed about the well-being of her own sons: 'To save my children from being corrupted I have not allowed them to sleep in the same bed, nor in the same room with other boys.'[19] It is not far-fetched to suggest that Ellen White was concerned that her sons (and the sons of Adventists) would engage in mutual masturbation, a form of adolescent homosexual activity, of which J. H. Kellogg had had clinical experience.[20] In his *Confidential Chats with Boys*, a certain Dr William Howard, who had no connections with Adventism, warned

Never sleep with another person, man or boy ... Sleeping with another person affects the organs ... and causes a feeling of attraction towards these delicate organs ... many boys will be tempted to talk and play with each other ... in the end it means self-abuse ... sleep on the floor, go without sleeping ... So never sleep with a man, except your father. If you ... find yourself in bed with a man, keep awake with your eyes on something you can hit him with.[21]

There is further evidence to suggest that in the world at large it was feared that masturbation might lead on to homosexual activity, and even that the term 'secret sin', or its synonyms, were sometimes used to denote homosexual activity as well.[22] While this may have been a genuine concern, it remained subsidiary, for Ellen White's major fear was that masturbation would so stimulate the sexual appetite of young men and women that they would seek heterosexual experience prematurely.[23]

In 1851, Amelia Bloomer pioneered a new sort of outfit for women, consisting of a short dress with trousers underneath, which became a subject of considerable interest in the USA. While Ellen White recognized that it had the virtue of being simple, warm, hygienic, and convenient, she could not encourage the wearing of the 'American Costume' by Adventists as it tended to blur the distinction between the sexes:

I was referred to Deuteronomy 22:5: 'The woman shall not wear that which pertaineth unto a man, neither shall a man put on a woman's garment: for all that do so are abomination unto the Lord thy God.' God would not have His people adopt the so-called reform dress. It is immodest apparel, wholly unfitted for the modest, humble followers of Christ. There is an increasing tendency to have women in their dress and appearance as near like the other sex as possible, and to fashion their dress very much like that of men, but God pronounces it abomination.[24]

Ellen White was further disturbed by the fact that Seventh-day Adventists would be confused with Spiritualist women who had, to a considerable extent, adopted the new style of dress. Such an identification would destroy the influence of Adventists, and should be avoided.[25]

By the mid 1860s, however, Ellen White was becoming very involved in health reform generally and advocated some innovation in dress styles for Adventist women. She objected to the style of dress traditionally worn by women of the time on a number of counts: the skirts brushed the floor and therefore attracted a lot of dirt and germs, they left the limbs largely unprotected from the cold, the corsets squeezed the waist, injuring various important organs of the body, and dresses were often extravagantly decorated. Ellen White therefore undertook to design a dress which retained the virtues of the Bloomer dress while remaining modest and feminine: 'We shall never imitate Miss Dr Austin or Mrs Dr York. They dress very much like men ... We shall institute a fashion which will be both economical and healthful.'[26] She in fact wore a dress similar to, but longer than, the fashionable costume in September 1865. So much controversy was generated in denominational publications, however, that finally Ellen White conceded that 'Because that which was given as a blessing was turned into a curse, the burden of advocating the reform dress was removed'.[27]

While the issue of dress reform is, in a sense, peripheral, it does illustrate Ellen White's fear of disturbing traditional sexual roles in any way, and strengthens suspicions concerning her probable views on homosexual activity. Ellen White and her contemporaries in the church would no doubt have been appalled by the notion that homosexuality would one day become a life-style preference affirmed openly by some of their spiritual heirs. The little statistical evidence which exists concerning the general incidence of homosexuality suggests that there would probably have been a few among the early Adventists who would themselves have coveted this kind of freedom.

14 · Homosexuality in Adventism: sin, disease or preference?

Homosexuality in the United States

In the inter-war years, some small groups of homosexuals were organized, for example, the Chicago Society for Human Rights in 1934–5, but these were ephemeral. Most homosexuals chose to conceal their sexual orientation on account of the incomprehension and hostility of the general public. Literary efforts to deal with the subject were soon suppressed. While members of the public continued to regard homosexuality variously as a sin, a crime, or, at least, a repulsive moral aberration, for some doctors it had graduated to the status of illness, for which a number of radical cures were tried.[1] A minority which opposed the view of homosexuality as a disease, took its lead from the German, Dr Magnus Hirschfeld, who regarded it as an unchangeable inborn sexual variation, neither to be treated nor punished. However, the general recodification of law which many states undertook around 1950 reflected a public opinion which was still firmly opposed to homosexuality; heavy fines and prison sentences were imposed on offenders.[2]

A principal agency in the modification of attitudes towards homosexuality was the massive research carried out by Alfred Kinsey and his associates at the Institute for Sex Research at the University of Indiana. His research, published as *Sexual Behavior in the Human Male* (1948), and *Sexual Behavior in the Human Female* (1953), was the most comprehensive of its type ever carried out. One of the major contributions of this work was to challenge the idea that an individual was distinctly heterosexual or homosexual in orientation; Kinsey rather sought to establish a person's predominant sexual orientation along a continuum of preference. Kinsey himself confessed surprise at the basic conclusion of his research, namely that homosexual practice was much more widespread than was generally believed, and that more people would have sought homosexual experience had the social sanctions been less rigid. The research showed that 37 per cent of the large male sample had had some homosexual experience between adolescence and old age, that 10 per cent had been 'more or less exclusively homosexual' for at least three years, and that 4 per cent had been 'exclusively homosexual' from adolescence.

However, the hostility of the American public to homosexuality was not to be easily eroded. Not long after the publication of Kinsey's first volume, there followed a prolonged and determined purge of suspected homosexuals and Communist sympathizers occupying positions in federal government. A Senate sub-committee found that the 'emotional instability' and 'weak moral fiber' of homosexuals made them susceptible to inducements offered by agents of foreign powers.[3] On a lower bureaucratic level, a witch-hunt of suspected homosexuals in Boise, Idaho, in 1955 was a classic example of an attempt to seek political preferment by smearing the reputation of others.[4]

Homosexuals began to recognize the need of organizing to inform the public on the nature of the condition, to create for themselves a sense of identity, and to generate political action designed to secure certain human rights. 1950 saw the creation of the Mattachine Foundation in Los Angeles, the first significant homosexual organization in the United States, by Henry Hay, who was, incidentally, a long-standing member of the Communist party. In 1955, the Daughters of Bilitis, an organization of lesbians, was formed in San Francisco. In 1958, the Supreme Court ruled that *One Magazine*, a homosexual publication, could be mailed without threat of prosecution to the publishers. In the 1950s, organizations of homosexuals tended to be secretive and introspective, concerning themselves primarily with aetiology and counselling.

As the 1960s progressed, however, the campaign for legal reform gathered momentum, deriving strength from the Wolfenden Report, published in Britain in 1957, the ALI Model Penal Code (1955), and Kinsey's research. There is considerable evidence of the growing strength of the homosexual lobby and of the slow erosion of prejudice against homosexuals. In 1962, Illinois became the first state to legalize consensual homosexual relations between adults in private. In 1964, the predominantly middle-class Society for Individual Rights was formed to protect the rights of homosexuals, while, three years later, New York State revoked legislation banning the treatment of homosexual themes in its theatres. In 1969, the Court of Appeals in Washington, DC, ruled that enquiries concerning the sexual orientation of an applicant for public employment was a denial of due process, and in so doing set a precedent for the rest of the country.

However, historians of homosexuality tend to date the beginning of the 'gay liberation movement' from 27 June 1969, when police raided the Stonewall Inn, a bar popular among homosexuals in Greenwich Village.[5] The riots which occurred on that and succeeding nights had the effect of galvanizing homosexuals into action. The conflict was commemorated the following year by the Christopher Street parade, which became the model for similar demonstrations in other American cities thereafter. The primary significance of these events was that they encouraged a large number of homosexuals to make public their sexual preference.

In 1972, *The Final Report and Background Papers* of the government's National Institute of Mental Health Task Force on Homosexuality urged an end to discrimination against homosexuals generally, and the decriminalization of homosexual practice between consenting adults. In 1973, the American Bar Association took a similar position, while in the same year the American Psychiatric Association voted to remove homosexuality from its official list of mental disorders; a number of other national professional organizations adopted similar policies. In 1973, the National Gay Task Force was formed, now the largest homosexual civil rights organization in the United States. Progress towards liberalization of laws and attitudes did not, however, go unimpeded. The successful and well-publicized crusade led by Anita Bryant in the Miami elections of 1977, preserving the right of an individual to deny housing or employment to homosexuals, was evidence of that. Nevertheless, the fact that International Gay Pride Week could be celebrated, in 1979, was testimony to the enormous change in public opinion and policy which had taken place in the previous decade.

The attitudes of the churches

In Britain it was discussion within the Church of England which stimulated debate in the political arena, leading to the establishment, in 1957, of the Wolfenden Committee, whose report ultimately prompted legal reform. A highly influential role in the debate was played by D. Sherwin Bailey, chairman of the Moral Welfare Council, whose *Homosexuality and the Western Christian Tradition* (1955) was then the most authoritative volume available on the subject, a volume which seemed to justify homosexuality as a sexual preference. In 1958, churchmen were instrumental in forming the Homosexual Law Reform Society. It is important to emphasize that churchmen were agitating for legal reform, and not necessarily seeking to justify the morality of homosexual behaviour.

In the United States, there was no counterpart to the Church of England's initiative to generate legal reform in the area of homosexuality. Kinsey's research had apparently gone unnoticed by the churches, which kept silence during the purges of the early 1950s. In 1964, the Methodist church made several innovative gestures in an attempt to make a bridge between itself and the homosexual community.

H. Kimball Jones, in *Toward a Christian Understanding of the Homosexual* (1966), acknowledging the permanency of a genuine homosexual orientation, sought to promote sympathetic understanding of homosexuals and to provide counselling resources for them. However, on the whole, the churches seemed content with the view that, since homosexuality was regarded by the medical profession as a sickness, they could most properly fulfil their responsibilities towards homosexuals by referring them for therapy. Failure to respond to therapy might then be regarded as a culpable failure to exert the requisite moral effort. Many homosexual Christians met this incomprehension on the part of the church either by the often painful method of concealing their orientation, or by leaving the church entirely. An alternative was provided in the 1960s by the network of Metropolitan Community Churches which welcomed homosexuals into their fellowship, while avoiding an exclusively homosexual membership.

As a generalization, it is fair to say that, by 1970, Protestants had said very little about the issue but felt an increasingly uneasy conscience about the traditional position as it became clear that it was founded on an inadequate scholarly basis, and was instrumental in causing human suffering. As homosexuals became progressively more active in pursuing their rights, and public awareness of their condition grew, many churches re-examined their own positions. Among the first communities to do so was the Lutheran Church in America which, in 1970, demanded an end to discrimination against homosexuals, who were 'sinners only as are all other persons'. In the same year, the Unitarians took a similar resolution, and urged the legalization of consensual acts in private between adults. Most churches which did pronounce on the subject expressed their solidarity with homosexuals in their common sinfulness, though with varying degrees of warmth. Official statements revealed policy-makers attempting to perform delicate balancing acts. In 1974, the Moravian church welcomed homosexuals to join them 'in a common search for wholeness before God'. The Disciples of Christ affirmed in 1977 that 'God's grace does not exclude persons of differing life styles or sexual preferences.' In the same year, the Presbyterians went further and advocated the 'need for the Church to stand for just treatment of homosexual persons in our society in regard to their civil liberties, equal rights, and protection under the law from social and economic discrimination'.[6]

On the other hand, some communions like the Lutheran Church – Missouri Synod, in 1973, continued to regard 'homophile behavior as intrinsically sinful'. In 1976, the Southern Baptist Convention urged member churches 'not to afford the practice of homosexuality any degree of approval through ordination, employment, or other designations of normal lifestyle'. The United Methodist church, in the same year, declared more circumspectly that it could 'not condone the practice of homosexuality' which it considered 'incompatible with Christian teaching'.[7] Those sectarian groups with which Adventism is usually bracketed, maintained traditional positions while evincing greater sympathy for those 'afflicted with the condition'.[8]

Official Roman Catholic teaching has, predictably, remained staunchly opposed to any move likely to lessen the moral culpability of homosexual practice. Various pronouncements made in the 1960s, while omitting specific reference to homosexuality, insisted on procreation as being the true end of the sexual act. The *Declaration on Sexual Ethics*, issued in 1975, made that condemnation explicit.

So much has been said by churchmen on the subject since 1970 that it is difficult to make useful generalizations. One can say with certainty, however, that there remains a wide range of views both within the churches and between them. One of the principal reasons for divergence of opinion is that so little is known about the aetiology of homosexuality that it becomes difficult to make sound judgements concerning the matter of moral responsibility. A number of communions tolerate the existence of a homosexual organization in their midst. A report produced by the United Presbyterian church in 1977 showed administrators to be more liberal in their attitudes than clergymen, whose views were nevertheless more sympathetic to homosexuals than were those of the laity.[9] A similar incongruence is often to be found between scholars and members of church hierarchies. The view expressed by the Jesuit scholar, John McNeill, in *The Church and the Homosexual* (1976), that monogamous homosexual relationships were licit, was, of course, a radical departure from traditional Catholic teaching.

Published Adventist opinion

The first explicit references to homosexuality in Adventist literature came relatively early, in 1951, in Harold Shryock's twin volumes of advice to teenagers, *On Becoming a Man* and *On Becoming a Woman* (pp. 42–6 and pp. 40–5). These suggested that the exchange of physical intimacies between persons of the same sex typically involved an innocent victim and an older person. The cause of homosexual behaviour was said to be arrested personality development often occasioned by some traumatic experience in the teenage years. Frequent reference was made to the dangers existing in a dormitory situation, where, in fact, many young Adventists would find themselves at some stage. The references were remarkable in that they appeared at an early stage in the development of public awareness of the issue, were quite frank, and lacked a hostile tone while clearly condemning the practice.

The first volume of the *Seventh-day Adventist Bible Commentary*, published in 1953, touched on the matter of homosexuality. The comment on Genesis 19:5 was brief and unequivocal: 'On the meaning of "to know" see ch. 4:1. The term here is used with reference to the abominably immoral practice Paul describes in Rom. 1:27, known as sodomy' (vol. 1, p. 333). Comment on the similar passages in Judges 19 was equally hostile:

These men were worse than brutes. Their unnatural lust and infamy were recalled with horror for centuries. (See Hosea 9:9; 10:9) ... Folly. This was frequently used for an outrage against the laws of nature, particularly of a sexual nature (Gen. 34:7; Deut. 22:21, 1 Sam. 13:12).

(vol. 2, pp. 410–11)

The reference to homosexuality in Leviticus 18:22 received no comment, while 20:13 was covered by the following statement: 'Verses 10–21 do not make pleasant reading. Nor were they intended to. The things mentioned are shameful things, wicked things. Hence the judgement is generally death' (vol. 1, p. 794). The commentary on Romans 1:26–7, contained in a volume published four years after the first, used the term 'homosexuality' for the first time:

Paul here refers euphemistically to the depraved practices of sodomy and homosexuality. The recompense for their error of idolatry was physical, mental and spiritual degradation. This was the inevitable penalty for what they had done.   (vol. 6, p. 480).

Similarly the comment on 1 Corinthians 6:9 ran thus:

Effeminate. Gr. *malakoi*, meaning basically 'soft of nature', 'delicate', or 'tender'. When used in connection with terms expressive of sensual vice as those found in v. 9, it designates homosexuals, more particularly those who yield themselves to be used for such immoral purposes. Abusers of themselves among mankind. Gr. *arsenokoitai*, another term describing homosexuals. The list of sins found in vs. 9, 10 includes most of the common sins of the flesh (see Gal. 5:19–21; Eph. 5:3–7). If a man persists in cherishing any of these evil habits, he will be excluded from the kingdom of God. He who lives a life of slavery to the sins of the flesh not only forfeits his own chance of a share in the glorious inheritance of the saints but passes on to his offspring a legacy of weakness, both physical and spiritual ...   (vol. 6, p. 699)

The reference in 1 Timothy to 'them that defile' was also seen as an allusion to homosexuals. Other texts which have some bearing on the subject elicited very little response in the *Commentary*. Passages in

Deuteronomy and the Books of the Kings were taken to refer to cultic prostitution, and received only a passing mention, while references in 2 Peter, Jude, and Revelation were not connected with homosexual practice. Commentaries produced by other denominations, which first appeared at approximately the same time, adopted similar attitudes but were more inclined to distinguish between perversion and inversion, orientation and practice.[10] Each volume of the *Seventh-day Adventist Commentary* has since gone through several revisions, but all comments about homosexuality have remained unchanged since the first edition.

The question of homosexuality was taken up in Adventist literature at much the same time as other denominations were awakening to the problem. A *Review* editorial in 1971 set the tone for later contributions. Homosexuality was apparently regarded as a disease for, it stated, Christians should relate to homosexuals 'with kindness and love, even as they would treat patients in a hospital'.[11] There followed a quotation from Ellen White which was judged to be apt: 'Christ has given His Spirit as a divine power to overcome all hereditary and cultivated tendencies to evil, and to impress His own character upon His church.'[12] It concluded:

Let Christians, then, continue to hold moral standards high. Let them call sin by its right name. At the same time let them point to the all-powerful Christ as the One who can meet every need, and let them reflect His warm understanding, loving spirit to every repentant sinner, whether his problem be inherited or cultivated.[13]

The editorial was significant in that it at least brought to the attention of a large Adventist readership the idea that a homosexual life-style was not always the result of a deliberate and perverse choice.

The Adventist youth magazine *Insight* carried its first article on homosexuality later the same year. The editorial board found it necessary to preface the article with a statement from a senior church administrator who, anticipating the disapproval of some readers, or perhaps parents of readers, argued that young people needed to be aware of the issue in view of the increased activism of the gay movement. The article recorded the fact that the president of the Adventist church had opposed the request of an American representative to a UN Human Rights Commission for liberalization on the question of homosexual marriages. Indeed, the institution of the family emerged as the major concern of the writer:

The Biblical view of sex is that it is a positive and purposeful gift to maintain the unity of the family structure. Whenever it becomes isolated from its role in family solidarity, it ceases to be meaningful and by definition becomes sinful ... Homosexuality is thus *an artificial form of sexuality*, since it does not, and indeed cannot serve as the foundation of a family unit ... It consists in detaching certain physical functions from their productive (not necessarily reproductive) context.[14]

One response to the article complained that the analysis was over-simplified and failed to do justice to the struggle engaged in by many believing homosexuals:

There are many homosexuals right in the church who are trying to establish a personal relationship with Christ as much as anyone ... Being a homosexual does not make one 'lost' or a sinner, for attraction to his own sex is just as inbred in him as attraction to the opposite sex in the heterosexual, and is just as unchangeable.[15]

The letter marked perhaps the earliest murmurings of the Adventist homosexual voice.

In 1972, the church made a bold attempt to reach the homosexual subculture in the shape of an attractive brochure produced by the Voice of Prophecy, an Adventist evangelistic agency based in California. *Two of a Kind* adopted a very sympathetic tone, lamenting the stereotypes with which the general public operated, and the suffering thereby inflicted. It reflected that this lack of understanding often precipitated frenzied participation in the 'gay life-style', which always failed to yield satisfaction, although it provided at least a measure of acceptance. It located the origins of homosexual behaviour in difficulties arising in the early stages of personality development. It made an attempt to create solidarity between 'gays' and 'straights' by asserting that the dislocation of the modern family unit meant that everyone suffered some sort of sexual tension, of which homosexuality was merely one example. While acknowledging that homosexuals could not be blamed for their orientation, the brochure did contain a clear call to responsible behaviour. The message of liberation was a simple religious one: that God gave anyone the power to overcome his condition. A later revision of the brochure (1977) conveyed essentially the same message although in a somewhat more restrained style. The brochures were imaginative, and significant in that, while they upheld traditional Christian teaching, they made clear in a way unprecedented in Adventist circles the distinction between inversion and perversion, and between orientation and practice, in addition to gently reproaching the general public for its hostility, ignorance, and complacency.

An equally frank discussion was contained in Wittschiebe's controversial *God Invented Sex* (1974), which was probably the fullest discussion of the subject yet to come before the general Adventist public, since *Two of a Kind* reached a young, to some extent non-Adventist, predominantly west-coast readership. The author adopted a traditional Adventist position: 'It would be our understanding as Adventists that a converted homosexual would not engage in any sexual relationship with another male (or a woman with another woman)' (p. 186). However, this view was prefaced by the plea that Adventists, instead of regarding homosexuality as a type of 'moral leprosy', should minister to those who experienced it. Furthermore,

... the church should remember that Scripture classifies homosexuality with a number of more common and less shocking sins. The church has a responsibility to explore more deeply the psychological and emotional causes, to become more sensitively aware of the blending of sin and sickness, and of culpability and non responsibility. (pp. 184–5)

The brief consideration of secular aetiological evidence Wittschiebe found compatible with Ellen White's exhortation:

Encourage the expression of love toward God and toward one another. The reason why there are so many hard-hearted men and women in the world is that true affection has been regarded as weakness, and has been discouraged and repressed.[16]

As for the role of religious experience in the 'cure' of homosexuality, Wittschiebe remained fairly realistic:

We cannot underestimate the power of prayer, yet one rarely hears of a homosexual who has had his nature changed to heterosexual by it alone ... More commonly one sees strength to meet continued temptation given in response to prayer. (p. 187)

The book contained a plea to Adventists to offer the warmth and understanding so vital to a homosexual for his emotional well-being, together with a request that Adventist scholars and medical personnel study the phenomenon from all angles, and that ministerial training should prepare men to counsel homosexuals.

Wittschiebe's book contained reference to research done by Ray B. Evans, then associate professor of psychiatry at Loma Linda School of Medicine, which suggested that aetiological explanations in terms of parent–child relationships were not exhaustive, and that there was a need for re-examination of the discredited biological theory. However, since Evans was not an Adventist, and since his work was not completed at Loma Linda, detailed examination of it will be omitted. Suffice it to say that it provoked no adverse reaction amongst his colleagues or the university administration.[17]

A major influence on Adventist thinking about homosexuality has been the work of Colin Cook, himself a homosexual. His first contribution to the debate was a series of three articles in *Insight*, in 1976. Basic to his position was the view that homosexuality must be faced squarely as sin. It was a manifestation of fundamental alienation from God: 'Nothing but the gospel reaches the real problem behind homosexuality.'[18] The profound fears and guilt experienced by all, heterosexuals as well, could, in Cook's view, only be dissolved by an acceptance of God's love. All aetiological explanations and varieties of therapy must be secondary to this. Despite the feelings which the homosexual might experience in the withdrawal period, he had to assert by faith that victory had been obtained; moral failures did not invalidate that. He claimed: 'You are heterosexual because Christ has declared you so, by creation and redemption.'[19] He did not wish to imply, however, that one immediately experienced heterosexual attraction. The withdrawal process was to be aided by the sympathetic help of a support group, with which the homosexual was to maintain regular contact. Cook concluded:

Increasingly it will dawn upon you that you have been delivered from one of the worst distortions of the truth about God ever inflicted on man by Lucifer. For when people confuse their sexuality, they lose within themselves and their partners the greatest yardstick this side of faith with which to know something of the image of God.[20]

Cook's three articles contained the germ of a ministry which was later to receive official church approval, and which will be examined in detail below.

Predictably, Cook's articles produced a variety of reactions. One homosexual correspondent, who remained anonymous for fear of losing his job in an Adventist institution, saw the publication of the articles as evidence of a maturing process within the church. The individual feared, however, that those homosexuals who had not experienced the sort of change described by Cook, would be regarded, and would even regard themselves, as insincere or undisciplined. The letter contained what was probably an accurate description of the plight of the typical young Adventist homosexual:

Few gay people set out to be gay. We wake up in our young adulthood to the fact that our emotions and drives have a different pattern from those of our friends. Most of us experience profound shock and dismay. Some submerge this by marrying the first person of the opposite sex who comes along – and then have unhappy marriages, if not divorce, as a result. Some leave the church because of their guilt feelings and fear of what the church will do to them. Others commit suicide.[21]

Another homosexual denominational employee condemned Cook's articles as projecting an image of God whose grace extended only to those with the same sexual orientation as the majority. The letter welcomed, however, treatment of 'a topic that is important to more SDA's than any of the leadership can ever know'.[22] Another letter confirmed this view:

There are a significant number of homosexuals in the church, and the reason we are not witnessing openly is that there is a stereotyped idea of homosexuality that is hampering our work to help individuals with this problem.[23]

Discussion of the subject spread beyond the youth magazine. One letter to the *Review* enquired whether Adventist theologians had undertaken any research on the biblical references to homosexuality, whether Adventist scholars had analysed the research available, and whether the church had communicated with homosexuals within its ranks. The writer believed that homosexuals, far from wanting to flaunt their condition, sought 'refuge from a hostile world in which, paradoxically, Christians are often in the forefront'.[24] Another letter argued that the judgemental spirit of the majority of Adventists was born of ignorance.[25]

Further evidence of hostility towards homosexuality appeared in 1977. An anthology of Ellen White's counsel on mental health designated homosexuality 'Sodom's Particular Sin', although, as previously argued, the evidence did not entirely support that judgement.[26] In the same year, church leaders pronounced on the problems arising where a homosexual married:

Homosexual practices are recognized as a misuse of sexual powers, and disapproved in Scripture. As a violation of the divine intention in marriage, they thus become just cause for divorce.[27]

This was the first time that such a policy had been adopted by the church. The *Sabbath School Lessons* also bore witness to a growing awareness of the issue in the denomination. On the basis of biblical references and citations from Ellen White's books, one author opined, under the heading 'homosexuality':

Jesus said that one of the signs of His near return would be a condition of morality similar to that among the antediluvians and Sodomites. Not only have the same deviant sexual patterns become prominent in our times, being pursued with open boldness, but some professed ministers now defend such practices, organize churches for persons of this life-style, and ordain some to the ministry. Such sinful brazenness indicates again the eroding morality of our times and the approaching end of the age.[28]

Expressions of support for Anita Bryant's campaign to oppose liberalization of laws on homosexuality in Miami appeared in Adventist periodicals late in 1977. The writer of a *Review* article said:

I don't think we can take the position that a homosexual is beyond the love of God ... Yes, I do believe that homosexuality is a sin ... I have to state unequivocally that at this point I cannot understand churches that are composed of 'gay' people. This is not to say that a 'gay' person might not be a church member, if he were aware of his problem and striving to over-come it, but a whole 'church' of homosexuals flaunting their sickness, and declaring it to be the norm boggles the mind ... Who wants to live in the tragic half-world of homosexuality when with God's grace he can come out into the sunshine of a full and happy life?[29]

In the summer of 1977, the General Conference president, Robert Pierson, released a statement condemning the homosexual life-style, which caught the attention of the national press. It came in response to official municipal celebration of 'gay pride week' in Seattle. As a clear statement of official denomination thinking, it is worth quoting at length:

The gay movement strikes at the very heart of family life. It encourages and makes acceptable a destructive lifestyle, rather than one that contributes to healthy, growing families, communities and nation ... It is proverbial that the wickedness of Sodom and Gomorrah prompted devastating judgments. Christ put Himself on record that He would personally pass judgment on such perversion when he returned. This is not to say that salvation is unavailable to those who practice homosexually. Holy Scripture promises power from God to transform and completely change personality, enabling the sinner to perfectly know the will of God. (Romans 12:2) The tendency to homosexuality may be one of the more difficult traits to erase. But through the power and grace of God, the strength of human will, and encouragement from human associates salvation is attainable for the repentant homosexual. (1 Cor. 6:9–15.) The Bible unequivocally labels homosexuality a sin. The church is full of sinners but it is for sinners who are looking for a better life. They are changing, through a process known as sanctification – a process that recognizes and accepts Christ's sacrifice for them. The very vocal and highly visible portion of the gay movement today do not want change, but bluntly demand acceptance as they are. The church earnestly, eagerly cares about the sinner, and anxiously wants to help that sinner grow and put sin out of his life.

Scripture does not condemn the homosexual, but denounces the practice. In keeping with this principle, the Seventh-day Adventist church members are urged to pray that those who call upon God for relief from their aberrant drives will find deliverance, peace and forgiveness.[30]

Adventist spokesmen found themselves in a little difficulty concerning the political dimensions of the issue, when they refused to extend the same cautious recognition to the 'gay rights movement' as they had to the civil rights and feminist movements. Some found it to be inconsistent with the church's commitment to religious liberty.[31]

Evidence concerning the way in which the church actually handled homosexuals who were discovered in its midst was provided by the case of a young man whose orientation was discovered while he was a student at Columbia Union College, Maryland. He was requested to withdraw following his refusal to renounce his homosexual practice. This administrative action appeared to attract the support of the student body, which was predominantly Adventist.[32]

Interest in the subject of homosexuality, fuelled by the Anita Bryant crusade, continued into 1978, when a spate of articles appeared in denominational publications. One originated from the mother of a homosexual who had married and had children. She claimed that her son had been miraculously healed; becoming heterosexual was a gift of God, not the result of great moral effort. She catalogued the hurts inflicted by uncomprehending members. Some were apparently unaware that they were rejecting one who needed acceptance. Others saw her son as a threat to their children, yet others did not wish to offend God by seeming to condone homosexuality. Many clearly regarded sexual sins as being the most heinous.[33] In an editorial accompanying this article, it was observed, perhaps a little surprisingly, that those guilty of pride, embezzlement, or sins of omission were no less culpable before God than the homosexual.[34]

Predictably, the two articles provoked an impressive response. Much of it was sympathetic, expressing appreciation that the matter had been raised in open forum, and exhorting church members to show understanding to those homosexuals in their midst. Some correspondents confirmed that there was a large number of Adventist homosexuals, many of whom had already left the church because of the unsympathetic response of members.[35] Some homosexual correspondents had apparently found a cure, others had not, in spite of great effort.[36]

Insight magazine continued the debate. In a further contribution, Cook challenged Wolfenden's claim that homosexual orientation was unalterable.[37] Another article suggested that Kinsey's work as an entomologist had distorted his renowned research on human sexuality.[38] A letter welcomed the church's attempt to grapple with the issue, but feared that change would be difficult for someone who rated high on the Kinsey scale.[39] Another letter contained a plea for the acceptance of a monogamous homosexual relationship.[40]

While expression of sympathy and understanding predominated in Adventist periodical literature of the time, hostile reactions also surfaced occasionally:

Rather than asking if the church has talked to the homosexuals within its ranks, it might be well to ask the homosexual if he has sought to know how to be saved from his predicament ... Gay people may be within the church, but if they are practicing this sin, they are not of the church. When the recording angel's book brings to light all behavior, unnatural, sinful practices will be seen for what they are. Those who practice them and who have not been transformed by divine grace will turn in shame and dismay from the presence of a sinless Redeemer.[41]

In the period 1978–80, three leading Adventist scholars produced significant contributions to the debate. Jack Provonsha took issue with the allegedly victimless nature of homosexuality.[42] If the fact that there were no victims was a sufficient ground for slackening the law, he said, then the law on incest might properly be revoked where the possibility of procreation was eliminated by contraception. The incest taboo was maintained, Provonsha argued, because the behaviour posed a serious threat to family structure and social stability. Moreover, a clear sense of personal identity was vital for the maintenance of mental health. Neither incest nor homosexuality was a victimless crime; they both constituted a threat to the social order itself. In his opinion, there existed the danger that sexuality could cease to be a symbol for family trust and permanence. It was therefore important to resist that which tended to undermine the basic social unit, for it was vital to the future health of society. A clear picture of the ideal of an enduring family unit had to be communicated to the next generation. While Provonsha believed that discrimination against homosexuals should be eliminated generally, and that those who suffered through no fault of their own had a right to acceptance and support, he nevertheless believed that society had the right to deny them access to role-modelling positions which facilitated public advocacy of their life-style.

James Londis' public lecture given at Loma Linda University in the following year was calculated to disturb any complacency on the matter.[43] He estimated that Adventist homosexuals in North America must number 'tens of thousands', and believed it to be 'a pastoral problem of profound significance'. Reading from letters received from Adventist homosexuals, he described what one correspondent called 'years of personal hell in a private world of guilt'. The same writer continued:

For years I thought I was the only Seventh-day Adventist who knew this struggle. I could not confront my nature or feelings directly enough to acknowledge them until the last two or three years. I have gone the route of psychiatry, psychology and even voluntary hospitalization in efforts either to deny my homosexuality or to find the 'cure' that the church seems to assume exists, but they cannot seem to effect it, at least not for me.[44]

Londis described the sense of rejection felt by homosexuals within the church, and the agonizing choice between leaving the church which was so much a part of their life, or denying their nature. Others faced the unhappy or ruined marriages which followed an attempt to deny their homosexuality. Londis suggested that a life of sexual abstinence was an option only for a minority, for it often produced emotional disorders which served to underline the profound loneliness which many homosexuals suffered. Londis regarded the matter of cure as the central issue in Adventist circles. If one believed that cure did indeed exist, then those who had not experienced it stood accused of not trying hard enough. Londis wondered whether cure was available to all, as the church seemed to assume. He further challenged Adventist orthodoxy by reviewing some modern scholarship which seemed to cast doubt on the traditional understanding of relevant biblical passages. The lecture concluded with a plea to the church's scholars in all disciplines to undertake a thorough study of the evidence so that the church could come to a mature position on the subject, and equip itself to minister to those who experienced social isolation.

After reviewing the theological and aetiological evidence, Sakae Kubo affirmed, in his *Theology and Ethics of Sex*, that one should hesitate to condemn homosexual practice among inverts. In the final analysis, however, he insisted that homosexuality be regarded as abnormal since the element of complementarity, central to biblical teaching on sexual relations, was absent. He concluded that it must be regarded as evil in the sense that disease, rather than sin, was evil. He held that

The homosexual may not be able to do anything about his attraction for his own sex, but by God's grace he can control his impulses. He may not have had any real choice regarding his condition, but he has choice about his actions. (p. 83)

The church had the important responsibility of helping inverts to live with their condition.

In this still rather cautious climate, it was perhaps a little surprising that an Adventist publisher should produce an autobiographical account of homosexual experience as explicit as that in *Out of the Closet – Into the Light* (1980). The author, Michael Munger, not himself an Adventist at the time of publication, described in considerable detail the experiences he had had as a homosexual, from childhood experimentation to adolescent prostitution. He traced the causes of his condition to unfortunate experiences in childhood and adolescence, and recounted the enormous internal struggles facing one who tried to reconcile his own sexual orientation with his Christian aspirations. The book concluded apparently with a claim to healing through the power of the Christian gospel and the support of Christian friends. The bold editorial decision to publish such a book was made in response to a perceived need for the church to address itself to the problem in a non-academic fashion.

That such a need existed was confirmed by another contribution to the debate by Cook, in which he estimated that

There may be between 10,000 and 20,000 homosexuals within the Adventist Church in the United States alone. Thousands of these suffer in deep conflict, longing for help, looking for a solution, needing at the very least an ear to talk into.[45]

Cook acknowledged the slowness of the Adventist church to enter this field:

It is painful to admit, but our Adventist church is at least a decade behind the Holy Spirit's work on the question of homosexuality. In the past ten years a whole network of ministries for homosexuals has risen, bringing love, acceptance, and healing ... (*ibid.*)

The church's first responsibility to homosexuals, then, was 'to make confession that we have failed to minister to the aching needs of so many, and to request that they will forgive us' (*ibid.*). It should, he believed, undertake a widespread counselling ministry which would seek to help individuals towards a life of heterosexual fulfilment. It was not a problem which should or could be tackled by specialists alone. On the contrary, he believed

We have ... fallen prey to a professionalism in our denomination that denies the doctrine of the priesthood of all believers and the gifts of the Spirit among us ... Christian communities have great potential as healing communities ...[46]

The problem, in Cook's view, was a spiritual one; homosexuality was just one manifestation of a failure to find wholeness. He rejected the view that it was an alternative form of sexual behaviour which was acceptable to God if used in a responsible way, in a monogamous relationship.

By 1980, it had become clear that thinking on the homosexual question within the Seventh-day Adventist church had become polarized. The church establishment predictably favoured Cook's philosophy that the gospel offered the homosexual the power to realize his own heterosexuality. In various forums Cook's philosophy received a good deal of favourable attention. Inevitably, however, it produced a reaction on the part of homosexuals brought up in an Adventist context who had failed to change, or thought it unnecessary to seek to change, their sexual orientation. The next two sections document that ideological struggle.

Quest learning center

Colin Cook, an English pastor, lived for many years in a private world of guilt produced by his attraction to members of the same sex. After acknowledging publicly his homosexual orientation, he left the ministry and became a counsellor at Green Hills Health Center in Reading, Pennsylvania, established in the early 1970s for the practice of preventive medicine. While there, Cook wrote a number of articles (already examined) which, in the late 1970s, Adventist journals seemed increasingly willing to publish. The fruit of Cook's reading, counselling, and personal struggle was the publication, in 1978, of ten hour-long taped lectures entitled *Homosexuality and the Power to Change*.

In these lectures, Cook acknowledged immediately that he was without formal training in the counselling of homosexuals; his programme for change, he conceded, would be regarded by many as naive, lacking as it did any complex therapy. The authority for his programme lay in his knowledge of homosexuals who had become heterosexual, in the clinical work of Lawrence Hatterer[47] and, most importantly, in his own claim to homosexual healing. He regarded homosexuality as abnormal behaviour whose aetiology was essentially spiritual rather than biological or environmental, although he acknowledged that such factors played an important secondary role. Basing his diagnosis on the book of Romans, he judged homosexuality to be one among many manifestations of alienation from God. It was an expression of self-love, and a desire to find sufficiency within oneself. It arose from a fear of what was other, whether that other was female, or divine. In religious circles that fear often produced an attempt to find salvation by the performance of good works, since the sort of unqualified acceptance extended by God towards humans was instinctively mistrusted by them.

Vital to the process of healing was an acceptance of the fact that homosexuality was a deviant form of behaviour, and that it fell short of the biblical ideal where humans were made male and female in the image of God. Cook maintained that, while one might acknowledge that our depersonalized modern society was productive of many kinds of behavioural deviance, the individual homosexual had ultimately to accept responsibility for his own acts and acknowledge his need for help. He had to assert his own God-given heterosexuality in the midst of homosexual temptation. He had to recognize that the experience of such temptation did not bring upon him the condemnation of God, and even that bowing to temptation did not automatically staunch the flow of divine grace. Homosexual desires often disappeared only gradually, Cook claimed, and relationships with women would at first probably be based on *agape* rather than *eros*. Initially, the homosexual might well experience indifference to women sexually. Relationships might be mechanical until the individual realized that he was particularly prized by a member of the opposite sex. Churches had often made a great mistake in recommending a celibate life to homosexuals; their behaviour was indicative of emotional arrest. It was necessary to promote emotional growth, not to stunt it. There must therefore be development towards heterosexuality.

Cook's analysis was perhaps welcomed by some Adventist homosexuals to the extent that it regarded homosexuality as one among many manifestations of alienation. His demand that all homosexual practice be renounced was likely to produce hostility among those who, unlike himself, did not claim to have experienced release from their condition. Furthermore, the call for the church to support homosexuals who sincerely sought cure, and to disfellowship those who promoted gay liberationist ideals, was a serious affront to a minority within the church.

Cook's counselling ministry to homosexuals grew to such an extent that, in 1980, he founded the Quest Learning Center, devoted entirely to the needs of homosexuals. A major breakthrough for that institution came in September 1981 when a lengthy and very frank interview with Cook was published in *Ministry* (pp. 4–13), which reaches a large number of clergy within and beyond Adventism. The interview covered much the same ground as his previous articles and taped lectures, but contained more autobiographical detail. Cook regretted the fact that Adventists had shown themselves to be insensitive to the needs of homosexuals, and ineffectual in helping them.

The interview produced a flood of enquiries and a blossoming in Quest's activities. The response encouraged the church, through the General Conference and the Columbia Union Conference, to provide funding for the centre. If publishing Cook's interview in *Ministry* was an acknowledgement of its work, the provision of funds was a positive endorsement. Cook urged, however, that Quest 'not now become the "official" church program for people in homosexuality. There must also be other ways of speaking the same word of hope.'[48] The fact is, however, that Quest remained the only option available within Adventism for homosexual 'healing'.

In its brief existence, the Quest Learning Center has helped hundreds of homosexuals through individual counselling sessions, seminars, and series of taped lectures.[49] It began to work in conjunction with Exodus International, a non-sectarian umbrella organization of ministries to homosexuals, and had a considerable influence beyond the confines of Adventism. Adventists constituted about half of Quest's clients for individual counselling but they showed a reluctance to attend public functions. Male clients outnumbered female in a ratio of approximately four to one. Quest was soon placed on a more stable financial footing with the allocation by the General Conference of an annual grant of $40,000, half of the centre's annual budget. Quest was not officially connected with the Adventist church, although the majority of its board of directors were members.

Perhaps the boldest of Quest's initiatives was the foundation of the Homosexuals Anonymous programme. Over twenty chapters of this organization based on Quest's philosophy were established in the United States. Anyone who attended one of Quest's seminars had the right to establish a chapter. Cook devoted considerable time to producing literature for the use of these chapters.[50] In Cook's opinion, the attitudes of Adventist administrators have softened as a result of the activities of the Quest Learning Center, while the views of rank-and-file members stand in need of considerable education.[51] The work of Quest, however, did not go unopposed.

SDA Kinship

While Cook's work may have aroused suspicion among some conservative heterosexual church members, it has met with hostility from other Adventists claiming their right to assert their homosexuality. There was a considerable response to an advertisement placed in a widely circulated 'gay' magazine, *The Advocate*, in 1976, requesting correspondence from homosexuals with Adventist connections. Many had either concealed their orientation or sought fellowship in a more receptive communion, such as the Metropolitan Community Church. In early 1977, the first gathering of Adventist homosexuals took place in Palm Desert, California.

The group, operating from Los Angeles, soon erected basic organizational structures, taking the name 'SDA Kinship' and publishing periodically a 'newsletter of Gay Seventh-day Adventists and their friends'. By the end of 1979, three chapters existed in Los Angeles, San Diego, and Phoenix, with another half-dozen or so in the process of formation across the nation. Despite these signs of growth, the organization experienced considerable early growth pangs, with the financial and administrative burden for the organization being borne by a very few people.[52]

The concerns of Kinship seem to have been threefold: first, to create a context in which Adventist homosexuals could worship without feeling isolated; secondly, to provide opportunity for social contact between those whose perspective on life was similar; thirdly, to organize Adventist homosexuals and give expression to their concerns. For the most part, they met only occasionally but the concern for spiritual fellowship was clearly expressed. The *Newsletter* recorded many requests for prayers for those suffering as a a result of their sexual orientation. Inevitably, some members felt resentment at the rejection they had faced in the church. The hurt continued as some members faced being disfellowshipped because of the public declaration of their proclivity which Kinship membership constituted. The *Newsletter*, however, urged on members a sense of responsibility towards the church, together with a pride in being homosexual.[53] Opposition to the notion of healing was clear:

Homosexuality and heterosexuality are two aspects of sexuality, neither being the counterfeit of the other, both being right or wrong depending upon the context of their expression ... Both the homosexual and the heterosexual are capable of lusting or loving, worshipping the creature or the Creator, and of seeking salvation by works or accepting it as a gift of God.[54]

Initially the group was content simply to organize for survival. Only nineteen attended the general meeting in January 1980, although some 300, the large majority of whom were male, were recorded on the mailing list in the middle of that year. Kinship received help in its efforts to organize from other Christian homosexual groups, like Dignity, and was thus enabled to establish contact with small groups of Adventist homosexuals in Florida and New England.

A major advance, however, was made by Kinship in August 1980 when it held its first 'kampmeeting' in Arizona. The fact that thirty-five homosexuals with Adventist connections convened for a week was evidence enough of growth. Far more significant, however, was the presence of six observers with the approval of the General Conference administration. It was an attempt on the part of the church hierarchy to respond to the issue of homosexuality, and took place after careful negotiation, to the admitted surprise of Kinship leaders themselves. The papers, presented by three professors from the Seventh-day Adventist Theological Seminary at Andrews University in Michigan, tended to the view that a 'simplistic reading of the few scriptural references to homosexual acts would not suffice to determine the Lord's will for homosexual persons today'.[55] Two pastors with experience in counselling homosexuals underlined the need to understand those homosexuals in the church. Cook drew on his own experience of homosexual 'healing'. Opportunity was given to those homosexuals attending to speak, and many testified to the hurt they had experienced as they grew up as homosexuals in an Adventist context. The experience was regarded by all who attended as a valuable one which fostered mutual understanding.

The Pacific Union Conference of Adventists, in whose territory the meeting was held, felt it necessary to release a press statement to clarify the situation:

Seventh-day Adventists hold that a homosexual lifestyle opposes Biblical principles. Moreover, we view a 'gay' relationship as a union contrary to both nature and God's expressed will.

... Any deviation from this divine pattern that weakens the foundation upon which a Christian home or Christian nation is built cannot be accepted by the Church.

... On the other hand, we also believe that while the Bible condemns the practice of homosexuality, it does make provision for the person ...

For this reason Church leaders have been in attendance with those at the Kinship Kampmeeting. Recognizing that the Lord loves all people, some ministers have met to reaffirm with them God's ideal.[56]

In reporting to the General Conference leaders, the six observers submitted the following nine proposals:

1 That the officers of the Biblical Research Institute be asked to set up a special subcommittee to study thoroughly the whole question of homosexuality and the church;
2 That balanced and responsible articles dealing with the Biblical, theological, and pastoral aspects of said topic be prepared for publication in the *Adventist Review* and *Ministry*;
3 That programs on sex education taught in our academies and colleges, seminaries and extension schools, church seminars and continuing education courses, and the like, include a unit on homosexuality;
4 That balanced and responsible reading lists be prepared for all levels of education indicated under item 3;
5 That guidelines (similar to those voted by the Fall Councils of 1976 and 1977 with respect to divorce and remarriage) be drawn up for the benefit of the pastors, teachers, and administrators as they try to handle wisely, graciously, and redemptively the particular cases of homosexuality that come under their care;
6 That we identify a number of informed and understanding pastors, teachers, counselors and other professionals, to whom our youth, on

discovering that they might have a homosexual orientation, may turn with confidence;

7 That vehicles, such as hotlines, be set up so that youth in our academies, colleges, and universities may contact such persons, assured of full confidentiality;

8 That the church recognize Kinship as a vehicle by which other young SDAs discovering that they have a homosexual orientation, may find the help they seek. (Both the officers and the general members of Kinship with whom we have been in contact assured us that they are (a) opposed to proselytizing and (b) committed to referring those who call on them for help to those professionals who can give them the help they seek);

9 That Josephine Benton and Larry Geraty be asked to serve as chaplains to the Kinship group.[57]

While the first seven of the proposals were accepted, the last two were rejected since it was felt that these would imply denominational recognition of Kinship, to which church leaders remained firmly opposed. It was decided, however, that, while not appointing chaplains to Kinship, the church would not oppose individuals serving in this capacity if their employing organizations did not object.

The success of the 'kampmeeting' seemed to inject new energy into the organization. The call for members to make their homosexuality public, and for recognition of the propriety of monogamous relationships attracted considerable attention in the *Newsletter*. Although the organization was clearly gaining in strength, some signs of fragility were evident. There was, however, unity in rejecting the idea of 'deliverance' as championed by Cook.

The next significant event in the life of Kinship was its incorporation as a non-profit-making, religious organization. In order to achieve this status Kinship had to produce a statement of beliefs and objectives. Fundamental among the beliefs were the following:

We believe that intimate love expressed between people of the same gender can be positive, beautiful, and healthy experience to the glory of God; and We affirm the rights of gay and lesbians as children of God to live in our church and society as citizens with the full respect and priviledges [sic] that go with it, and pledge ourselves to work towards that goal.[58]

Its objectives were basically fourfold:

1 to bear witness to Jesus Christ in the homosexual community;
2 to provide guidance to Seventh-day Adventists and other Christians who discovered themselves to be homosexuals;
3 to promote understanding of homosexuals among the Adventist community;
4 to 'facilitate through education, advocacy and reconciliation, the acceptance of gay and lesbian Seventh-day Adventists within the Seventh-day Adventist institutions and churches'.

It was a matter of no great surprise that such a clear statement of Kinship's position swiftly elicited an equally clear statement of the church's view. In a letter to administrators in key positions, the president of the General Conference, Neal Wilson, confessed

disappointment and dismay at the apparent direction in which Kinship is moving, as noted in their newsletter. They indicate that they intend to obtain the church's recognition of their lifestyle as an acceptable alternative within the church's fellowship. With these objectives, which appear clearly to ignore the real possibility of change and deliverance by Jesus Christ through the provisions of the gospel, we cannot be in agreement.[59]

Wilson further requested administrators to advise their employees not to attend Kinship meetings if invited, since it might be a source of confusion for lay members, and 'the cause of the truth of the gospel' would not be served. The issue, clearly a matter of real concern to administrators in the United States, was raised at the spring meeting of Adventist leaders in 1981. The church affirmed that it was unable to accept the view that homosexual relationships be considered a legitimate alternative life-style. Moreover, the church felt it could not negotiate with organized groups of homosexuals; the efforts of the church had to be directed towards individuals in need. Especially, the church could have no dealings with a group which described itself as 'Seventh-day Adventist gays', and it was in fact seeking legal advice about denying it the right to use the denominational name.[60] The establishment's response to Kinship's statement of its position meant that the fragile relationship between the two parties was effectively broken. It seems that both had misread the signals being given by the other; from the spring of 1981 a sharp division of opinion existed between the two.

The June edition of the *Newsletter* contained critical, though restrained, reaction to the General Conference pronouncements. One writer traced the breakdown in communication between the church hierarchy and Kinship to a number of causes. The church was currently experiencing a serious theological crisis unassociated with these moral issues, which had brought sharp division between members. The church leadership, it was said, was under great pressure from conservatives within the church to affirm traditional positions. The incorporation of Kinship may also have been regarded as a threat by the leadership. The church leaders were sensitive to the adverse reaction of some members to the General Conference efforts to relate to Kinship. Finally, an article apparently condoning homosexual promiscuity may, wrongly, have been taken as typifying Kinship opinion.[61] Representatives of both camps attempted privately to mend the breach, and agreement was reached that church employees would be allowed to attend Kinship meetings if they felt that it was part of their ministry to do so, provided they remained anonymous, and that Kinship did not claim their presence as a sign of official endorsement. Kinship regretted the apparent reversal of church policy when it was ministering so successfully to Adventists, many of whom had long been alienated from the church.

The second 'kampmeeting' took place in August 1981 with sixty in attendance, including ministers. A Pacific Union Conference policy statement, similar to that produced in 1980, recorded that

Though the Seventh-day Adventist Church does not recognize 'Seventh-day Adventist Kinship International, Inc.' as a viable adjunct to the Church, it does accept responsibility for ministry to the homosexual on a one-to-one basis just as it does to the wanton heterosexual.[62]

Throughout 1981, there were signs that Kinship was beginning to flourish; the *Newsletter* claimed a mailing list of 500,[63] some living outside the United States. In the United States, Kinship had organized into eight regional groups. The range of interests and activities recorded in the *Newsletter* broadened during the year; Kinship, with a rather more stable organization, was becoming less introspective. Its future was in some measure influenced by the decision that officers should not only be Adventist homosexuals but should also have publicly acknowledged their orientation.

Kinship continued in much the same vein in 1982 with a gradual expansion of its activities. The *Newsletter* announced the establishment of a telephone 'crisis counselling service', and even news of an embryonic Kinship group in Australia. However, at the third 'kampmeeting', which seventy-five attended, a split developed in the leadership of the group. The president resigned, criticizing a certain faction for being more interested in pursuing political objectives than in providing support for homosexuals who felt lonely and isolated. Allegations of dishonesty and mismanagement were made. A power struggle, similar to that experienced by the Mattachine Foundation, seems to have taken place in the organization over a period of months. The departing president, in an open letter,[64] announced his intention to found a new organization, Orion Fellowship Alliance, Inc., which he believed more accurately represented the early ideals of Kinship. A brochure published by Orion contained a philosophy and intended range of activities similar to those of Kinship. January 1983 saw the publication of the first edition of *Lifeline*, a magazine very similar in style to Kinship's *Newsletter* but which comprised largely news gleaned from non-Adventist homosexual sources. The publication was full of aspirations but little else; a second edition did not appear. It seemed very unlikely that there was room for a second Adventist homosexual organization, particularly when Kinship was relatively well established. The split in the ranks of Adventist homosexuals did, however, indicate the fragility of the situation.

The change in the leadership of Kinship certainly seemed to work to its advantage. The magazine, which in December 1982 assumed the name *Kinship Connection*, became a much more sophisticated publication both in terms of production and content. It gave evidence of a small but flourishing organization. Between December 1982 and May 1983, the mailing list showed an increase from 366 to 443 subscribers, although rather less than half of these were active members. Kinship was organized in nine regions, with chapters supporting an increasing number of activities. Kinship spread its activities beyond the United States by officially opening a chapter in Australia in July 1983. It maintained contacts with Dignity and Integrity, its Catholic and Episcopalian equivalents, which referred Adventists to them whenever they presented themselves. Although Kinship advertised widely in gay publications and meeting places, there was not a significant response from what it claimed to be a large hidden Adventist constituency. The posture of the organization certainly became mildly militant. The January 1983 edition of *Kinship Connection* was devoted largely to the virtues of 'coming out'. The long-term good of homosexuals in the Adventist community would be served, it claimed, primarily by Kinship members making their voices heard. Gradually Kinship members found that they were receiving invitations to address Adventist groups concerning their orientation. The most ambitious move in the attempt to 'educate' Adventists on the subject came in July 1983, when some packages of well-produced reading material about homosexuality were sent to 650 selected pastors and counsellors.

Kinship has not been without its difficulties; the newsletter has recorded the financial problems which the group has regularly faced and the generosity of a few dedicated members. Just as threatening potentially was the debate generated by the question of the use of alcohol at Kinship functions. Those who believed that the leadership should avoid legislating on such matters of practice, accepting all-comers whatever their present opinions and practice, found themselves opposed by those who believed that Kinship should uphold the standards of that church whose name it bore.

Kinship did much to consolidate its position after the publicity campaign of July 1983. In September 1984, subscribers to *Kinship Connection* totalled nearly 700, an increase of almost 300 over the twelve months,[65] nearly a fifth being lesbians. It instituted a plan for regular donations which made the organization more stable financially.[66] In an attempt to inform the Adventist membership, it sent out further sets of information packages, and maintained an unofficial presence at the General Conference session in New Orleans, in 1985. It sought to establish contacts with homosexuals with Adventist connections in Europe, South America, and Australasia.[67] While the church administration has refused to recognize the group, Kinship has gradually succeeded, in a limited way, in dispelling ignorance about homosexuality. Yet its main concern has remained the provision of support and friendship for Adventist homosexuals. Kinship has championed the cause of homosexual monogamy and given thought to a rite of 'couple affirmation'.[68] *Kinship Connection* has provided a regular diet of devotional articles, features on the pain of being an Adventist homosexual, on AIDS, and general developments within the church. The organization has remained very closely identified with the ethos of Adventism in many ways, although *Kinship Connection* periodically carried expressions of resentment towards the church.[69] Relationships with Quest have remained distinctly cool, although expression of opposition has been restrained.[70]

Kinship had its fair share of teething troubles during its infancy. With a more professional and sophisticated leadership, it has given evidence of being able adequately to represent the homosexual cause to the Adventist community. The future success of the organization really depends on whether the numbers of Adventist homosexuals are as large as Kinship has projected, whether those who have felt wounded by attitudes within the church wish to maintain their contact with it, and whether those who are currently concealing their sexual orientation within the church believe that the effort involved in declaring it publicly would be worthwhile.

Recent developments

Adventist periodicals have continued to address the subject of homosexuality from time to time. Certainly, the most significant contribution was a *Review* editorial, which constituted the first official acknowledgement of the existence of Kinship.[71] While it defended a traditional position by recommending celibacy to those who were homosexual in their orientation, it adopted a compassionate tone which Kinship members found encouraging.[72] It gave them grounds for feeling that their attempts to 'educate' their co-religionists were succeeding.

If Adventist leaders needed any encouragement to recognize that homosexuality was a problem within the church, they received it in disclosures that two of their own number had been arrested, on separate occasions, on charges of homosexual solicitation. In October 1983, the president of Andrews University was accused of propositioning an undercover police officer, and was obliged to resign as a consequence.[73] The following year, the pastor of the church at Adventist headquarters in Washington, DC, was arrested on a similar charge.[74] Such incidents confirmed the belief of Kinship members that many homosexuals reside anonymously in the Adventist church, and strengthened them in their resolve to defend the interests of such members.

Towards the end of 1984, the General Conference established a committee of enquiry into sexual problems being experienced in Adventist academies and colleges. Consideration was given to homosexuality, as it was in a larger study project on human sexuality undertaken by the Biblical Research Institute of the General Conference. A historical and biblical study of homosexuality tended to reaffirm traditional views, while a sociological analysis was more sympathetic to the plight of homosexuals.[75] Neither enquiry has yet produced any recommendations, but the fact that such studies have been undertaken suggests that administrators have identified a problem of significant proportions.

Factors affecting homosexuality in Adventism

While Kinsey's work is still taken as authoritative regarding the incidence of homosexuality in society at large, there is little evidence to indicate whether his findings can be applied to the Christian church in general, or Adventism in particular. Certainly, talk of the existence of 20,000 Adventist homosexuals in North America[76] is mere speculation based on Kinsey's work. It assumes, among other things, that homosexuals are evenly distributed throughout the population, and that religious commitment has done nothing to alter or mute such tendencies. Since there is a distinct lack of understanding of the aetiology of homosexuality generally, only very tentative suggestions can be offered concerning factors likely to cause a homosexual orientation among Adventists.

Sociological factors

There is little reliable sociological research which would permit an assessment of the probable levels of incidence of homosexuality in Adventism. There is a consensus that homosexual relations do not predominate in any one social group, although Kinsey did suggest that frequency among American males was greater among those who had not received a college education.[77] This would tend to depress the incidence of male homosexuality among

Adventists, but it would be unwise to make any rigid application to the Adventist situation.

Kinsey found a higher incidence of homosexual activity among city-dwellers,[78] probably simply because of the opportunities and anonymity afforded by the metropolis. Adventists have tended to regard cities as places which encourage morally corrupt behaviour but have nevertheless sensed a responsibility to their inhabitants. They have resolved this dilemma by living in suburban areas or in fairly densely populated Adventist communities. They tend less and less to live in rural districts, where Kinsey found homosexual activity at its lowest.

Kinsey found a reduced level of lesbian activity within the churches.[79] Among males, he found that

... homosexual contacts occur most frequently among the males who are not particularly active in their church connections. They occur less frequently among devout Catholics, Orthodox Jewish groups, and Protestants who are active in the church. The differences are not always great, but lie constantly in the same direction.[80]

It seems likely that those who maintain some connection with the Adventist church engage less in homosexual activity than do members of the general public. This may be because traditional hostility to homosexuals within the church has forced some to leave; it may be that Adventists are strongly motivated to suppress or conceal their homosexual orientation because of the considerable implications for their social and occupational lives.

Weinberg and Williams found that religious homosexuals were less experienced in homosexual practices than their unchurched peers. Furthermore, they noted that those who were high in religiosity were more likely to believe that their condition was inborn. Those who regarded religion as important, and who perceived homosexual behaviour to be a violation of it, showed a greater tendency to depression, but generally Weinberg and Williams found no marked pathology among religious homosexuals.[81] Kinsey found that '... differences between religiously devout persons and religiously inactive persons of the same faith are much greater than the differences between two equally devout groups of different faiths'.[82] If true, this represents a source of possible instability within a group like Kinship, where religious affiliation needs to be a force sufficiently potent to overcome other social differences. Since lesbianism seems to be correlated with parental separation and divorce, rates of female homosexuality within the church could reasonably be expected to be below average because Adventist divorce rates have been lower, and marriages perhaps happier.

It must be acknowledged that the lack of serious sociological research into the relationship between religious affiliation and homosexuality makes it impossible to pronounce with any certainty on the phenomenon within Adventism.

Psychological factors

It is possible to construct a Freudian explanation of homosexuality within Seventh-day Adventism. Adventists believe that 'sanctification' – the living of a progressively more devout and virtuous life – is the product of 'justification' – acceptance by God the Father through the merits of Jesus Christ. This may create the sort of tendency towards perfectionism which Colin Cook identified within himself.[83] At the same time, Adventist fathers are exhorted to be the priests of the household, creating a religious ambience in the home and upholding high standards of behaviour. It may be that Adventist fathers, tending to be rigorous in the demands made on themselves and on their children, are sometimes perceived to be hostile and remote by their offspring; such relationships are thought to be productive of homosexuality. Where a mother tries to compensate for a poor father–son relationship, the risk may be augmented. Furthermore, where only one parent is an Adventist, that parent is likely to be the mother. Such mothers, concerned that their children remain in the church, may become possessive, creating a negative response capable of initiating a homosexual tendency in sons.

Adventists traditionally have been distrustful of emotions, as the following sentiments of Ellen White indicate: 'Pure religion has to do with the will ... your emotions, are not to be trusted, for they are not reliable.'[84] Cook confirmed the view that such an attitude produces a great deal of emotional repression among Adventists, which in his case, and probably that of others, creates problems of sexual adjustment, such as homosexuality.[85]

267

There remains within Adventism a strain of American Puritanism which regards the sexual nature as dangerous and not a source of pleasure. The church has always expended considerable effort to ensure propriety in heterosexual relationships among its young members. Such moralizing may have created sexual fears among some young people, who subsequently sought relationships only, or primarily, with those of the same sex.[86] It is conceivable also that ignorance about their sexual nature may have given rise to unexpressed and destructive fears among young Adventists. Furthermore, it could be argued that Adventists, tending to promote the passive virtues, provide the young males in their congregations with role models which are less than 'masculine'.

It is currently impossible to confirm the view that a conservative religious group like Adventists is likely to produce a relatively high proportion of homosexuals.[87] All the foregoing must remain highly speculative until such time as some serious study is undertaken on the incidence and aetiology of homosexuality in the Seventh-day Adventist community, or one like it.

Adventist theology

Hostility towards homosexuals is probably not significantly greater among Adventists than among other conservative Christians. Nevertheless, it is worthwhile to attempt to trace some causes of that hostility in Adventist theology.

The fact that many Adventist rank-and-file members, and administrators, remain fundamentalist in their outlook means that they are very suspicious of the use of the various tools of biblical criticism. They would therefore reject an analysis of the relevant biblical material of the sort done by D. Sherwin Bailey and other apologists. They would regard this as tampering with the Scriptures, an evidence of bad faith. Some Adventist scholars, probably a majority, would also regard the contemporary explications of the Sodom narrative, and the Levitical and Pauline references, as unacceptable. Adventists are unlikely to accept that the Bible contains anything other than outright condemnation of homosexuality; recognition of distinctions between inversion and perversion, orientation and practice, private consensual acts and prostitution, are unlikely to sway them.

Adventists further believe that the gospel is sufficiently powerful to transform any person's life, whatever his/her history. Most would see no reason to exempt homosexuals. The fact that Adventists have in their midst one who claims to have found healing is likely to confirm them in their views, particularly since his philosophy has been championed by the church establishment. Most others who remain sceptical about Cook's claim would probably advocate celibacy for the homosexual. The church is likely to continue to resist staunchly the kinds of moves for recognition being made by Kinship.

The point is often made that the prohibitions against homosexual behaviour made by the Hebrews, and later by the early Christians, were not primarily sexual in nature but constituted a means of distinguishing true religion from paganism. The same would be true of Adventists; regarding themselves as a 'remnant', a repository for the truth in the 'last days', they would see in the liberalizing of moral standards, particularly by the other churches, a confirmation of their role.

Adventists, believing as they do in a literal reading of the creation narrative, hold clear views about what is natural, or God-given. The Genesis account leaves them in little doubt that homosexuality is a perversion of God's ideal for human relationships, and, as such, is to be avoided. Moreover, Adventists would find it hard to accept that any behaviour is entirely private. All are parts of 'the body of Christ', and to the extent that one 'member' malfunctions, the life of the whole body is affected. The notion of 'sanctification', that each believer grows in virtue and devotion, reaches its culmination in 'harvest theology',[88] the view that Christ delays his return to the earth until there is a perfect church ready to receive him. Such a view is a source of controversy within Adventism, but it is clear that any church which contains a strain of perfectionism such as this must find it difficult to tolerate in its bosom those who are so far from the alleged biblical ideal of sexuality.

Adventist theological structures are such that there is scant room for a liberalization of views on homosexual practice. Adventists are likely to become more open to helping homosexuals as they come to understand their plight more fully. But they will continue to be regarded as candidates for therapy, and those who fail to show evidence of some change may be held responsible for inadequate effort, a prospect sufficient to daunt some from seeking help in the first place.

The ethos of Adventism

It is perhaps worth considering three other aspects of the issue of homosexuality as it currently affects the Seventh-day Adventist church. It must be seen as a political issue both within the church and beyond it; it must be viewed in relation to the family unit; and it must be seen in the context of American culture.

Homosexuality has become an issue in the Adventist church at a time when it has been experiencing considerable trauma in other areas. The validity of certain distinctive features of Adventist theology has been seriously called into question and minor schisms have resulted. Serious allegations about the authority of Ellen White's writing have been made. Confidence in the church administration has been weakened by its handling of an affair involving a major loss of funds through unwise investment. When the church is in the midst of such turmoil, administrators are unlikely to open up further controversial issues for debate. Indeed, the adoption of a firm stand on an issue on which there is broad agreement is likely to have a unifying effect. From that point of view, the efforts of Adventist homosexuals to seek some kind of recognition are ill-timed. This is not to suggest that Adventist homosexuals might have chosen a more propitious time to wage their campaign. It was natural that the adoption of a more open style of church government in the last decade would encourage groups to pursue their various vested interests at roughly the same time.

Furthermore, 'gay liberation' has become a highly politicized issue in the United States generally. In the last decade or so, the Adventist church has experienced considerable difficulties with other groups seeking their rights, notably blacks and women. Church leaders no doubt wanted to avoid a further debilitating and protracted internal struggle, and judged that the damage done to the denomination by making concessions to Kinship would have been far greater than any good achieved by modifying present policy.

There is a considerable body of evidence to show that homosexuality has been traditionally linked in the public mind with idolatry, treason, and heresy. The McCarthy purge is but one example of that.

Homosexuality has frequently been regarded as a manifestation of a radical conspiracy against the existing social structure. As Arno Karlen observed:

Through much of western history, if a person seemed to reject any of society's treasured norms or values – sexual, religious, or political – he was suspected of rejecting the others.[89]

The Adventist church had recent experience of this when one of its leading theologians was accused of being either homosexual himself, or sympathetic to homosexuals, because of his occasional attempts to minister at Kinship functions.[90]

The centrality of the family unit in Adventism is another significant factor in the equation. There exists within the Adventist church a very strong pressure to marry. Singleness is only just becoming an option for its young people. Presumably, it is believed that singleness may breed a certain lack of commitment, while marriage and the responsibilities it brings produce the kind of solid units on which the church is best built. The young must fulfil their responsibility to produce new generations of Adventists. Furthermore, the unattached male may be regarded as a potential threat to congregational arrangements. Some conferences long required their pastors to be married before they entered the ministry.[91] The church champions heterosexuality, marriage, parenthood, and traditional sexual roles since these all represent permanence. Anything short of these ideals constitutes a threat. The fact that in sexual relationships generally the emphasis has shifted from the procreative to the relational dimension makes no difference in the present case.

Adventist hostility to homosexuality may also be peripherally attributed to the church's deep roots in American culture. Kinsey's observation that few cultures have become so disturbed about male homosexuality was confirmed by the comparative research of Weinberg and Williams.[92] It may be that homosexual acts represent an overt and ultimate disavowal of the puritan belief that sex is for the purpose of procreation rather than pleasure. The fact that a majority of states still retain legislation on 'unnatural vice' may be a reflection of this attitude.

Conclusion

There is evidence that hostility towards homosexuality among members is gradually diminishing. A recent survey showed Adventist young people somewhat less willing than their parents to describe homosexual behaviour as 'sin'.[93] It reflects an increasing willingness of Adventists to view the plight of individual homosexuals sympathetically while not conceding what they would regard as points of principle. However, the fact that 83 per cent of the young respondents to the survey regarded homosexual behaviour as 'sinful' suggests that attitudes are not likely to change radically in the foreseeable future. Homosexuality will continue to be regarded as a condition to be cured, a sin to be renounced, rather than a preference to be asserted.

Seventh-day Adventism is, in many respects, an extremely systematized religion. Its theology is highly structured and specific. Its behavioural norms are codified in considerable detail. Its administration is highly stratified. Sexual and occupational roles are still clearly defined. The fundamental threat posed by homosexuality to Adventism is its challenge to a nexus of familiar and prized classification systems.

IV

POSTSCRIPT

15 · Adventism in transition

The renewal of Adventism

One hundred and forty years have now passed since the 'Great Disappointment' of 1844. During the last decade, a period of great turmoil in the Adventist church, two principal mechanisms for coping with the unexpectedly long delay of the advent have emerged. According to an official church statement, '... the crisis is brought on by our inexcusable delinquency in failing to adopt God's plan for finishing the work'.[1] On this account, the church has not been true to its charter, and must now do all within its power to 'preserve the landmarks'.[2] It is a call to restore primitive Adventism. Others would invoke the authority of Ellen White to argue that, in the history of Adventism, calls to 'preserve the landmarks' have left people's minds 'sealed against the entrance of light'.[3] They fear that an undue preoccupation with the past will make the Adventist church an irrelevance in modern society.[4] They believe that each generation of Adventists must discover its own 'present truth' and not simply remember the 'former truth'.[5] One such attempt to seek renewal calls for Adventists to embrace a more radical form of discipleship by rediscovering their roots in Anabaptism.[6] Among the ethical consequences of such a move would be a greater commitment to non-violence, a clearer separation of Adventism and the state, a diminished concern for status, and more concerted effort to remove inequalities between men and women, blacks and whites, clergy and laity, in order to create a greater sense of community. Sceptics might see any such attempt at renewal as an occasion for further secularization of the movement.

It has been observed that the younger generations, in the western world at least, have little sense of history.[7] If this is true of Adventists, it seems likely that they will be more concerned with the practical

275

value of their faith than with its continuity with primitive Adventism. Where the church fails to meet the demand for relevance and meaning, it faces the prospect of losing its young members, and in view of dominant affiliation patterns it can scarcely afford to do that. The conservative impulse in the church is strong, however.

Several eventual outcomes seem possible. Historically, Adventists have been successful at resisting schism, and serious fragmentation seems unlikely now. It may be that those disappointed with the pursuit of renewal will forsake the movement, leaving a predominantly conservative residue. It may be that the defence of traditional Adventist values and the search for contemporary relevance will create a healthy tension. The fear lingers that the recent turmoil in the church has been so debilitating that Adventists will 'have little energy to undertake bold, new tasks — or ignite the enthusiasm of the next generation'.[8]

Conclusion

The disinterested observer would regard the value system peculiar to Adventism as a function of certain historical and sociological conditions. Wilson has observed that new sectarian movements are conditioned more 'than they know or care to acknowledge by the prevailing secular facilities' and 'the anxieties felt at the time of their emergence'.[9] It is a view which some Adventists have not been unwilling to apply to themselves. One writer, describing early Adventist reactions to labour unions, commented:

More than they realized, Adventist writers and theologians conformed to the prevailing values, fears and prejudices of rural America.[10]

Another Adventist has observed that

In her illustrious 87 years (1827–1915), Ellen White virtually personified the Protestant period of American culture, and her writings offer a perspective on every major issue and event of the era.[11]

Even a more conservative source like *A Critique of 'Prophetess of Health'*, while rejecting a purely naturalistic explanation of Ellen White's ministry, quite readily acknowledged that 'she did not live in a vacuum' (p. 11). Adventists are not unduly distressed by suggestions that their church's identity is, to a significant extent, a product of historical forces, because they believe that divine providence determined the social matrix of Adventism. Nor are they disturbed by allegations that many of Ellen White's ideas reflected the spirit of the age, because they believe that her genius lay, at least partly, in the God-given ability to distil the wisdom of the age.

Niebuhr has said that

Each religious group gives expression to that code which forms the morale of the political or economic class it represents.[12]

There is considerable evidence to repudiate Clark's description of Adventism as a 'typical cult of the disinherited and suffering poor'.[13] Graybill has shown that many early Adventists were 'occupationally independent, distributed in a wide spectrum of economic statuses, but favoring the upper side of that spectrum'.[14]

He has also confirmed the view that Adventism encourages upward social mobility towards, though not beyond, middle-class status. On Niebuhr's account, therefore, the set of moral commitments for which Adventism stands is a function of the socioeconomic class of its members, particularly in the United States. Such a view is unlikely to trouble those Adventists who see economic success as an accompaniment of godliness, and middle-class moral values as a basically sound articulation of the Christian ethic. It will disturb those who believe that Adventism has so accommodated to the socio-economic order of which it is part that it has become 'Laodicean',[15] an epithet reserved, at the birth of Adventism, for other churches.

Today, Adventism is rather like a new model of a motor car produced by one of the long-standing manufacturers. A new shell has been fitted to an old chassis powered by a standard engine, without much having been done in the way of redesigning the engineering of the vehicle. Consequently, there are fears as to whether the car will function efficiently in modern road conditions, and indeed as to whether it will sell well in large numbers. It is not, however, a problem peculiar to this manufacturer; it is a problem encountered by the whole industry as potential customers turn to other forms of transport, though without obvious signs of satisfaction. Some observers believe that the future for the vehicle lies in the export market. Others believe it will become a collector's item. Adventists are inclined to believe that a discerning public will always create a demand for a reliable product, whatever the price.

Notes

MH	*Ministry of Healing*, Washington, DC: Review & Herald, 1905
MM	*Medical Ministry*, 2nd edn, Mountain View, Calif.: Pacific Press, 1963
MYP	*Messages to Young People*, Nashville, Tenn.: Southern Publishing Association, 1930
PK	*Prophets and Kings*, Mountain View, Calif.: Pacific Press, 1917
PP	*Patriarchs and Prophets*, Battle Creek, Mich.: Review & Herald, 1890
SD	*Sons and Daughters of God*, Washington, DC: Review & Herald, 1955
1SG, 2SG, etc.	*Spiritual Gifts*, 4 vols., Battle Creek, Mich.: vols. 1 and 2, James White, 1858, 1860; vols. 3 and 4, Seventh-day Adventist Publishing Association, 1864; facsimile reproduction, Washington, DC: Review & Herald, 1945
SL	*The Sanctified Life*, Washington, DC: Review & Herald, 1937
1SM, 2SM, etc.	*Selected Messages*, 3 vols., Washington, DC: Review & Herald, 1958 and 1980
1T, 2T, etc.	*Testimonies for the Church*, 9 vols., Mountain View, Calif.: Pacific Press, 1948
Te	*Temperance*, Mountain View, Calif.: Pacific Press, 1949
TM	*Testimonies to Ministers*, 3rd edn, Mountain View, Calif.: Pacific Press, 1962
WM	*Welfare Ministry*, Washington, DC: Review & Herald, 1952

1 Confrontation with the issues

1. See, for example, A. W. Spalding, *Origin and History of Seventh-day Adventists*, 4 vols., and L. E. Froom, *Movement of Destiny.*
2. See W. R. Cross, *The Burned-over District.*
3. Revisionist historians wish to correct the view that such optimism was ubiquitous. See R. Sandeen, 'Millennialism', in E. S. Gaustad (ed.), *The Rise of Adventism*, pp. 116–17.
4. *Seventh-day Adventist Yearbook 1916*, p. 282.
5. *122nd Annual Statistical Report 1984*, p. 2.
6. See *Seventh-day Adventists Answer Questions on Doctrine*, pp. 341–445.
7. *122nd Annual Statistical Report 1984*, p. 2.
8. *Ibid.*, pp. 39–40.

9. Begun in 1850 as the *Second Advent Review and Sabbath Herald*, it has seen continuous publication since then, although with slight changes in name. It will be referred to in the text and in the endnotes as the *Review*.
10. For comment on its role see R. Graybill, 'Kenneth Wood on the state of the church', *Spectrum*, vol. 13, no. 2, pp. 19–24, and E. Anderson, 'Johnsson on the future of the "Adventist Review" ', *Spectrum*, vol. 13, no. 4, pp. 43–8.
11. See B. R. Wilson, *Religion in Sociological Perspective*, pp. 17–26.

2 Advent and remnant: two major doctrinal influences

1. Cited in E. S. Gaustad, *A Religious History of America*, p. 151.
2. *Seventh-day Adventist Encyclopedia*, p. 793; P. G. Damsteegt, *Foundations of the Seventh-day Adventist Message and Mission*, p. 99.
3. J. White letter to Bro. Collins, 26 August 1846.
4. *LS*, p. 105.
5. *1T*, p. 72; *LS*, pp. 86–7.
6. Concerning the 'shut-door' theory, see above, p. 19; see also R. Branson, 'Adventism between the Times: The Shift in the Church's Eschatology', *Spectrum*, vol. 8, no. 1, pp. 14–26.
7. G. Storrs, in *The Midnight Cry*, 15 February 1844, pp. 237–8.
8. See C. Teel, 'Withdrawing Sect, Accommodating Church, Prophesying Remnant: Dilemmas in the Institutionalization of Adventism', pp. 14–23.
9. *The Social Sources of Denominationalism*, pp. 3–25.
10. *1T*, p. 358.
11. *1T*, pp. 359–60.
12. A. W. Spalding, *Origin and History of Seventh-day Adventists*, vol. 1, p. 315.
13. Cited in *ibid.*, p. 29.
14. Edwin Gaustad, *Historical Atlas of Religion in America*, p. 115.
15. C. C. Crider and R. C. Kistler, *The Seventh-day Adventist Family*, pp. 64–5.
16. B. R. Wilson, unpublished lecture given at Andrews University, March 1974.
17. For example, B. Casey, 'Let the Wilderness Be Glad! The Apocalypse and the Environment', *Spectrum*, vol. 13, no. 3, pp. 40–51; C. Scriven, 'Radical Discipleship and the Renewal of Adventist Mission', *Spectrum*, vol. 14, no. 3, pp. 11–20.
18. H. E. Douglass, *Why Jesus Waits*. See also Annual Council proposal 'Evangelism and Finishing God's Work', 1976.

19. 'Toward an Adventist Ethic', *Spectrum*, vol. 12, no. 2, p. 2.
20. 'The World of Ellen G. White and the End of the World', *Spectrum*, vol. 10, no. 2, p. 10.
21. B. Wilson, 'Sect or Denomination: Can Adventism Maintain its Identity?' *Spectrum*, vol. 7, no. 1, pp. 34–43.
22. *Seventh-day Adventist Encyclopedia*, pp. 1068–9.
23. See Ellen White's book with this title.
24. 'Politics', *Review*, 11 September 1856, p. 152, and 10 March 1859, p. 124.
25. *Review*, 12 August 1862, p. 84.
26. *1T*, pp. 356–62.
27. See J. Butler, 'Adventism and the American Experience', in Gaustad (ed.), *The Rise of Adventism*, p. 185.
28. Spalding, *Origin and History of Seventh-day Adventists*, vol. 2, pp. 257–62.
29. *Ibid.*, vol. 3, pp. 80–1.
30. R. C. Kistler, *Adventists and Labor Unions in the United States*; E. T. Russell, *The Conflict between Capital and Labor*.
31. W. Johnsson, 'An Ethical People', *Review*, 22 January 1981, p. 13; E. Vick, 'Against Isolationism: The Church's Relation to the World', *Spectrum*, vol. 8, no. 3, pp. 38–40; T. Dybdahl, 'We Should Be Involved in Politics', *ibid.*, pp. 33–7.
32. C. Teel, 'Withdrawing Sect, Accommodating Church, Prophesying Remnant', p. 42.
33. B. Schantz, 'The Development of Seventh-day Adventist Missionary Thought', pp. 509–12.
34. K. Seltman, 'Christian Brotherhood: The Foundation of the Church', *Spectrum*, vol. 12, no. 1, pp. 15–18; J. Craven, 'The Wall of Adventism', *Christianity Today*, 19 October 1984, pp. 20–5.
35. *So Much in Common*; C. Rubencamp, 'The Seventh-day Adventists and the Ecumenical Movement', *Spectrum*, vol. 2, no. 4, pp. 5–18; R. Dederen, 'An Adventist Response', *ibid.*, pp. 19–25; B. Schantz, 'The Development of Seventh-day Adventist Missionary Thought', pp. 144–96.
36. H. E. Douglass, 'Men of Faith', in *Perfection – The Impossible Possibility*, pp. 9–56.
37. R. H. Pierson, 'An Earnest Appeal From the Retiring President of the General Conference', *Review*, 26 October 1978, pp. 10–11.
38. W. J. Hackett, 'Preserve the Landmarks', *Review*, 26 May 1977, p. 2.
39. R. Branson, 'Celebrating the Adventist Experience', *Spectrum*, vol. 12, no. 1, p. 5.
40. E. Troeltsch, *The Social Teaching of the Christian Churches*, vol. 2, p. 999.

41. R. Wallis, *The Elementary Forms of the New Religious Life*, pp. 4–5.
42. R. Graybill, 'Millenarians and Money: Adventist Wealth and Adventist Beliefs', *Spectrum*, vol. 10, no. 2, pp. 31–41.
43. Manuscript 76, 1905; Letter 182, 1902.
44. 'North American Division Church Size and Membership Distribution', Review & Herald Publishing Association document, 1 September 1983.
45. R. W. Schwarz, 'Adventism's Social Gospel Advocate – John Harvey Kellogg', *Spectrum*, vol. 1, no. 2, pp. 15–28.
46. 'Our Duty to the Poor and Afflicted', *Review*, 18 December 1894, pp. 785–6; *5T*, p. 369.
47. *8T*, p. 185.
48. *Annual Report 1983–4*, pp. 20–1.
49. Cf. 'Report on Financial Statements 1981'.
50. 'Evangelism and Finishing God's Work', 1976 Annual Council proposal cited in *Spectrum*, vol. 8, no. 2, p. 55.
51. *Spectrum*, vol. 14, no. 3, p. 44; *Seventh-day Adventist Yearbook* for 1983, p. 10, and for 1984, p. 4.
52. J. Wilson, 'Hospital Chains Struggle to Stay in the Pink', *Businessweek*, 14 January 1985, p. 112.
53. *Spectrum*, vol. 13, no. 2, pp. 69–70.
54. *1T*, pp. 421–2.
55. D. E. Robinson, *The Story of our Health Message*, pp. 143–55.
56. For example, *6T*, p. 450.
57. R. Hammill, 'The Church Does Need a Law School', *Spectrum*, vol. 1, no. 3, p. 11.
58. B. Wilson, 'Sect or Denomination: Can Adventism Maintain its Identity?', *Spectrum*, vol. 7, no. 1, p. 43.
59. G. Oosterwal, 'Seventh-day Adventist Mission in the Seventies', *Spectrum*, vol. 2, no. 2, pp. 5–20; 'The New Shape of Adventist Mission', *Spectrum*, vol. 7, no. 1, pp. 44–54.

3 Keeping the family together: stable homes and a united church

1. L. Tarling, *The Edges of Seventh-day Adventism*.
2. B. R. Wilson, 'Becoming a Sectarian: Motivation and Commitment', in D. Baker (ed.), Studies in Church History, vol. 15, *Religious Motivation: Biographical and Sociological Problems for the Church Historian*, p. 483.
3. About 2.5 per cent. See *Seventh-day Adventist Yearbook 1984*, p. 4.
4. R. Hammill, 'The Church Does Need a Law School', *Spectrum*, vol. 1, no. 3, pp. 5–11.

5. B. R. Wilson, *Religion in Sociological Perspective*, pp. 148–79; D. Martin, *A General Theory of Secularization*.
6. See, for example, D. M. Canright, *Seventh-day Adventism Renounced*.
7. See, for example, W. Utt, 'Desmond Ford Raises the Sanctuary Question', *Spectrum*, vol. 10, no. 4, pp. 3–8.
8. N. C. Wilson, 'A Report to the Church', *Review*, 29 August 1982, pp. 4–6; N. C. Wilson, 'Report of the President's Review Commission', *Review*, 27 January 1983, pp. 8–10; 'Adventists Facing Financial Crisis', *The Washington Post*, 24 August 1981, B 1 and 7; T. Dybdahl, 'Bad Business: The Davenport Fiasco, *Spectrum*, vol. 12, no. 1, pp. 50–61.
9. See, for example, B. Reeves, 'The Call for Black Unions', C. B. Rock, 'Cultural Pluralism and Black Unions', and Lorenzo Grant, 'Ethical Implications of the Quest for Black Power', in *Spectrum*, vol. 9, no. 3, pp. 2–3, pp. 4–12, pp. 12–22 respectively. See also *Spectrum*, vol. 2, no. 2; D. McAdams, 'The 1978 Annual Council: A Report and Analysis', *Spectrum*, vol. 9, no. 4, pp. 3–5.
10. E. Anderson, J. Butler, M. Couperus, A. Zytkoskee, 'Must the Crisis Continue?', *Spectrum*, vol. 11, no. 3, pp. 44–52.
11. For example, Ellen White letter 6, 1881; *Review*, 15 October 1914, p. 1; *Review*, 8 November 1881, pp. 289–90.
12. 'The Temperance Cause in Battle Creek', *Review*, 11 April 1882, p. 232.
13. See, for example, F. M. Wilcox, 'The Church and Politics', *Review*, 13 September 1928, p. 3; Ellen White, 'Special Testimony Relating to Politics', 16 June 1899; James White, 'Politics', *Review*, 21 August 1860, p. 108; P. A. Gordon, 'To Vote or Not to Vote', *Review*, 12 September 1968, pp. 1, 5–6, and 19 September 1968, pp. 2–3.
14. See W. Johnsson, 'An Ethical People', *Review*, 22 January 1981, p. 13.
15. 'Seventh-day Adventists and the Millennium', in Michael Hill (ed.), *A Sociological Yearbook of Religion in Britain*, vol. 7, p. 126.
16. C. Y. Glock, B. B. Ringer, and E. R. Babbie, *To Comfort and to Challenge*, pp. 202–16.
17. *MH*, p. 349; Crider and Kistler, *The Seventh-day Adventist Family*, pp. 44–6.
18. *Mission Possible*, p. 55.
19. *Seventh-day Adventist Encyclopedia*, p. 925.
20. W. G. Johnsson, 'The Forgotten Third', *Review*, 8 July 1982, p. 12. According to the brochure *Welcome to Adventist Contact*, the figure is 162,000.
21. For example, J. R. Fay, 'Singles – What is the Church Doing?', 27 January 1983, pp. 11–12; 'Reading Resources for Singles', 22 December 1983, pp. 10–11.

22. 'You Are Not Alone' notebook. See also H. I. Smith, 'Ministering to One-Parent Families', *Ministry*, November 1981, pp. 4–6.
23. *Welcome to Adventist Contact* brochure; advertisement *Insight*, 4 August 1981, p. 16.
24. *PP*, p. 324.
25. Spalding, *Origin and History of Seventh-day Adventists*, vol. 2, p. 108.
26. Resolutions on Polygamy and Marriage Relationships, G. C. Committee Minutes, vol. 13, book 1, 6th meeting, 13 June 1926.
27. Resolution on Polygamous Marriages in Heathen Lands, 'Actions of the Autumn Council of the General Conference Committee', vol. 14, book 1, 59th meeting, 3 November 1930.
28. General Conference policy, voted 4 June 1941.
29. General Conference Working Policy on Polygamy, in *Constitution, Bylaws and Working Policy*, 1977 edition.
30. For example, *AH*, pp. 61–9.
31. Crider and Kistler, *The Seventh-day Adventist Family*, pp. 47, 51; R. Theobald, 'The Seventh-day Adventist Movement', pp. 286–7.
32. Manuscript 1, 1855.
33. Wilson, *Religion in Sociological Perspective*, p. 134.
34. *Ibid.*, p. 137.
35. *The Social Sources of Denominationalism*, p. 85.
36. See *Seventh-day Adventists Answer Questions on Doctrine*, pp. 402–45.
37. G. Vandeman, *Planet in Rebellion*, p. 36.
38. For example, *3T*, p. 183. See also *Comprehensive Index to the Writings of E. G. White*, vol. 3, pp. 3006–9.
39. I. Linden, *The Last Trump*, p. 253.
40. E. Chellis, 'The *Review and Herald* and Early Adventist Response to Organized Labor', *Spectrum*, vol. 10, no. 2, p. 25.
41. For example, *7T*, p. 84.
42. T. Shaw, 'Racism and Adventist Theology', *Spectrum*, vol. 3, no. 4, pp. 29–38.
43. T. Dybdahl and J. W. Chapman, 'Stewardship and Securities: A Study of Adventist Corporate Investment', *Spectrum*, vol. 5, no. 2, pp. 39–46; R. E. Osborn, 'Investment Practices of the General Conference', *ibid.*, pp. 47–59.
44. *DA*, p. 509.
45. *The Social Sources of Denominationalism*, p. 86.
46. See K. Dobbelaere, 'Professionalization and Secularization in the Belgian Catholic Pillar', *Japanese Journal of Religious Studies*, vol. 6, nos. 1 and 2 (March–June 1979), pp. 39–64.

4 A cultural legacy: Victorian and American

1. G. Schwartz, *Sect Ideologies and Social Status*, pp. 116–36, 172.
2. For example, alcohol, *Ed*, p. 202; tobacco, *MH*, pp. 327–30; dancing, *MYP*, pp. 398–400; tea and coffee, *CD*, pp. 420–31; meat, *CD*, pp. 373–416; condiments, *CH*, p. 114; novel reading, *2T*, p. 236; immodest dress, *4T*, p. 645; card-playing, *AH*, pp. 517–18; theatre, *MYP*, p. 380.
3. R. L. Phillips, 'Cancer among Seventh-day Adventists', *Journal of Environmental Pathology and Toxicology*, 3 (1980), pp. 157–69; N. C. Wilson, 'Scientific Studies Show Rewards of Temperate Living', *Review*, 17 October 1985, p. 19.
4. 'The World of E. G. White and the End of the World', *Spectrum*, vol. 10, no. 2, p. 10.
5. C. G. Tuland, 'Let's Stop Arguing over the Wedding Ring', *Spectrum*, vol. 8, no. 2, pp. 59–61; R. Churchman, 'That Wedding Ring', *Spectrum*, vol. 6, no. 1/2, pp. 74–6.
6. E. G. White, *Special Testimonies to Ministers and Workers*, series A, no. 3, pp. 6–7.
7. 'The Sons of Samuel', *Signs of the Times*, 26 January 1882, p. 37.
8. See prospectus and its publication *Update*.
9. See, for example, *Time*, 26 November 1984, pp. 50–1; 3 December 1984, pp. 38–9.
10. R. Graybill, 'An Interview with Robert H. Pierson', *Spectrum*, vol. 7, no. 1, p. 4.
11. C. F. Randolph, 'Rev. Louis Richard Conradi, DD – A Biographical Sketch', *The Sabbath Recorder*, 4 March 1940, supplement. Also 'Statement on Conradi Hearing', adopted by General Conference Committee, 16 October 1931.
12. Manuscript 177, 1905; Letter 12, 1890.
13. Letter 127, 1896.
14. For example, *Review*, 8 October 1867, pp. 260–1.
15. Letter 10, 1895.
16. Manuscript 107, 1909.
17. R. Graybill, 'The Power of Prophecy', p. 18.
18. Spalding, *Origin and History of Seventh-day Adventists*, vol. 1, p. 77.
19. W. P. Bradley, 'Ellen White and her Writings', *Spectrum*, vol. 3, no. 2, p. 59.
20. Manuscript 2, 1913.
21. A. L. White, *Ellen G. White*, vol. 6, p. 404.
22. Among the latest is *Mind, Character, and Personality*, published in 1977, whose two volumes contain nearly 900 pages.

23. 'To a Brother at Monroe, Wis.', *Review*, 17 March 1868, p. 220.
24. R. Branson and H. Weiss, 'Ellen White: A Subject for Adventist Scholarship', *Spectrum*, vol. 2, no. 4, p. 30.
25. *The Prophetess of Health*.
26. *The White Lie*.
27. Butler, 'The World of E. G. White and the End of the World', *Spectrum*, vol. 10, no. 2, pp. 2–13.
28. Manuscript 227, 1902. Letter 36, 1897; Graybill, 'The Power of Prophecy', pp. 78–81.
29. A. Thompson, 'From Sinai to Golgotha', *Review*, 3, 10, 17, 24, 31 December 1981, pp. 4–6, 8–10, 7–10, 7–9, 12–13 respectively.
30. J. Butler, 'Adventism and the American Experience', in Gaustad, *The Rise of Adventism*, p. 185.
31. Schantz, 'The Development of Seventh-day Adventist Missionary Thought', p. 690.
32. *Seventh-day Adventist Yearbook, 1984*, p. 4.
33. Spalding, *Origin and History of Seventh-day Adventists*, vol. 3, p. 289.
34. *Year Book of the Seventh-day Adventists, 1904*, p. 8; *Seventh-day Adventist Yearbook, 1963*, p. 4.
35 See J. M. Patt, 'Living in a Time of Trouble: German Adventists under Nazi Rule', and E. Sicher, 'Seventh-day Adventist Publications and the Nazi Temptation', in *Spectrum*, vol. 8, no. 3, pp. 2–10 and pp. 11–24 respectively.
36. *Ministry*, December 1984, p. 22; C. Scriven, 'The Oppressed Brother: The Challenge of the True and Free Adventists', *Spectrum*, vol. 13, no. 3, pp. 24–30.
37. Schantz, 'The Development of Seventh-day Adventist Missionary Thought', pp. iv–v.
38. H. John, 'SAWS Expands its Focus', *Spectrum*, vol. 12, no. 3, pp. 15–21.
39. Schantz, 'The Development of Seventh-day Adventist Missionary Thought', pp. 426–7.
40. 'Four Great Ideas in Adventism – An Evangelical's Testimony', *Spectrum*, vol. 14, no. 3, p. 4.
41. Wilson, *Religion in Sociological Perspective*, p. 152.
42. M. E. Marty, *The New Shape of American Religion*, pp. 45–89.
43. *Religion in Sociological Perspective*, p. 152.
44. B. Wilson, 'American Religious Sects in Europe', in C. Bigsby (ed.), *Superculture: American Popular Culture and Europe*, p. 114.
45. 'From Rural Populism to Practical Christianity: The Modernisation of the Seventh-day Adventist Movement', *Archives de Sciences Sociales des Religions*, no. 60/1 (July–September 1985), p. 114.

46. Butler, 'The World of E. G. White and the End of the World', *Spectrum*, vol. 10, no. 2, p. 7.
47. *TM*, pp. 200–3; A. L. White, *Ellen G. White*, vol. 4, pp. 183–6; see 'Solusi College', in *Seventh-day Adventist Encyclopedia*, pp. 1204–5.
48. A. L. Baker, 'Should Adventists Take Federal Aid for Their Schools?', *Spectrum*, vol. 1, no. 1, pp. 33–49; L. R. Simmons, 'Federal Support Is Intrusive', *Spectrum*, vol. 1, no. 4, pp. 45–52; C. Fleming, 'Federal Support Is Not Coercive', *Spectrum*, vol. 1, no. 4, pp. 53–60.
49. D. McAdams, 'The 1978 Annual Council: A Report and Analysis', *Spectrum*, vol. 9, no. 4, p. 6.

5 Marital relations among Adventists: the pursuit of purity

1. *Day Star*, 20 September 1845, pp. 24, 26.
2. Letter to Bro. Jacobs, published in *Day Star*, 11 October 1845.
3. Dennett, *Birth Control Laws*, p. 9, cited in Fryer, *The Birth Controllers*, p. 117.
4. *Ibid.*
5. H. F. Pringle, *Theodore Roosevelt*, p. 172, cited in Fryer, *The Birth Controllers*, p. 199.
6. *Report of the Conference of Bishops of the Anglican Communion* (1908), pp. 145, 147, 152, 153, 156.
7. *Review*, 24 March 1868, p. 236.
8. V. E. Robinson, 'Ernest Farnsworth', *Review*, 2 December 1965, p. 7; T. A. Davis, 'An Adventist for 100 Years', *Review*, 10 August 1972, pp. 14–15.
9. R. Graybill, 'Millenarians and Money: Adventist Wealth and Adventist Beliefs', *Spectrum*, vol. 10, no. 2, p. 35.
10. J. White letter to Brother Collins, 26 August 1846.
11. R. Graybill, 'The Courtship of Ellen Harmon', *Insight*, 23 January 1973, pp. 4–7; *5T*, p. 592; *8T*, pp. 292–3; *LS*, pp. 79–84; also see below, p. 70.
12. *1T*, p. 273.
13. *2T*, pp. 93–5.
14. *2T*, pp. 230, 329.
15. *2T*, p. 380.
16. *Ibid.*
17. *2T*, p. 477.
18. *Ibid.*
19. *2T*, pp. 474–5.

20. *2T*, p. 477.
21. *2T*, p. 475.
22. *2T*, p. 451.
23. For example, *Appeal to Mothers* (1864).
24. *Seventh-day Adventist Encyclopedia*, p. 649. See R. W. Schwarz, *John Harvey Kellogg, MD*.
25. Schwarz, *John Harvey Kellogg, MD*, p. 88.
26. *Plain Facts about Sexual Life*, p. 137.
27. *Ibid.*, pp. 106–9.
28. *Man the Masterpiece*, p. 419.
29. *Ladies' Guide in Health and Disease*, p. 347.
30. J. Money, *The Destroying Angel*, p. 84.
31. R. L. Numbers, *Prophetess of Health*, p. 159.
32. On Ellen White's severe experience of the menopause, see Letter 6 1869; F. D. Nichol, *Ellen G. White and her Critics*, p. 71; Numbers, *Prophetess of Health*, pp. 180–1, p. 252, note 7.
33. 'To our Missionary Workers', *Review*, 8 December 1885, pp. 753–4.
34. Manuscript 1, 1888.
35. For example, Manuscript 14, 1888.
36. Manuscript 17, 1891.
37. Purportedly written by Ellen White, 15 February 1885. A similar letter dated the next day also exists.
38. A. L. White, *Ellen G. White*, vol. 5, p. 49.
39. Letter from M. S. Boyd to W. C. White, 21 December 1921.
40. 8 December 1885, pp. 753–4.
41. *Review*, 25 October 1892, pp. 657–8; *CT*, pp. 326–8.
42. *2T*, p. 380.
43. Letter 50, 1895.
44. Letter 8, 1884.
45. Letter 73, 1886.
46. For example, *MH*, p. 356; Manuscript 126, 1904.
47. Letter, 10 August 1892.
48. *Ibid.*
49. A. L. White, 'Marital Relations', p. 3.
50. Letter 6a, 1894. See also Letter 4, 1893.
51. Letter 103, 1894.
52. *2SM*, p. 85, note.
53. E. G. White, 'Beware of Fanciful Delusions', *Review*, 21 January 1904, p. 9.
54. *Ibid.*
55. Letters from Hetty H. Haskell to Ellen White, 27 February 1900, and 1 July 1900.

56. Letter 103, 1894; *Southern Watchman*, 5 April 1904, p. 217.
57. Private communication from the White Estate, 7 April 1981.

6 Adventists and intimacy: the celebration of sex

1. *The Lambeth Conferences 1867–1930*, pp. 199–201.
2. R. M. Fagley, *The Population Explosion and Christian Responsibility*, p. 9.
3. 'Population Sampling Report of the Seventh-day Adventists in the United States'. This unpublished document was the statistical basis for *Seventh-day Adventist Youth at the Mid-Century*.
4. 'The Seventh-day Adventist Movement: A Sociological Study with Particular Reference to Great Britain', p. 413.
5. *Happiness for Husbands and Wives*, p. 159.
6. *Ibid.*, p. 47.
7. *Ibid.*, p. 182.
8. *A Study Guide to 'The Adventist Home'*.
9. See, for example, B. E. Seton, 'Christian Ideals for Modern Marriage', *Review*, 9 January 1969, pp. 2–4; J. R. Spangler, 'Adventists and Birth Control', *Ministry*, March 1969, pp. 3–5, and April 1969, pp. 17–19.
10. H. E. Douglass, 'How Large Should a Family Be?', *Review*, 4 February 1971, p. 14.
11. For example, 'Birth Control Pills', *Life and Health*, October 1972, p. 9.
12. For example, A. Mazat, *That Friday in Eden*, pp. 80–95.
13. For example, N. van Pelt, *The Compleat Marriage*, pp. 118–43.
14. For example, J. F. Knight, *What a Married Couple Should Know About Sex*, pp. 94–162.
15. For example, D. Jewett, *Sex is Not to Lose Sleep Over*. See R. G. Gravesen, 'A Physician Reviews Adventist Sexual Advice Books', *Spectrum*, vol. 15, no. 1, pp. 19–23.
16. For example, C. E. Wittschiebe, *Teens and Love and Sex*, pp. 28–31.
17. *Review*, 17 February 1977, pp. 14–19.
18. Mazat, 'Adventists and Sex: A Therapist's Perspective', *Spectrum*, vol. 15, no. 1, pp. 2–9. See also Wittschiebe, *God Invented Sex*, pp. 87–93.
19. For example, the Adventist Marriage Enrichment project, described in R. Dudley and P. Dudley, *Married and Glad of It*. See also private communication from Home and Family Service, 30 July 1981.
20. Appendix II, pp. 1–2, 7–8.
21. K. Dobbelaere, 'Professionalization and Secularization in the Belgian Catholic Pillar', *Japanese Journal of Religious Studies*, vol. 6, nos. 1 and 2 (March–June 1979), pp. 39–64.

22. Unpublished survey completed in September 1981, by J. Witzel, for the purposes of this research.
23. Private communications, various dates.
24. 'Program Feasibility Assessment – Kenya Private Sector Family Planning Project', 6 July 1983.
25. R. Theobald, 'Seventh-day Adventists and the Millennium', in Michael Hill (ed.), *A Sociological Yearbook of Religion in Britain*, vol. 7, p. 126.
26. M. J. Penton, *Apocalypse Delayed*, pp. 261–7; L. J. Arrington and D. Bitton, *The Mormon Experience*, p. 295.
27. W. Petersen, *Population*, p.538, cited in Andorka, *Determinants of Fertility in Advanced Societies*, p. 313.
28. G. Schwartz, *Sect Ideologies and Social Status*, p. 210.
29. R. Theobald, 'The Politicization of a Religious Movement', *British Journal of Sociology*, June 1981, pp. 214–16. See also L. W. Sargent, 'Occupational Status in a Religious Group', *Review of Religious Research*, 4:3 (1962), pp. 149–55.
30. Andorka, *Determinants of Fertility in Advanced Societies*, pp. 266–74.
31. Theobald, 'The Politicization of a Religious Movement', *British Journal of Sociology*, June 1981, p. 215; Crider and Kistler, *The Seventh-day Adventist Family*, pp. 131–3.
32. Andorka, *Determinants of Fertility in Advanced Societies*, pp. 259–61.
33. *Ibid.*, p. 344.
34. Schwartz, *Sect Ideologies and Social Status*, p. 184.
35. *Ibid.*
36. *Prophetess of Health*, p. 159.
37. Letter 59, 1904; letter from G. I. Butler to Ellen White, 28 January 1904.
38. *2T*, pp. 414–15.
39. J. N. Loughborough letter, 21 April 1907.
40. T. Dybdahl and M. Hansen, 'An Interview with Charles Wittschiebe', *Spectrum*, vol. 7, no. 3, p. 11.
41. Wittschiebe, *Teens and Love and Sex*, pp. 28–31.
42. Andorka, *Determinants of Fertility in Advanced Societies*, p. 336.

7 Adventists and abortion: early hostility

1. J. C. Mohr, *Abortion in America*, pp. 79–85.
2. H. L. Hodge, in Wharton and Stillé, *Medical Jurisprudence*, p. 270, cited in Mohr, *Abortion in America*, p. 97.
3. *Ibid.*
4. Cited in M. Potts, P. Diggory, and J. Peel, *Abortion*, p. 168.

5. Illinois State Medical Society Annual Meeting, 1871, cited in Mohr, *Abortion in America*, p. 194.
6. J. Todd, 'Fashionable Murder', *Congregationalist and Boston Recorder*, 52 (1867), p. 45, cited in Mohr, *Abortion in America*, p. 189.
7. *PP*, p. 516.
8. *MH*, p. 397.
9. Manuscript 43, 1900.
10. *CH*, p. 41.
11. *MH*, pp. 372–3.
12. *2T*, p. 378.
13. 'Mrs White's Department', *Health Reformer*, November 1871, p. 157.
14. Letter 16a, 1861.
15. 'Criminal Abortion', *Good Health*, October 1881, p. 315.
16. *How to Live*, no. 5, pp. 66–74.
17. *How to Live*, no. 2, p. 36.
18. *Health Reformer*, September 1871, p. 90.
19. *MH*, p. 117.
20. *2T*, p. 386.
21. *5T*, p. 348.
22. *MH*, p. 143.
23. *Signs of the Times*, 21 April 1890, p. 242.
24. For example, *MB*, p. 89.
25. *1T*, pp. 39–40.
26. *2T*, p. 351.
27. *Signs of the Times*, 10 September 1894, p. 691.
28. 'Quack medicines', reprint from *The Revolution*, in *Health Reformer*, August 1868, p. 27.
29. 'Foeticide on the Increase', from *New York Telegram*, in *Health Reformer*, September 1873, p. 267.
30. From *Michigan Tribune, ibid.*
31. A. K. Gardner, 'Physical Decline of American Women', reprint from *Knickerbocker Magazine*, in *Health Reformer*, September 1876, p. 258.
32. From *Michigan Tribune*, in *Health Reformer*, September 1873, p. 267.
33. Gardner, 'Physical Decline of American Women', reprint from *Knickerbocker Magazine*, in *Health Reformer*, September 1876, p. 258.
34. *Ibid.*
35. Reprint from *Western Rural*, in *Health Reformer*, December 1869, p. 107.
36. Gardner, 'Physical Decline of American Women', *Knickerbocker Magazine*, in *Health Reformer*, September 1876, p. 258.
37. *Health Reformer*, December 1869, p. 107.
38. *Health Reformer*, April 1869, p. 198.

39. Reprint from 'Quack Medicines' in *The Revolution*, in *Health Reformer*, August 1868, p. 27.
40. Reprint from the *Michigan Tribune*, in *Health Reformer*, September 1873, p. 267.
41. 'Criminal Abortion', *Good Health*, October 1881, pp. 315–16.
42. J. Todd, 'Fashionable Murder', *Review*, 25 June 1867; 'A Few Words Concerning Great Sin', *Review*, 30 November 1869.
43. *Plain Facts about Sexual Life*, p. 182.
44. For example, 'The State Medical Association', 'Beware of Quacks', *Health Reformer*, June 1877, pp. 180–2.

8 Abortion: tensions in the institutionalized church

1. R. Branson, 'Massacre at Sea', *Spectrum*, vol. 12, no. 3, pp. 22–4; G. M. Daffern, 'Adventist Layman Helps IndoChinese Refugees', *ibid.*, pp. 25–31.
2. Potts, Diggory and Peel, *Abortion*, pp. 87–8; D. W. Lonisell and J. T. Noonan, 'Constitutional Balance', in J. T. Noonan (ed.), *Morality of Abortion*, p. 241.
3. Its proceedings were published as W. O. Spitzer and C. L. Saylor (eds.), *Birth Control and the Christian*.
4. J. Taylor, 'Epistle of the First Presidency', 4 April 1885, cited in R. M. Nelson, 'Reverence for Life', address delivered to the General Conference, 6 April 1985, p. 16.
5. *General Handbook of Instructions*, 1983, p. 77, cited in *ibid.*, p. 17.
6. 'Interruption of Pregnancy – Statement of Principles: Recommendations to SDA Medical Institutions', Minutes of Officers' Meeting, 21 June 1971 (71–231–33).
7. Minutes of meetings, 14 February 1973 (73–51), and 7 June 1973.
8. W. R. Beach, 'Abortion?', *Ministry*, March 1971, pp. 3–6; R. F. Waddell, 'Abortion Is Not the Answer', *ibid.*, pp. 7–9.
9. 'An Appraisal of Therapeutic Abortion', pp. 29–36.
10. 'The Psychiatrist and Abortion', pp. 23–7.
11. 'Abortion in our Changing World', pp. 7–11, citation pp. 8–9.
12. 'A Sociologist Looks at Abortion', pp. 12–18.
13. 'A Christian Anthropological Base for Doing Bioethics', 'Seminar on Genetic Engineering', pp. 58–71.
14. 'The Abortion Problem Reviewed', *ibid.*, pp. 146–50.
15. 'Seventh-day Adventists and Abortion: The Search for a Principled Approach', *ibid.*, pp. 151–80.
16. 'Summary and Analysis of Abortion Presentations', *ibid.*, pp. 181–7.

17. W. G. Dick, 'A Look at Abortion', *Review*, 13 May 1971, p. 11.
18. M. Wood, 'Right to Live', *Review*, 7 September 1978, p. 12.
19. 'About Abortion', *Review*, 1 September 1983, pp. 13-14.
20. *DA*, p. 550.
21. *PP*, p. 308, cited in 'Abortion: A Moral Issue?', *Ministry*, January 1985, p. 20.
22. *Ibid.*
23. 'How Much Is a Foetus Worth?', *Ministry*, January 1984, pp. 15-17, 24.
24. D. Augsburger, 'Abortion: Don't Believe All You Hear', *Ministry*, September 1976, pp. 24-6.
25. See also L. McMillan, 'To Abort or Not to Abort: That Is the Question', *Ministry*, March 1978, pp. 11-13.
26. H. B. Gow, 'The Right to Life', *Insight*, 11 October 1977, pp. 4-7; 'Unborn Child's Humanity', 24 August 1976, pp. 14-15.
27. 14 April 1981, pp. 4-5.
28. J. L. Londis, 'Abortion: What Shall Christians Do?', 19 March 1974, pp. 12-17.
29. A. T. Serb, H. W. John, R. W. Nixon, 'Do We Need an Abortion Amendment?', March-April 1976, pp. 1-7; L. Ambrose, 'Abortion: The McRae Case', September-October 1978, pp. 10-15.
30. 'Adventists and Abortion: A Principled Approach', *Spectrum*, vol. 12, no. 2, pp. 6-17.
31. See also R. H. Dunn's unpublished compilation, 'The Nature of Man in the Early Stages of Life and our Responsibility', 1977.
32. 'Professionalization and Secularization in the Belgian Catholic Pillar', *Japanese Journal of Religious Studies*, vol. 6, nos. 1 and 2 (March-June 1979), pp. 39-64.
33. Policy statements of various institutions.
34. Private communications, various dates.
35. Private communications, various dates.
36. 'Adventists and Abortion: A Principled Approach', *Spectrum*, vol. 12, no. 2, p. 7.
37. A. L. Hall, 'The Woman and Abortion', *Spectrum*, vol. 3, no. 2, pp. 37-42.
38. *God Invented Sex*, p. 133.
39. Winslow, 'Adventists and Abortion: A Principled Approach', *Spectrum*, vol. 12, no. 2, p. 7.
40. Potts, Diggory and Peel, *Abortion*, pp. 454-504.
41. *Reproduction in the United States*, pp. 286-7.
42. See *Abortion and the Politics of Motherhood*.
43. *Abortion*, p. 119.

NOTES TO PAGES 128–37

44. P. G. Steinhoff, 'Background Characteristics of Abortion Patients', in H. J. Osofsky and J. D. Osofsky, *The Abortion Experience*, pp. 211–12.
45. D. Callahan, *Abortion: Law, Choice and Morality*, p. 298.
46. N. B. Ryder and C. F. Westoff, *Reproduction in the United States, 1965*, p. 279.
47. F. D. Nichol, *Answers to Objections*, p. 372.
48. Adventists practise adult baptism. Furthermore, Ellen White taught that the eternal welfare of those who die in early childhood will depend on the spiritual status of their parents. See *PK*, p. 239.
49. *Seventh-day Adventists Answer Questions on Doctrine*, pp. 511–19.
50. *Ibid.*, p. 512.
51. *Seventh-day Adventist Dictionary*, pp. 1036–7; see *Seventh-day Adventist Bible Commentary* on texts therein listed.
52. *Abortion*, p. 363.
53. *Ibid.*, pp. 3, 119–22, 545.
54. *Ibid.*, pp. 536–8.
55. B. Häring, 'A Theological Evaluation', in J. T. Noonan (ed.), *Morality of Abortion*, pp. 142–3.
56. British edition, p. 39.
57. 'Seminar on Genetic Engineering', p. 160.
58. Letter from F. W. Wernick to G. F. Gibson, 7 April 1977, Office of Archives and Statistics, General Conference, Washington, DC.

9 Early Adventist women: in the shadow of the prophetess

1. 'The Role of Charisma in the Development of Social Movements', *Archives de Sciences Sociales des Religions*, no. 49/1, 1980, p. 95.
2. S. S. Hale, in *Ladies' Magazine*, 1 (1828), pp. 422–3, cited in A. Douglas, *The Feminization of American Culture*, pp. 73, 71.
3. See M. T. Blauvelt, 'Women and Revivalism', in R. R. Ruether and R. S. Keller (eds.), *Women and Religion in America*, vol. 1, pp. 1–9.
4. N. Hardesty, L. S. Dayton, and D. W. Dayton, 'Women in the Holiness Movement', in R. Ruether and E. McLaughlin (eds.), *Women of Spirit*, pp. 224–54.
5. V. L. Brereton and C. R. Klein, 'American Women in Ministry', in J. W. James (ed.), *Women in American Religion*, pp. 171–90; R. P. Beaver, *All Loves Excelling*, pp. 107–8; H. B. Montgomery, *Western Women in Eastern Lands*.
6. 'The Feminization of American Religion', in M. S. Hartman and L. Banner (eds.), *Clio's Consciousness Raised*, pp. 137–57.

7. *Ibid.*, p. 138.
8. See *Comprehensive Index to the Writings of Ellen G. White*, vol. 2, pp. 1828–39.
9. *Ibid.*, vol. 1, pp. 999–1002.
10. *Signs of the Times*, 16 March 1891, p. 85. See also *MH*, pp. 377–8; *Good Health*, March 1880, pp. 76–7.
11. *Appeal to Mothers*, pp. 17–18; *Ed*, p. 196.
12. *Comprehensive Index to the Writings of Ellen G. White*, vol. 3, pp. 2998–3004, while the husband's role is described in considerable, though less, detail, *ibid.*, vol. 2, pp. 1305–9.
13. *MH*, pp. 376–7.
14. *Signs of the Times*, 13 September 1877, p. 286.
15. *5T*, p. 594.
16. *CTBH*, p. 77.
17. 2SG, pp. 107–8.
18. *LS*, p. 131; Letter 12, 1867.
19. See, for example, the dates of the original letters, manuscripts, and articles in the compilations *Child Guidance* and *The Adventist Home*, especially pp. 231–76 of the latter, and the *Subject Index to the Ellen G. White Periodical Articles*, pp. 610–13.
20. A. W. Spalding, 'A Mother in Israel', *Youth's Instructor*, 11 July 1939, p. 13.
21. *2SG*, pp. 107–8.
22. L. Sexton, *Autobiography of Lydia Sexton*, pp. 342–3, cited in Ruether and McLaughlin (eds.), *Women of Spirit*, p. 242.
23. *Review*, 2 January 1879, p. 1.
24. *Good Health*, June 1880, p. 175.
25. Letter 33, 1879.
26. Letter 133, 1898.
27. Letter 83, 1899.
28. Letter 231, 1899.
29. Letter 77, 1898.
30. Manuscript 43a, 1898.
31. Letter 13, 1893.
32. Manuscript 47, 1898.
33. Manuscript 149, 1899.
34. Letter 137, 1898.
35. *Review*, 9 May 1899, p. 293; see also Letter 169, 1900.
36. Manuscript 142, 1903.
37. Letter 164, 1902.
38. *GW*, p. 453.

39. *Ibid.*
40. *Review*, 9 May 1899.
41. *1T*, p. 421.
42. Letter 40a, 1874.
43. *3T*, p. 565.
44. See, for example, 'Special Testimony Relating to Politics', 16 June 1899, in *FE*, pp. 475–84.
45. *Review*, 8 November 1881, pp. 289–90.
46. 'The Temperance Cause in Battle Creek', *Review*, 11 April 1882, p. 232.
47. Letter 118, 1898.
48. Letter 61, 1896.
49. Manuscript 2, 1911.
50. 'Paul Says So', *Review*, 10 September 1857, p. 152.
51. J. White, 'Women in the Church', *Review*, 29 May 1879, p. 172.
52. M. W. Howard, 'Woman as a Co-Worker', *Review*, 18 August 1868, p. 133.
53. G. W. Morse, 'Women as Public Speakers', *Review*, 2 February 1886, p. 75.
54. G. C. Tenney, 'Woman's Relation to the Cause of Christ', *Review*, 5 June 1894, p. 360.
55. See J. G. Beach, *Notable Women of Spirit*, p. 50.
56. For a brief outline of the contribution of women see A. W. Spalding, *Origin and History of Seventh-day Adventists*, vol. 2, pp. 42–9.
57. M. R. White, *Whirlwind of the Lord*, p. 298.
58. A. M. Covington, *They Also Served*, p. 177.
59. For example, Letter 9, 1898; Letter 231, 1899.
60. The *Review* of 4 June 1901 was the last to carry the weekly feature.
61. J. H. Kellogg, *Ladies' Guide in Health and Disease*, pp. 190–1.
62. See Beach, *Notable Women of Spirit*, p. 66.
63. G. I. Butler, 'The Devout and Honorable Women Persecuted', *Review*, 28 May 1889, p. 344.
64. W. A. Colcord, 'Learning the Nature of the WCTU', *Review*, 17 March 1891, p. 171.
65. Mrs L. B. Priddy, 'Women and the Message', *Review*, 13 January 1910, p. 11.
66. R. Runck, 'Woman's Work', *Review*, 30 July 1914, pp. 12–13.
67. J. H. Egbert, 'The Model Woman', *Review*, 11 November 1902, p. 12.
68. L. B. Priddy, 'Woman's Gospel Work', *Review*, 5 November 1901, p. 718.
69. Mrs L. B. Priddy, 'Women and the Message', *Review*, 13 January 1910, p. 11.

70. L. B. Priddy, 'Woman's Gospel Work', *Review*, 5 November 1901, p. 718.
71. S. N. Haskell, 'Employment of Holy Women in Bible Times', *Review*, 13 November 1900, p. 726.
72. Mrs H. A. Morrison, 'Young Womanhood', *Review*, 6 January 1910, pp. 11–12.
73. M. O'Rell, 'Women Losing their Modesty', *Review*, 3 December 1901, p. 783.
74. *Review*, 17 December 1925, p. 13.
75. Letter 138, 1909.
76. *Review*, 9 July 1895, p. 2.
77. Letter from J. W. Watt to O. A. Olsen, 2 January 1896.
78. *PP*, p. 59, cited in H. Jemison, 'Our God-Appointed Roles', unpublished manuscript, n.d., p. 9.
79. James White, *Review*, 13 August 1867, p. 136.
80. *Review*, 20 December 1881, p. 392.
81. Minutes of the General Conference Committee, 30 March 1898, p. 17.

10 Adventist women in the modern church: the pain of liberation

1. *Century of Struggle*, p. 236.
2. K. Bennett and M. Hodge, *Causes of Unrest among the Women of the Church*, p. 11, cited in James, *Women in American Religion*, p. 182.
3. C. Marshall, *To Live Again*, p. 95.
4. C. Marshall, *A Man Called Peter*, p. 55.
5. S. Maitland, *A Map of the New Country*, p. 78.
6. *The Adventist Woman*, November 1984, p. 2. See also *Seventh-day Adventist Yearbook*.
7. B. Dasher, 'Leadership Positions: A Declining Opportunity?', *Spectrum*, vol. 15, no. 4, pp. 35–7.
8. *Review*, 29 February 1949, p. 13.
9. K. H. Wood, 'All Are Needed', *Review*, 14 December 1961, p. 9.
10. V. J. Johns, 'The Security of Togetherness', *Review*, 1 October 1959, pp. 12–13.
11. See, for example, B. Lunday, 'Please Stay Home with Me!', 26 May 1960, p. 12, and J. H. Lammerding, 'What It Means to Be a Christian Mother', 12 November 1959, pp. 12–13.
12. See also M. and J. Butler, 'Back to the Dollhouse: A Look at "Fascinating Womanhood"', *Spectrum*, vol. 7, no. 2, pp. 40–3.
13. H. E. Rice, 'Remember Lot's Wife', *Review*, 4 January 1968, p. 10.

NOTES TO PAGES 156–60

14. For example, 'How Do You Rate as a Wife?', *Review*, 29 May 1969, pp. 10–11; W.M. Booth, 'The Divine Purpose of Marriage', 19 June 1969, pp. 8–9; 21 December 1972, p. 10.
15. F. Taylor, 'God's Appointed Role for Women', *Ministry*, October 1973, pp. 42–4. See also, for example, R.R. Bietz, 'What about a Children's Lib?', *Review*, 26 August 1971, pp. 12–13.
16. L.K. Tobiassen, 'Training for Adventist Women', *Review*, 24 July 1969, p. 8. See also W.R. Beach, 'In Defense of Stable Motion', *Review*, 16 January 1975, pp. 4–5.
17. P. Newman, 'The Liberated Woman', *Review*, 20 November 1975, pp. 8–9.
18. B.J. Butka, 'Women's Liberation', *Spectrum*, vol. 3, no. 4, pp. 22–8.
19. K. Schwartz, ' "Uncle Arthur's Bedtime Stories": A Content Analysis of Sex-Stereotyping', in L. Richardson and V. Taylor (eds.), *Feminist Frontiers*, pp. 84–6. Interestingly enough, Ellen White opposed rigid sex-role stereotyping in children; see *Ed*, pp. 216–17.
20. C.L. Freeman and N.C. Maberly, 'Sexism in SDA Basal Readers', *The Journal of Adventist Education*, December 1980 – January 1981, pp. 14–15, 40–1.
21. Editorial and graphic criteria for content and illustration of 'Seventh-day Adventist reading series', 9 May 1980.
22. R.J. Moore, 'Fact and Fiction about Women and Work', *Spectrum*, vol. 7, no. 2, pp. 34–9.
23. Butka, 'Women's Liberation', *Spectrum*, vol. 3, no. 4, p. 23. See also H. Shryock, *On Becoming a Man*, and *On Becoming a Woman*.
24. E. Larsson, 'We Need More Women Physicians', *Review*, 8 March 1973, p. 14.
25. M. Shelgren, *Life and Health*, October 1975, p. 17.
26. C. Scriven, 'Christianity and Women's Lib', *Insight*, 18 January 1972, p. 18. See also H. Coe, 'The Power behind the Throne', *Ministry*, January 1977, pp. 38–9.
27. K.H. Wood, 'Toward Strengthening the Family', *Review*, 3 February 1977, pp. 2, 15.
28. I. Ross, 'Reaping the Whirlwind?', *Listen*, February 1967, pp. 3–5.
29. R.H. Pierson, 'True Christian Woman Power', *Review*, 4 February 1971, p. 2.
30. L.G. Running, 'The Status and Role of Women in the Adventist Church', *Spectrum*, vol. 4, no. 3, pp. 54–62.
31. K. Watts, 'You've Come a Long Way', *Liberty*, January 1972, p. 10.
32. M. McLeod, *Betrayal*.
33. See T. Dybdahl, 'Merikay and the Pacific Press: Money, Courts and

299

Church Authority', *Spectrum*, vol. 7, no. 2, pp. 44-53; T. Dybdahl, 'Merikay and the Pacific Press: An Update', *Spectrum*, vol. 8, no. 1, pp. 44-5; R. H. Pierson, 'When the Church is Taken to Court', *Review*, 24 March 1977, pp. 6--8; series of articles in *Spectrum*, vol. 8, no. 4, pp. 2-36; N. C. Wilson, 'Pacific Union Settles Litigation', *Review*, 5 January 1978, pp. 17-18; N. C. Wilson, 'Pacific Press Suit Settled out of Court', *Review*, 30 March 1978, p. 32; N. C. Wilson, 'New Information on Litigation', *Review*, 8 June 1978, p. 24; T. Dybdahl, 'Court Verdict on Pacific Press Case', *Spectrum*, vol. 11, no. 1, pp. 14-17; *Spectrum*, vol. 13, no. 3, p. 56.

34. 'Pacific Union Settles Litigation', *Review*, 5 January 1978, pp. 17-18.
35. K. H. Wood, 'Avoid Linguistic Sexisms', *Review*, 30 January 1975, p. 2.
36. 'The Role of Women in the Early Christian Church', unpublished manuscript, 1973.
37. 'Study of the Role of Women in Israel, in the Background of the Contemporary Near East', unpublished manuscript, 1973.
38. 'The Role of Women in the Seventh-day Adventist Church', unpublished manuscript, 1972.
39. 'The Role of Woman Today: A Theology of Relationship – Man to Woman', unpublished manuscript, 1973.
40. 'Survey of the Religious Issue (Role of Women) as Faced in Other Churches (Protestant, Roman Catholic, and Jewish groups)', unpublished manuscript, 1973.
41. B. Stirling, 'Social Change and Women's Liberation: An Evaluation', unpublished manuscript 1973; R. J. Moore, 'Woman-power: The View from down Here', unpublished manuscript, 1971; M. Wood, 'Discrimination and the Adventist Woman Employee', unpublished manuscript, n.d.; L. G. Running, 'Types of Role Available for Ordained Women in the Church', unpublished manuscript, 1973.
42. 'Man and Woman in Genesis 1-3', published as 'Equality from the Start: Women in the Creation Story', *Spectrum*, vol. 7, no. 2, p. 27.
43. 'The Role of Women in the Old Testament outside the Pentateuch', unpublished manuscript, 1976.
44. 'Jesus and the Status of Women', *Review*, 19 August 1976, pp. 7-9; 26 August, pp. 8-10; 2 September, pp. 7-9; 9 September, pp. 6-8.
45. 'Differently but Equally the Image of God: The Meaning of Womanhood according to Four Contemporary Protestant Theologians', unpublished manuscript, January 1976.
46. 'A Summary Report to BRIAD on Roles of Women in the Seventh-day Adventist Church', unpublished manuscript, n.d. [1976].

47. 'An Exegesis of 1 Timothy 2: 11 – 15, and its Implications', unpublished manuscript, 1976, p. 14.
48. 1974 Annual Council action on the role of women in the church, cited in *Ministry*, February 1978, supplement p. 24 0; see also G. Hyde, 'A Summary-Report to BRIAD', pp. 9 – 13.
49. Manuscript later appeared as R. Dederen, 'A Theology of Ordination', *Ministry*, February 1978, supplement 24K – 24P.
50. Cited in J. L. Nelson and Y. Carpenter, 'Breaking the Mold', *Insight*, 30 August 1977, p. 6. See also G. M. Hyde, 'The Ordination of Women', *Review*, 28 October 1976, pp. 12 – 13.
51. L. Neff, 'The Role of Women in American Protestantism, 1975'; manuscript later appeared in *Review*, 5 and 12 August 1976, pp. 1, 6 – 7, and pp. 6 – 8.
52. Correspondence to W. D. Eva, General Conference vice-president, 1974.
53. '175 – 85 GN Role of Women in the Church – Committee Report', pp. 49 – 52, General Conference Minutes.
54. L. Running, 'The Status and Role of Women in the Adventist Church', *Spectrum*, vol. 4, no. 3, pp. 54 – 62.
55. 'The Bible and the Ordination of Women: A Bibliographical Essay', *Spectrum*, vol. 7, no. 2, pp. 29 – 33.
56. A. L. Kwiram, 'How the General Conference Election Works', *Spectrum*, vol. 7, no. 1, pp. 17 – 22.
57. 'How Long Must Women Wait? Prospects for Adventist Church Leadership', *Spectrum*, vol. 12, no. 4, pp. 39 – 43.
58. *Review*, 21 April 1977, p. 18.
59. T. H. Blincoe, 'Needed – a Theology of Ordination', *Ministry*, February 1978, pp. 22 – 4, and R. Dederen, 'A Theology of Ordination', *Ministry*, February 1978, supplement, pp. 24K – 24P.
60. *Spectrum*, vol. 14, no. 3, p. 49.
61. 'Ministers – Both Male and Female?', *Review*, 10 March 1977, pp. 6 – 8.
62. 'The Ordination of Women', *Review*, 28 October 1976, pp. 12 – 13.
63. W. Eva and B. E. Seton, 'Should our Church Ordain Women?', *Ministry*, March 1985, pp. 14 – 22; M. Gordon and L. Rivers, 'Should Women Be Ordained to the Gospel Ministry?', *Review*, 7 March 1985, pp. 5 – 12.
64. J. R. Spangler, 'Ordination of Women', *Ministry*, March 1985, pp. 23 – 4.
65. 1976 edition, p. 86.
66. J. P. Nembhard, 'Women Pastors Begin Baptizing', *Spectrum*, vol. 15, no. 2, pp. 7 – 13.
67. '175 – 85 GN Role of Women in the Church – Committee Report', p. 61. See also '175 – 85 GNb Women's Participation in Church Work'; '175 – 85 NGd Ministerial Worker Functions in NAD – Clarification'.

68. *The Adventist Woman*, September 1984, pp. 6-7.
69. N. Carter and R. Ruether, 'Entering the Sanctuary: The Struggle for the Priesthood in Contemporary Episcopalian and Roman Catholic Experience', in R. Ruether and E. McLaughlin (eds.), *Women of Spirit*, p. 382.
70. Notably in *The Desire of Ages*.

11 Divorce in Adventism: a perennial problem

1. J. Bates, 'Business Proceedings of the Michigan State Conference', *Review*, 14 October 1862, p. 157.
2. Cited in N. M. Blake, *The Road to Reno*, p. 130.
3. *Ibid.*, p. 131.
4. L. C. Halem, *Divorce Reform*, p. 28.
5. Blake, *The Road to Reno*, p. 134.
6. Halem, *Divorce Reform*, pp. 28, 49.
7. *Review*, 26 January 1886, p. 50.
8. *4T*, p. 507. See also *7T*, p. 46.
9. Letter 17, 1896.
10. Manuscript 3, 1854.
11. Manuscript 2, 1863.
12. Letter 8, 1888.
13. Manuscript 2, 1863.
14. Letter 168, 1901. See also Letter 57, 1888.
15. Letter 14a, 1891.
16. *Signs of the Times*, 11 November 1903, p. 10.
17. Letter 50, 1895.
18. Letter 8, 1888. See also Letter 76, 1896.
19. Manuscript 9, 1868. See also Letter 145, 1900.
20. Letter 23, 1871.
21. Letter 51, 1886.
22. Letter 30, 1887.
23. Manuscript 24, 1900.
24. *Review*, 24 March 1868, p. 236.
25. *2T*, p. 100.
26. Letter 34, 1890.
27. Letter 51, 1889.
28. Letter 14, 1895.
29. Letter 175, 1901. See also Letter 109, 1894.
30. Letter 5, 1891.
31. Letter from W. C. White, 21 February 1927.

32. *IT*, p. 215.
33. *Review*, 24 March 1868, p. 236.
34. Letter 41, 1902, and Letter 7a, 1894, and a letter from W. C. White, 21 February 1927.
35. Letter 16, 1887.
36. *Ibid.*
37. Letter 95, 1893.
38. Letter 73, 1886.
39. Letter 40, 1888.
40. Manuscript 2, 1913.
41. *IT*, pp. 215–16.
42. *TM*, pp. 427–8.
43. W. C. White letter, 6 January 1931.
44. *IT*, p. 216.
45. See R. Graybill, 'The Power of Prophecy', pp. 25–53; A. L. White, *Ellen G. White*, vol. 3, pp. 72–83, 130–80.
46. 'Divorce', *Review*, 15 April 1862, p. 160.
47. Bates, 'Business Proceedings of the Michigan State Conference', *Review*, 14 October 1862, p. 157.
48. J. Clarke, 'Divorces', *Review*, 14 July 1874, p. 35.
49. *Review*, 4 September 1879, p. 84.
50. 'Divorce', *Review*, 6 March 1879, p. 79.
51. U. Smith, 'Divorce in America', *Review*, 20 March 1883, p. 184.
52. G. I. Butler, 'Marriage and Divorce', *Review*, 18 December 1883, pp. 785–6.
53. 'Divorce and Marriage', *Review*, 11 January 1887, p. 32.
54. U. Smith, 'Divorce and Marriage', *Review*, 8 February 1887, p. 89.
55. *Ibid.*
56. G. C. Tenney, 'Marriage and Divorce', *Review*, 30 October 1894, p. 681 and G. C. Tenney, 'To Correspondents', *Review*, 31 March 1896, p. 201.
57. *Ibid.*
58. W. C. White letter, 21 February 1927.
59. *Review*, 30 October 1894, p. 681.
60. G. C. Tenney, 'Timely Decision', *Review*, 29 December 1896, p. 825.
61. 'Passing Events and Comments', *Review*, 14 April 1896, p. 231. See also 'Loose Notions about Marriage', *Review*, 13 August 1889, p. 519.
62. G. C. Tenney, 'Marriage and Divorce', *Review*, 30 October 1894, p. 681.
63. 'Influence of Divorce Evil', *Review*, 5 March 1914, p. 9.
64. F. M. Wilcox, 'The Divorce Evil', *Review*, 20 January 1916, p. 5.

12 Divorcing and enforcing: problems with principles and procedures

1. L. C. Halem, *Divorce Reform*, pp. 92, 112.
2. See, for example, 'The God of Love Hates a Divorcing', *The Watchtower*, 1 July 1981, pp. 17–22.
3. A. J. Cherlin, *Marriage, Divorce, Remarriage*, pp. 26, 50.
4. 'On Divorce', *Review*, 26 November 1925, p. 14.
5. *Review*, 26 September 1940, p. 8; *Review*, 10 October 1940, p. 11; *Review*, 28 March 1940, p. 12.
6. F. M. Wilcox, 'Questions from the Field', *Review*, 19 August 1943, p. 2. See also T. E. Bowen, 'The Question of Divorce', *Review*, 28 March 1929, p. 5.
7. F. Lee, 'Divorce: Social Enemy Number One', *Review*, 18 April 1946, p. 5.
8. C. B. Haynes, 'Divorce', *Review*, 8 January 1942, p. 4.
9. *Ibid.*, p. 6.
10. 'Divorce', *Review*, 3 December 1942, p. 10.
11. F. M. Wilcox, 'The Question of Divorce', *Review*, 15 January 1948, p. 4.
12. A. V. Olson, 'The Divorce Question', 5 April 1949, p. 2.
13. 'Proceedings of the General Conference', *Review*, 23 July 1950, p. 228.
14. See *Spectrum*, vol. 7, no. 2, pp. 2 and 10, endnote 1.
15. 'The Minister's Calling, Work and Responsibility', *Ministry*, September 1954, p. 17.
16. R. O. Williams and M. S. Williams, *God's Seventh Commandment*, p. x. This publication was a later and enlarged version of earlier more ephemeral material.
17. *3T*, p. 265, cited in R. R. Bietz, 'Church Standards on Divorce and Remarriage', *Review*, 3 May 1956, p. 9.
18. See, for example, *Review*, 17 June 1965, p. 15; 11 November 1965, p. 13; L. G. Storz, 'Two = One in God's Mathematics', *Review*, 11 August 1966, pp. 1, 7–8.
19. For example, K. H. Wood, 'A Bit of Heaven or a Bit of Hell?', *Review*, 25 March 1971, p. 2; A. L. Campbell, 'The ʻIʼ in Divorce', *Review*, 12 August 1976, pp. 10–11; C. D. Henri, 'Homeless Houses', *Review*, 30 August 1979, pp. 7–8.
20. For example, R. M. Bradshaw, 'Happiness Is Not Divorce', *Review*, 13 June 1974, pp. 10–12.
21. For example, W. R. L. Scragg, 'The Inside Outsiders', *Review*, 10 February 1977, p. 10.
22. C. E. Wittschiebe, *God Invented Sex*, p. 218.
23. M. Moore, 'Divorce, Remarriage and Church Discipline', *Spectrum*, vol. 10, no. 1, pp. 20–2.

24. 'What Does the New Testament Say about Divorce?', *Spectrum*, vol. 13, no. 4, pp. 15–21.
25. N. C. Wilson, *Review*, 17 February 1977, p. 19.
26. 'Annual Council Passes Actions on Conciliation, Divorce and Remarriage', *Review*, 17 February 1977, pp. 12–18.
27. *Review*, 21 April 1977, p. 12.
28. 'Divorce and Remarriage', set of twenty-four tapes, Study Tapes, Redlands, California, 1978–9.
29. 'A Proposed Policy for Marriage, Divorce and Remarriage – The Loma Linda University Church'. This document went through numerous versions but by October 1981 the form had become fairly settled. The definitive version, *Guidelines Regarding Marriage and Divorce*, was published in 1982.
30. Indeed the term 'indissoluble' was used, a description rare if not unique in Adventist literature; see version produced on 1 July 1980, pp. 1–2.
31. Garden ceremonies are popular in the United States.
32. See R. L. Dudley and M. G. Dudley, *Married and Glad of It*.
33. Unpublished statistical report, 1982.
34. Private communication from Home and Family Service, 13 September 1985.
35. For example, F. I. Nye, 'Child Adjustment in Broken and Unhappy Unbroken Homes', *Journal of Marriage and the Family* 19 (1957), pp. 356–61. J. T. Landis argued on the other hand that only 22 per cent of children from broken homes regarded their pre-divorce homes as discordant and were most injured by the shock of the divorce; see 'The Trauma of Children When Parents Divorce', *Journal of Marriage and the Family*, 22 (1960), pp. 7–13.
36. *Marital Breakdown*, p. 141.
37. See, for example, Ellen G. White, *Mind, Character and Personality*, vol. 1, pp. 3–55; vol. 2, pp. 697–728, 755–810. 'Adventist Concepts of Psychology', pp. 180–95.
38. *MH*, p. 361.
39. Dominian, *Marital Breakdown*, p. 142.
40. *Ibid.*, pp. 62–9.
41. *Marriage, Divorce and the Church*, p. 110. See also *Spectrum*, vol. 13, no. 4, pp. 15–21.
42. J. R. Udry, 'Marital Stability by Race, Sex, Education, Occupation, and Income Using 1960 Census Data', in R. F. Winch and L. W. Goodman (eds.), *Selected Studies in Marriage and the Family*, pp. 572–8. M. Rheinstein, *Marriage Stability, Divorce and the Law*, p. 426.
43. *Marriage Stability, Divorce and the Law*, p. 426.

44. See *Divorce Reform*, p. 285.
45. See, for example, W. J. Goode, 'Family Disorganization', in R. K. Merton and R. A. Nisbet (eds.), *Contemporary Social Problems*, pp. 498–500; G. Levinger, 'Marital Cohesiveness and Dissolution: An Integrative Review', in Winch and Godman (eds.), *Selected Studies in Marriage and the Family*, pp. 579–92.
46. *Marriage Stability, Divorce and the Law*, pp. 251–2.
47. K. H. Wood, 'A Bit of Heaven or a Bit of Hell?', *Review*, 25 March 1971, p. 2.
48. See W. J. Goode, 'Family Disorganization', in Merton and Nisbet (eds.), *Contemporary Social Problems*, pp. 524–7.
49. *Marriage, Divorce and the Church*, p. 13.
50. *Ibid.*

13 Homosexuality: the sin unnamed among Adventists

1. J. Katz *Gay American History*, pp. 36–9.
2. *Ibid.*, p. 51.
3. 'The Conception of Homosexuality', *Journal of the American Medical Association*, vol. 6, 2 August 1913, see pp. 335–40, cited in Katz, *Gay American History*, pp. 148–51.
4. Letter from A. L. White, 26 August 1974. In a section of *A Solemn Appeal* not written by Ellen White, there is condemnation of 'effeminacy' (p. 10).
5. See *Plain Facts for Old and Young*, pp. 231, 247.
6. *PP*, pp. 156–70.
7. *PP*, p. 156.
8. *PP*, p. 159.
9. *PP*, p. 160.
10. *Signs of the Times*, 2 September 1875, p. 342.
11. Manuscript 19a, 1886.
12. A. L. White letter, 26 August 1974.
13. *Mind, Character, and Personality*, vol. 1, p. 232.
14. *GC*, pp. 270–1.
15. *PP*, p. 165.
16. See J. Money, *The Destroying Angel*.
17. *2T*, p. 469.
18. See, for example, *2T*, pp. 390–411.
19. *A Solemn Appeal*, p. 14.
20. *Plain Facts for Old and Young*, p. 247.
21. Pp. 102–4, cited in Katz, *Gay American History*, p. 642.

22. See V. Bullough, *Sexual Variance in Society and History*, p. 547; V. Bullough and M. Voght, 'Homosexuality and its Confusion with the "Secret Sin" in Pre-Freudian America', in *Journal of the History of Medicine and Allied Sciences*, vol. 28 (April 1973), pp. 143–55, cited in R. L. Numbers, *Prophetess of Health*, p. 245.
23. *4T*, p. 96.
24. *1T*, p. 421.
25. *Ibid.*
26. Letter 1a, 1864.
27. Manuscript 167, 1897.

14 Homosexuality in Adventism: sin, disease or preference?

1. Katz, *Gay American History*, pp. 129–207.
2. M. S. Weinberg and C. J. Williams, *Male Homosexuals*, pp. 17–30.
3. Katz, *Gay American History*, pp. 95–9.
4. See J. Gerassi, *The Boys of Boise*.
5. V. L. Bullough, *Homosexuality: A History*, p. 63.
6. Statements cited in E. Batchelor, *Homosexuality and Ethics*, pp. 237–41.
7. *Ibid.*, pp. 240–2.
8. The Jehovah's Witnesses' position is made clear in *Awake*, 8 June 1976, pp. 5–12, and 22 June 1980, pp. 17–23; that of the Salvation Army appears in *Positional Statements*, pp. 9–10.
9. S. Hiltner, 'Homosexuality and the Churches', in J. Marmor (ed.), *Homosexual Behavior*, p. 225.
10. For example, *The Interpreter's Bible* (1953), vol. 2, p. 103; vol. 10, p. 72.
11. K. H. Wood, 'Power to Counter All Deviations', *Review*, 15 July 1971, p. 2.
12. *DA*, p. 671.
13. *Review*, 15 July 1971, p. 2.
14. 14 December 1971, p. 10. Emphasis in original.
15. 11 April 1972, p. 2.
16. *DA*, p. 516, cited p. 181.
17. For example, 'Biological Factors in Male Homosexuality', *Medical Aspects of Human Sexuality*, July 1973, pp. 12–27; 'Physical and Biochemical Characteristics of Homosexual Men', *Journal of Consulting and Clinical Psychology*, vol. 39, no. 1, pp. 140–7; 'Adjective Check List Scores of Homosexual Men', *Journal of Personality Assessment*, vol. 35, no. 4, pp. 344–9.
18. 14 December 1976, p. 8.

19. 21 December 1976, p. 15.
20. *Ibid.*, p. 16.
21. *Insight*, 12 April 1977, pp. 2–3.
22. *Ibid.*, 6 September 1977, p. 2.
23. *Ibid.*, p. 3.
24. *Review*, 10 November 1977, p. 3.
25. *Ibid.*
26. *Mind, Character, and Personality*, vol. 1, p. 232.
27. *Review*, 17 February 1977, p. 18.
28. October 1977, p. 48 (330) (British edition).
29. M. Wood, 'Anita Bryant and Homosexuality', *Review*, 6 October 1977, p. 8; see also *These Times*, December 1977, p. 8.
30. Dated 24 June 1977.
31. See *The New York Times*, 22 August 1977, p. 17; *Washington Star*, 22 August 1977, p. E-7; *The National Courier*, 16 September 1977, p. 25.
32. *Montgomery County Sentinel*, 24 November 1977, p. A-11.
33. Meg True, 'Homosexuality in the Family', *Review*, 23 February 1978, pp. 6–8, and 2 March 1978, pp. 7–10.
34. *Review*, 2 March 1978, p. 18.
35. *Review*, 13 April 1978, p. 13.
36. *Review*, 6 April 1978, p. 21.
37. 'Homosexuality: The Lie', *Insight*, 21 March 1978, pp. 11–16.
38. G. F. Will, 'How Far Out of the Closet?', *Insight*, 21 March 1978, pp. 20–3.
39. 20 June 1978, p. 3.
40. 30 May 1978, p. 3.
41. *Review*, 6 July 1978, p. 14.
42. 'The Christian, Homosexuals, and the Law', *Spectrum*, vol. 9, no. 2, pp. 45–50.
43. In D. F. Bigger, 'Marriage and the Family', F 1–10.
44. *Ibid.*, F 2.
45 'The Church's Responsibility to Homosexuals', *Insight*, 16 December 1980, p. 9.
46. *Insight*, 21 July 1981, p. 15.
47. For example, *Changing Homosexuality in the Male*.
48. *Spectrum*, vol. 12, no. 3, p. 48.
49. Recent productions include one series called 'The Healing of Homosexuals', and another entitled 'Homosexuality: Christian Basics for Recovery'.
50. 'Homosexuals Anonymous Policy and Advisory Manual', a regular newsletter, and a book which is in preparation.

51. See private communication from Cook dated 28 September 1984, and issues of *Quester* and *Homosexuals Anonymous News*. Ultimately the work of Quest had to cease because of alleged indiscretions on the part of Cook towards some of his clients. See *Ministry*, September 1987, pp. 4–9.
52. *SDA Kinship Newsletter*, December 1979, pp. 2, 7.
53. August–September 1979, p. 2.
54. J. Stuart, 'Counterfeits', May 1980, p. 4.
55. E. Benton, 'Adventists Face Homosexuality', *Spectrum*, vol. 12, no. 3, p. 35.
56. Dated 1 August 1980.
57. *Newsletter*, October 1980, pp. 1, 11.
58. Seventh-day Adventist Kinship, International Inc., 'Objectives, Purposes, and Beliefs'.
59. Dated 23 April 1981.
60. *Review*, 21 May 1981, p. 15. Such a move was actually made in 1985, although Kinship did not immediately respond to it.
61. 'Gay Ethics', *Newsletter*, January–February 1981, pp. 8–10.
62. Dated 1 May 1981, p. 2.
63. November 1981, p. 5.
64. Dated 19 August 1982.
65. *Kinship Connection*, September 1984, p. 10.
66. *Ibid.*, April 1985, p. 9.
67. *Ibid.*, April 1984, p. 9; January 1985, p. 6.
68. *Ibid.*, March 1984, p. 1.
69. *Ibid.*, August 1984, p. 5.
70. *Ibid.*, January 1984, p. 3.
71. 'The Church and the Homosexual', *Review*, 26 April 1984, pp. 11–12.
72. *Kinship Connection*, June 1984, pp. 2, 4–7.
73. *South Bend Tribune*, 23 October 1983, M-1, p. 23; *The Washington Post*, 3 November 1983, C3. In the early 1950s, V. E. Hendershot was obliged to leave his post as president of the Adventist Theological Seminary, in a similar case; compare *Seventh-day Adventist Yearbook 1952*, p. 266, with that for 1953, pp. 272, 481.
74. *The Washington Post*, 21 July 1984, B3.
75. R. Springett, *Homosexuality in History and the Scriptures*, Washington DC: Biblical Research Institute, 1988; D. Larson, 'Homosexuality', unpublished manuscript, 1983.
76. *Spectrum*, vol. 12, no. 3, p. 38.
77. *Sexual Behavior in the Human Male*, pp. 630–6.
78. *Ibid.*, p. 630.

79. *Sexual Behavior in the Human Female*, pp. 463-6.
80. *Sexual Behavior in the Human Male*, p. 631.
81. *Male Homosexuals*, pp. 248-59.
82. *Sexual Behavior in the Human Male*, p. 486.
83. *Ministry*, September 1981, p. 6.
84. *5T*, p. 513. See also *MYP*, p. 136; *ISM*, p. 328.
85. *Ministry*, September 1981, p. 4.
86. See M. Munger, *Out of the Closet – Into the Light*, pp. 9-11.
87. *Spectrum*, vol. 12, no. 3, p. 38.
88. H. E. Douglass, *Why Jesus Waits*.
89. 'Homosexuality in History', in Marmor (ed.), *Homosexual Behavior*, p. 88.
90. *The Australasian Record*, 26 March 1983, p. 12.
91. *Seventh-day Adventist Encyclopedia*, p. 925.
92. Kinsey *et al.*, *Sexual Behavior in the Human Female*, p. 83; Weinberg and Williams, *Male Homosexuals*, pp. 84-5.
93. R. L. Dudley and M. G. Dudley, 'Adventist Values: Flying High?', *Ministry*, April 1985, p. 7.

15 Adventism in transition

1. 1976 Annual Council resolution, 'Evangelism and Finishing God's Work', cited in *Spectrum*, vol. 8, no. 2, p. 54.
2. W. J. Hackett, 'Preserve the Landmarks', *Review*, 26 May 1977, p. 2.
3. Manuscript 13, 1889.
4. A. Kwiram, 'Can Intellectuals Be at Home in the Church?', *Spectrum*, vol. 8, no. 1, pp. 36-9.
5. F. Guy, 'The Church and its Future: Adventist Theology Today', *Spectrum*, vol. 12, no. 1, pp. 6-14.
6. C. Scriven, 'Radical Discipleship and the Renewal of Adventist Mission', *Spectrum*, vol. 14, no. 3, pp. 11-20.
7. B. R. Wilson, *Contemporary Transformations of Religion*, pp. 4-5.
8. R. Branson, 'A Time for Healing', *Spectrum*, vol. 13, no. 2, p. 2.
9. *Religion in Sociological Perspective*, pp. 106, 125.
10. Chellis, 'The *Review and Herald*, and Early Adventist Response to Organized Labor', *Spectrum*, vol. 10, no. 2, p. 20.
11. Butler, 'The World of E. G. White and the End of the World', *Spectrum*, vol. 10, no. 2, p. 3.
12. *The Social Sources of Denominationalism*, p. 24.
13. E. T. Clark, *The Small Sects in America*, p. 25.
14. R. Graybill, 'Millenarians and Money: Adventist Wealth and Adventist Beliefs', *Spectrum*, vol. 10, no. 2, pp. 31-2
15. Revelation 3: 14-17.

Select bibliography

Books

Adventist sources

Ball, B. W., *The English Connection*, Cambridge: James Clarke, 1981

Beach, J. G., *Notable Women of Spirit*, Nashville, Tenn.: Southern Publishing Association, 1976

Canright, D. M., *Seventh-day Adventism Renounced*, Chicago: Fleming H. Revell, 1889

Church Manual, Washington, DC: General Conference of Seventh-day Adventists, 1932; rev. edns 1934, 1940, 1951, 1963, 1972, 1976, 1981 British edn, Watford, Herts.: British Union Conference of Seventh-day Adventists, 1940

Comprehensive Index to the Writings of Ellen G. White, 3 vols., Mountain View, Calif.: Pacific Press, 1962–3

Covington, A. M., *They Also Served*, Washington, DC: Review & Herald, 1940

Crider, C. C., and R. C. Kistler, *The Seventh-day Adventist Family: An Empirical Study*, Berrien Springs, Mich.: Andrews University Press, 1979

Crisler, C. C., *Organization: Its Character, Purpose and Development in the Seventh-day Adventist Church*, Washington, DC: Review & Herald, 1938

A Critique of 'Prophetess of Health', Washington, DC: Ellen G. White Estate, 1976

Damsteegt, P. G., *Foundations of the Seventh-day Adventist Message and Mission*, Grand Rapids, Mich.: Eerdmans, 1977

Douglass, H. E., *Why Jesus Waits*, Washington, DC: Review & Herald, 1976

Douglass, H. E., E. Heppenstall, H. K. Larondelle, and C. M. Maxwell, *Perfection – the Impossible Possibility*, Nashville, Tenn.: Southern Publishing Association, 1975

Dudley, R., and P. Dudley, *Married and Glad of It*, Washington, DC: Review & Herald, 1980

Emmerson, W. L., *The Reformation and the Advent Movement*, Washington, DC: Review & Herald, 1983

Evans, N., P. T. Magan, and G. Thomason (eds.), *The Home Physician and Guide to Health*, Mountain View, Calif.: Pacific Press, 1923; rev. edn 1931

Ford, H., *No Guns on Their Shoulders*, Nashville, Tenn.: Southern Publishing Association, 1968

Froom, L. E., *Movement of Destiny*, Washington, DC: Review & Herald, 1971
The Prophetic Faith of Our Fathers, 4 vols., Washington, DC: Review & Herald, 1961

Jewett, D., *Sex is Not to Lose Sleep Over*, Mountain View, Calif.: Pacific Press, 1979

Johnsen, C., *God, the Situation Ethicist*, Mezien, Sisteron, France: Untold Story Publishers, n.d.

Kellogg, J. H., *The Home Handbook of Domestic Hygiene and Rational Medicine*, Des Moines, Iowa: W. D. Condit, 1882
Ladies' Guide in Health and Disease, 2nd edn, Battle Creek, Mich.: Modern Medicine Publishing Co., 1893
Man the Masterpiece, rev. edn, Battle Creek, Mich.: Modern Medicine Publishing Co., 1894
Plain Facts about Sexual Life, Battle Creek, Mich.: Office of the *Health Reformer*, 1877
Plain Facts for Old and Young, rev. edn, Burlington, Iowa: I. F. Segner, 1886

Kellogg, J. H., and E. E. Kellogg, *Social Purity / A Talk with Girls*, Battle Creek, Mich.: Good Health Publishing Company, 1891

Kistler, R. C., *Adventists and Labor Unions in the United States*, Washington, DC: Review & Herald, 1984

Knight, J. F., *What a Married Couple Should Know about Sex*, Mountain View, Calif.: Pacific Press, 1979

Kubo, S., *Theology and Ethics of Sex*, Nashville, Tenn.: Review & Herald, 1980

Linden, I., *The Last Trump*, Frankfurt: Peter Lang, 1978

Londis, J., *Abortion: Mercy or Murder?* Nashville, Tenn.: Southern Publishing Association, 1980

Loughborough, J. N., *The Second Great Advent Movement*, Battle Creek, Mich.: General Conference Association of Seventh-day Adventists, 1892

McLeod, M., *Betrayal*, Loma Linda, Calif.: Mars Hill Publications, Inc., 1985

Manual for Ministers, Washington, DC: General Conference of Seventh-day Adventists, 1925

Marriage Education, Washington, DC: Home and Family Service of the General Conference of Seventh-day Adventists, 1979

Maxwell, A. S., *Uncle Arthur's Bedtime Stories*, British edns., Watford, Herts., and Grantham, Lincs.: Stanborough Press, various dates

Mazat, A., *That Friday in Eden*, Mountain View, Calif.: Pacific Press, 1981

Munger, M. S., *Out of the Closet – Into the Light*, Mountain View, Calif : Pacific Press, 1980

Nichol, F. D., *Answers to Objections*, rev. edn, Washington, DC: Review & Herald, 1952

  Ellen G. White and Her Critics, Washington, DC: Review & Herald, 1951

Numbers, R. L., *Prophetess of Health*, New York: Harper & Row, 1976

Oliphant, C. J., *Considering Divorce?*, Washington, DC: Review & Herald, 1975

Olsen, M. E., *A History of the Origins and Progress of Seventh-day Adventists*, Washington, DC: Review & Herald, 1926

Olsen, V. N., *The New Testament Logia on Divorce*, Tübingen: J. C. B. Mohr, 1971

Oosterwal, G., *Mission Possible*, Nashville, Tenn.: Southern Publishing Association, 1972

Pelt, N. van, *The Compleat Marriage*, Nashville, Tenn.: Southern Publishing Association, 1979

Porter, D. S., *A Century of Adventism in the British Isles*, Grantham, Lincs.: Stanborough Press, 1974

Rea, W. T., *The White Lie*, Turlock, Calif.: M. & R. Publications, 1982

Ricchiuti, P. B., *Ellen*, Mountain View, Calif.: Pacific Press, 1977

Robinson, D. E., *The Story of Our Health Message*, 3rd edn, Nashville, Tenn.: Southern Publishing Association, 1965

Robinson, V., *James White*, Washington, DC: Review & Herald, 1976

Russell, E. T., *The Conflict between Capital and Labor*, Washington, DC: Review & Herald, 1912

Schwarz, R. W., *John Harvey Kellogg MD*, Nashville, Tenn.: Southern Publishing Association, 1970

Seventh-day Adventist Bible Commentary, 7 vols., Washington, DC: Review & Herald, 1953–7; rev. edn, 1976; rev. edn, 1977–80

Seventh-day Adventist Dictionary, Washington, DC: Review & Herald, 1960

Seventh-day Adventist Encyclopedia, Washington, DC: Review & Herald, 1966, rev. edn, 1976

Seventh-day Adventist Yearbook, Washington, DC: General Conference of Seventh-day Adventists, formerly *Year Book of the Seventh-day Adventists*

Seventh-day Adventists Answer Questions on Doctrine, Washington, DC: Review & Herald, 1957

Shryock, H., *Happiness for Husbands and Wives*, Washington, DC: Review & Herald, 1949

  On Becoming a Man, Washington, DC: Review & Herald, 1951

  On Becoming a Woman, Washington, DC: Review & Herald, 1951

Spalding, A. W., *Makers of the Home*, Mountain View, Calif.: Pacific Press, 1928

  Origin and History of Seventh-Day Adventists, 4 vols., Washington, DC: Review & Herald, 1962

Spalding, A. W., and B. Wood-Comstock, *The Days of Youth*, Mountain View, Calif.: Pacific Press, 1932

  Growing Boys and Girls, Mountain View, Calif.: Pacific Press, 1931

  Through Early Childhood, Mountain View, Calif.: Pacific Press, 1930

Springett, R., *Homosexuality in History and the Scriptures*, Washington, DC: Biblical Research Institute, 1988

A Study Guide to 'The Adventist Home', Nashville, Tenn.: Southern Publishing Association, 1965

Subject Index to the Ellen G. White Periodical Articles, Washington, DC: Review & Herald, 1977

Tarling, L., *The Edges of Seventh-day Adventism*, Bermagui South, NSW: Galilee, 1981

Vandeman, G., *Planet in Rebellion*, Nashville: Tenn.: Southern Publishing Association, 1960

Weeks, H. B., *Adventist Evangelism in the Twentieth Century*, Washington, DC: Review & Herald, 1969

White, A. L., *Ellen G. White*, 6 vols., Washington, DC: Review & Herald, 1981–5

White, E. G., *The Adventist Home*, Nashville, Tenn.: Southern Publishing Association, 1952

  Appeal to Mothers, Battle Creek, Mich.: Seventh-day Adventist Publishing Association, 1864

  Child Guidance, Nashville, Tenn.: Southern Publishing Association, 1954

  Christ's Object Lessons, Washington, DC: Review & Herald, 1900

  Counsels on Diet and Foods, Washington, DC: Review & Herald, 1938

  Counsels on Health, Mountain View, Calif.: Pacific Press, 1951

  Counsels to Parents, Teachers and Students, 2nd edn, Mountain View, Calif.: Pacific Press, 1943

  The Desire of Ages, Washington, DC: Review & Herald, 1898

  Education, Mountain View, Calif.: Pacific Press, 1903

BIBLIOGRAPHY

Evangelism, Washington, DC: Review & Herald, 1946
Fundamentals of Christian Education, Nashville, Tenn.: Southern
  Publishing Association, 1923
Gospel Workers, 2nd edn, rev. and enlarged, Washington, DC: Review
  & Herald, 1948
The Great Controversy, rev. and enlarged edn, London, Pacific Press, 1893
Life Sketches of Ellen G. White, Mountain View, Calif.: Pacific Press, 1915
Medical Ministry, 2nd edn, Mountain View, Calif.: Pacific Press, 1963
Messages to Young People, Nashville, Tenn.: Southern Publishing
  Association, 1930
Mind, Character, and Personality, 2 vols., Nashville, Tenn.: Southern
  Publishing Association, 1977
Ministry of Healing, Washington, DC: Review & Herald; Oakland,
  Calif.: Pacific Press Publishing Assoc., 1890
Patriarchs and Prophets, Battle Creek, Mich.: Review & Herald, 1890
Prophets and Kings, Mountain View, Calif.: Pacific Press, 1917
The Sanctified Life, Washington, DC: Review & Herald, 1937
Selected Messages, 3 vols., Washington, DC: Review & Herald, 1958 and
  1980
A Solemn Appeal, London: Signs Publishing Company, n.d.
Sons and Daughters of God, Washington, DC: Review & Herald, 1955
Special Testimonies to Ministers and Workers, 2 vols., Payson, Ariz.:
  Leaves of Autumn Books; Series A, 1976, Series B, n.d., reprint edn,
  of pamphlets
Spiritual Gifts, 4 vols., Battle Creek, Mich.: vols. 1 and 2, James White,
  1858, 1860; vols. 3 and 4, Seventh-day Adventist Publishing Association,
  1864; facsimile reproduction, Washington, DC: Review & Herald, 1945
Temperance, Mountain View, Calif.: Pacific Press, 1949
Testimonies for the Church, 9 vols., Mountain View, Calif.: Pacific Press,
  1948
Testimonies to Ministers, 3rd edn, Mountain View, Calif.: Pacific Press,
  1962
Thoughts from the Mount of Blessing, London: International Tract
  Society, 1900
Welfare Ministry, Washington, DC: Review & Herald, 1952
White, E. G., and J. White, *Christian Temperance and Bible Hygiene*, Battle
  Creek, Mich.: Good Health Publishing Company, 1890; reprint edn,
  Payson, Ariz.: Leaves of Autumn Books, 1976
White, E. G., *et al.*, *How to Live*, Battle Creek, Mich.: Seventh-day Adventist
  Publishing Association, 1865
White, J. (ed.), *A Solemn Appeal Relative to Solitary Vice and the Abuses*

and Excesses of the Marriage Relation, Battle Creek, Mich.: The Seventh-day Adventist Publishing Association, 1870; reprint edn, R. L. Numbers (ed.), *Health Reform and Hydrotherapy in Nineteenth Century America*, a Reprint Collection, Bryn Mawr, Calif.: Religion and History Press, 1976

White, M. R., *The Whirlwind of the Lord*, Washington, DC: Review & Herald, 1953

Williams, R. O., and M. S. Williams, *God's Seventh Commandment*, 2nd edn, Sedona, Ariz.: publ. by the authors, 1977

Wittschiebe, C. E., *God Invented Sex*, Nashville, Tenn.: Southern Publishing Association, 1974

Teens and Love and Sex, Washington, DC: Review & Herald, 1982

Your Teens and Sex, Washington, DC: Review & Herald, 1983

Wood-Comstock, B., *All about the Baby*, Mountain View, Calif.: Pacific Press, 1930

Woolsey, R. H., *Christian Sex and Family Planning*, Washington, DC: Review & Herald, 1974

Year Book of the Seventh-day Adventists, Washington, DC, General Conference of Seventh-day Adventists (currently *Seventh-day Adventist Yearbook*)

Zurcher, J. R., *The Nature and Destiny of Man*, New York: Philosophical Library, 1969

Other sources

Ahlstrom, S. E., *A Religious History of the American People*, New Haven, Conn.: Yale University Press, 1972

Andelin, H. B., *Fascinating Womanhood*, Santa Barbara, Calif.: Pacific Press, 1965

Anderson, R. M., *Vision of the Disinherited*, New York: Oxford University Press, 1979

Andorka, R., *Determinants of Fertility in Advanced Societies*, London: Methuen, 1978

Arrington, L. J., and D. Bitton, *The Mormon Experience*, London: Allen & Unwin, 1979

Bailey, D. S., *Homosexuality and the Western Christian Tradition*, London: Longmans, Green & Co., 1955

The Mystery of Love and Marriage, London: SCM Press, 1952

Baker, D. (ed.), *Religious Motivation: Biographical and Sociological Problems for the Church Historian*, Studies in Church History, vol. 15, Oxford: Blackwell, 1978

Banks, J. A., *Prosperity and Parenthood*, London: Routledge & Kegan Paul, 1954

Banks, O., *Faces of Feminism*, Oxford: Martin Robertson, 1981

Barnett, W., *Homosexuality and the Bible*, Wallingford, Pa.: Pendle Hill, 1979

Barnhouse, R. T., *Homosexuality: A Symbolic Confusion*, New York: Seabury Press, 1977

Batchelor, E., *Homosexuality and Ethics*, New York: Pilgrim Press, 1980

Beaver, R. P., *All Loves Excelling*, Grand Rapids, Mich.: Eerdmans, 1968

Beckford, J. A., *The Trumpet of Prophecy*, Oxford: Blackwell, 1975

Bigsby, C., *Superculture: American Popular Culture and Europe*, London: Elek, 1975

Blake, N. M., *The Road to Reno*, New York: Macmillan, 1962

Bliss, K., *The Service and Status of Women in the Churches*, London: SCM Press, 1948

Blodgett, G. (ed.), *Victorian America*, Philadelphia: University of Pennsylvania Press, 1976

Boswell, J., *Christianity, Social Tolerance and Homosexuality*, Chicago: University of Chicago Press, 1980

Boyd, K. M., *Scottish Church Attitudes to Sex, Marriage and the Family 1850–1914*, Edinburgh: John Donald Publishers, 1980

Budd, S., *Sociologists and Religion*, London: Collier-Macmillan, 1973

Bullough, V. L., *Homosexuality: A History*, New York: New American Library, 1980

  Sexual Variance in Society and History, New York: Wiley, 1976

Burridge, K., *New Heaven, New Earth*, Oxford: Blackwell, 1969

Callahan, D., *Abortion: Law, Choice and Morality*, London: Macmillan, 1970

Cherlin, A. J., *Marriage, Divorce, Remarriage*, Cambridge, Mass.: Harvard University Press, 1981

Clark, E. T., *The Small Sects in America*, rev. edn, New York: Abingdon Press, 1949

Coleman, P., *Christian Attitudes to Homosexuality*, London: SPCK, 1980

Cox, F. D., *Human Intimacy*, St Paul, Minn.: West Publishing Co., 1981

Cross, W. R., *The Burned-over District*, New York: Harper & Row, 1950

Daly, M., *Beyond God the Father*, Boston, Mass.: Beacon Press, 1973

  The Church and the Second Sex, New York: Harper & Row, 1968

Davies, C., *Permissive Britain*, London: Pitman, 1975

Dominian, J., *Make or Break*, London: SPCK, 1984

  Marital Breakdown, Harmondsworth, Middlesex: Penguin, 1968

  Marriage, Faith and Love, London: Darton, Longman & Todd, 1981

Donninson, H., *Midwives and Medical Men*, London: Heinemann, 1977
Douglas, A., *The Feminization of American Culture*, New York: Knopf, 1977
Duvall, E.M., *Marriage and Family Development*, New York: J.B. Lippincott, 1977
Ellis, H., and J.A. Symonds, *Sexual Inversion*, London: Wilson & Macmillan, 1897; 3rd edn, revised and enlarged, Philadelphia, Penn.: F.A. Davis, 1915
Ellisen, S.A., *Divorce and Remarriage in the Church*, Grand Rapids, Mich.: Zondervan, 1980
Fagley, R.M., *The Population Explosion and Christian Responsibility*, New York: Oxford University Press, 1960
Flexner, E., *Century of Struggle*, rev. edn, Cambridge, Mass.: Belknap Press, 1975
Foster, L., *Religion and Sexuality*, New York: Oxford University Press, 1981
Fryer, P., *The Birth Controllers*, London: Secker & Warburg, 1965
Gardner, R.F.R., *Abortion: The Personal Dilemma*, Exeter: Paternoster Press, 1972
Gaustad, E.S., *Historical Atlas of Religion in America*, rev. edn, New York: Harper, 1976
A Religious History of America, 2nd edn, New York: Harper & Row, 1974
Gaustad, E.S. (ed.), *The Rise of Adventism*, New York: Harper & Row, 1974
Gay, P., *Bourgeois Experience*, vol. 1, Oxford: Oxford University Press, 1984
Gerassi, J., *The Boys of Boise*, New York: Collier, 1968
Glock, C.Y., and R.N. Bellah, *The New Religious Consciousness*, Berkeley and Los Angeles: University of California Press, 1976
Glock, C.Y., B.B. Ringer, and E.R. Babbie, *To Comfort and to Challenge* Berkeley, Calif.: University of California Press, 1967
Glock, C.Y., and R. Stark, *Religion and Society in Tension*, Chicago: Rand McNally & Co., 1965
Goode, W.J., *After Divorce*, Glencoe, Ill.: Free Press, 1956
Women in Divorce, New York: Free Press, 1969
Hageman, A.L. (ed.), *Sexist Religion and Women in the Church — No More Silence*, New York: Association Press, 1974
Halem, L.C., *Divorce Reform*, New York: Free Press, 1980
Hall, R.E., *Abortion in a Changing World*, 2 vols., New York: Columbia University Press, 1970
Hansen, K.J., *Mormonism and the American Experience*, Chicago: University of Chicago Press, 1981
Hartman, M.S., and L. Banner (eds.), *Clio's Consciousness Raised: New Perspectives on the History of Women*, New York: Harper & Row, 1974

BIBLIOGRAPHY

Hatterer, L. J., *Changing Homosexuality in the Male*, New York: McGraw-Hill, 1970

Heron, A. (ed.), *Towards a Quaker View of Sex*, London: Friends Home Service Committee, 1963

Hill, M. (ed.), *A Sociological Yearbook of Religion in Britain*, vol. 7, London: SCM Press, 1974

Himes, N. E., *Medical History of Contraception*, New York: Schocken Books, 1970

Hirschfeld, M., *Die Homosexualität des Mannes und des Weibes*, Berlin: L. Marcus, 1914.

The Holy Bible, authorized King James' version

Hovey, A., *The Scriptural Law of Divorce*, Philadelphia: American Baptist Publication Society, 1866

Hyde, H. M., *The Other Love*, London: Heinemann, 1970

The Interpreter's Bible, 12 vols., New York: Abingdon Press, 1951-7

James, J. W. (ed.), *Women in American Religion*, Philadelphia: University of Pennsylvania Press, 1980

Jones, H. K., *Towards a Christian Understanding of the Homosexual*, New York: Association Press, 1966

Katz, J., *Gay American History*, New York: Thomas Y. Crowell Co., 1976

Kelsey, G. D., *Social Ethics among Southern Baptists*, Metuchen, NJ: Scarecrow Press, 1973

Kinsey, A. C., W. B. Pomeroy, C. E. Martin, and P. H. Gebhard, *Sexual Behavior in the Human Female*, Philadelphia: W. B. Saunders Co., 1953

Kinsey, A. C., W. B. Pomeroy, and C. E. Martin, *Sexual Behavior in the Human Male*, Philadelphia: W. B. Saunders Co., 1948

The Lambeth Conferences 1867-1930, London: SPCK, 1948

Leathard, A., *The Fight for Family Planning*, London: Macmillan, 1980

Lifton, R. J., *The Woman in America*, Boston, Mass.: Houghton Mifflin, 1965

Lovelace, R. F., *Homosexuality and the Church*, London: Lamp Press, 1979

Luker, K. *Abortion and the Politics of Motherhood*, Berkeley, Calif.: University of California Press, 1984

McCormick, E. P., *Attitudes toward Abortion*, Lexington, Mass.: D. C. Heath & Co., 1975

McLoughlin, W. G., *Modern Revivalism*, New York: Ronald Press, 1959

McNeill, J. J., *The Church and the Homosexual*, Shawnee, Kan.: Sheed, Andrews & McNeel, 1976

Macourt, M., *Towards a Theology of Gay Liberation*, London: SCM Press, 1976

Maitland, S., *A Map of the New Country: Women and Christianity*, London: Routledge & Kegan Paul, 1983

Marmor, J. (ed.), *Homosexual Behavior: A Modern Reappraisal*, New York: Basic Books, 1980

Marshall, C., *A Man Called Peter*, New York: McGraw-Hill, 1951
To Live Again, New York: McGraw-Hill, 1957

Martin, D., *A General Theory of Secularization*, Oxford: Blackwell, 1978

Marty, M., *The New Shape of American Religion*, New York: Harper, 1959

May, E. T., *Great Expectations: Marriage and Divorce in Post-Victorian America*, Chicago: University of Chicago Press, 1980

Merton, R. K., and R. A. Nisbet (eds.), *Contemporary Social Problems*, New York: Harcourt Brace, 1961

Mohr, J. C., *Abortion in America*, New York: Oxford University Press, 1978

Money, J., *The Destroying Angel*, Buffalo, NY: Prometheus Books, 1985

Montgomery, H. B., *Western Women in Eastern Lands*, New York: Macmillan, 1910

The New English Bible, Oxford and Cambridge: Oxford University Press, and Cambridge University Press, 1970

The New International Commentary on the New Testament, Grand Rapids, Mich.: Eerdmans, 1953–

Niebuhr, H. R., *The Social Sources of Denominationalism*, Cleveland, Ohio: World Publishing Co., 1957

Noonan, J. T., *Contraception: A History of its Treatment by the Catholic Theologians and Canonists*, New York: Mentor-Omega Books, 1967

Noonan, J. T. (ed.), *Morality of Abortion: Legal and Historical Perspectives*, Cambridge, Mass.: Harvard University Press, 1970

O'Dea, T. F., *The Mormons*, Chicago: University of Chicago Press, 1957
The Sociology of Religion, Englewood Cliffs, NJ: Prentice-Hall, 1966

Osofsky, H. J., and J. D. Osofsky, *The Abortion Experience*, Hagerstown, Md.: Harper Row, 1973

Packard, V., *The Status Seekers*, Harmondsworth, Middlesex: Penguin, 1965

Paxton, G. J., *The Shaking of Adventism*, Wilmington, Del.: Zenith Publishers, 1977

Penton, M. J., *Apocalypse Delayed*, Toronto: University of Toronto Press, 1985

Petersen, W., *Population*, New York: Macmillan, 1969

Pittenger, N., *Time for Consent*, London: SCM Press, 1976

Positional Statements, London: Salvation Army, 1980

Potts, M., P. Diggory, and J. Peel, *Abortion*, Cambridge: Cambridge University Press, 1977

Rentoul, R.R., *The Causes and Treatment of Abortion*, Edinburgh: Pentland, 1889

Rheinstein, M., *Marriage Stability, Divorce and the Law*, Chicago: University of Chicago Press, 1972

Rice, F.P., *Contemporary Marriage*, Boston: Allyn & Bacon, 1983

Richardson, L., and V. Taylor (eds.), *Feminist Frontiers*, Reading, Mass.: Addison-Wesley Publishing Co., 1983

Ruether, R.R., *Liberation Theology*, New York: Paulist Press, 1972
New Woman, New Earth, New York: Seabury Press, 1975

Ruether, R.R. (ed.), *Religion and Sexisms*, New York: Simon & Schuster, 1974

Ruether, R.R., and R.S. Keller (eds.), *Women and Religion in America*, vol. 1, San Francisco: Harper & Row, 1981

Ruether, R., and E. McLaughlin (eds.), *Women of Spirit*, New York: Simon & Schuster, 1979

Ryder, N.B., and C.F. Westoff, *Reproduction in the United States, 1965*, Princeton, NJ: Princeton University Press, 1971

St John Stevas, N., *Life, Death and the Law*, London: Eyre & Spottiswoode, 1961

Scanzoni, L., and V.R. Mollenkott, *Is the Homosexual my Neighbour?*, London: SCM Press, 1978

Schwartz, G., *Sect Ideologies and Social Status*, Chicago: University of Chicago Press, 1970

Shaner, D.W., *A Christian View of Divorce*, Leiden: Brill, 1969

Sider, R., *Rich Christians in an Age of Hunger*, London: Hodder & Stoughton, 1978

Smith, T., *Revivalism and Social Reform*, New York: Harper & Row, 1965

Spitzer, W.O., and C.L. Saylor (eds.), *Birth Control and the Christian*, Wheaton, Ill.: Tyndale House, 1969

Stephenson, A.M.G., *Anglicanism and the Lambeth Conferences*, London: SPCK, 1978

Thielicke, H., *The Ethics of Sex*, Grand Rapids, Mich.: Baker Book House, 1975

Troeltsch, E., *The Social Teaching of the Christian Churches*, 2 vols., trans. by O. Wyon, London: Allen & Unwin, 1931

Wallis, R., *The Elementary Forms of the New Religious Life*, London: Routledge & Kegan Paul, 1984

Weinberg, M.S., and C.J. Williams, *Male Homosexuals: Their Problems and Adaptations*, New York: Oxford University Press, 1974

Whelpton, P., A.A. Campbell, and J.E. Patterson, *Fertility and Family Planning in the United States*, Princeton, NJ: Princeton University Press, 1966

Whiteley, C.H., and W.M. Whiteley, *Permissive Morality*, London: Methuen, 1964

Whitworth, J.M., *God's Blueprints*, London: Routledge & Kegan Paul, 1975

Wilson, B.R., *Contemporary Transformations of Religion*, Oxford: Clarendon Press, 1976

Religion in a Secular Society, London: C.A. Watts, 1966

Religion in Sociological Perspective, New York: Oxford University Press, 1982

Sects and Society, London: Heinemann, 1961

Wilson, B.R. (ed.), *Patterns of Sectarianism*, London: Heinemann, 1967

Winch, R.F., and L.W. Goodman (eds.), *Selected Studies in Marriage and the Family*, Chicago: Holt, Rinehart & Winston, 1968

Winnett, A.R., *The Church and Divorce*, London: Mowbray, 1968

Divorce and Remarriage in Anglicanism, London: Macmillan, 1958

Wood, C., and B. Suitters, *The Fight for Acceptance*, Aylesbury, Bucks.: Medical and Technical Publishing Co., 1970

Wright, D.F. (ed.), *Essays on Evangelical Social Ethics*, Exeter: Paternoster Press, n.d.

Periodicals

Adventist sources

Adventist Health Ministry
Adventist Heritage
The Adventist Woman
The Australasian Record
Day Star
Forum
Good Health
Health Reformer
Homosexuals Anonymous News
Insight
The Journal of Adventist Education
Liberty
Life and Health
Lifeline
Listen
Message Magazine
The Midnight Cry
Ministry

Quester
Review and Herald, also known during its history as the *Second Advent Review and Sabbath Herald*, *The Advent Review and Sabbath Herald*, the *Adventist Review*, and *The Review*
Sabbath School Lessons
SDA Kinship Connection, formerly *Newsletter*
Signs of the Times
Southern Watchman
Spectrum
These Times
Update
Youth's Instructor

Other sources

Archives de Sciences Sociales des Religions
Awake
British Journal of Psychology
British Journal of Sociology
Businessweek
Christianity Today
The Christian Science Monitor
Discover
International Review of Social History
Japanese Journal of Religious Studies
Journal of Consulting and Clinical Psychology
Journal of Environmental Pathology and Toxicology
Journal of Marriage and the Family
The Journal of Pastoral Counselling
Journal of Personality Assessment
Medical Aspects of Human Sexuality
Montgomery County Sentinel
The Montgomery Journal
The National Courier
Newsletter of the Movement for the Ordination of Women
Newsweek
The New York Times
Review of Religious Research
The Sabbath Recorder
The South Bend Tribune
The Sunday Times

BIBLIOGRAPHY

Time
The Times
The Washington Post
Washington Star
The Watchtower

Unpublished material

Adventist sources

The majority of titles listed here will be found in the Office of Archives and Statistics, General Conference. The remainder are in the author's own collection

'Adventist Concepts of Psychology', Washington, DC: Department of Education, General Conference of Seventh-day Adventists, 1977
Anderson, E. M., 'The Roles of Women in the Seventh-day Adventist Church – A Study of E. G. White Writings', 1976
Benton, J., 'A Survey of Current Trends Which Have Raised the Issue of the Role of Women in the Church', 1973
Bigger, D. F., 'Marriage and the Family', n.d.
'Consultation II', General Conference of Seventh-day Adventists, 1981
'Counsels from the Spirit of Prophecy on Labor Unions and Confederacies', n.d.
Dederen, R., 'The Role of Women Today: A Theology of Relationship – Man to Woman', 1973
'A Theology of Ordination', 1976
Delafield, D. A., 'Pornography and Homosexuality', n.d.
Dudley, R. L., and M. G. Dudley, 'Values and the Adventist Family', 1984
Dunn, R. H., 'The Nature of Man in the Early Stages of Life and our Responsibility', 1977
Gladson, J. A., 'The Role of Women in the Old Testament outside the Pentateuch', 1976
Graybill, R. D., 'The Power of Prophecy: Ellen G. White and the Women Religious Founders of the Nineteenth Century', Ph.D. Thesis, The Johns Hopkins University, 1983
Guy, F., 'Differently but Equally the Image of God: The Meaning of Womanhood according to Four Contemporary Protestant Theologians', 1976
Haldeman, M., 'The Role of Women in the Early Christian Church', 1973
Henderson, R., 'The Role of Seventh-day Adventist Women in the Women's Rights Movement', 1972

Holbrook, R. B., 'The Pauline Concept of the Roles of Women', 1975

'Homosexuals Anonymous Policy and Advisory Manual', Reading, Penn.: Quest Learning Center, 1984

Howard, C., 'Ordination Now: Women and the Seventh-day Adventist Church', n.d.

Hyde, G. M., 'A Summary-Report to BRIAD on Roles of Women in the Seventh-day Adventist Church', n.d. [1976]

'Interruption of Pregnancy – Statement of Principles: Recommendations to SDA Medical Institutions', Minutes of Officers' Meeting, 21 June 1971

Jemison, H., 'Our God-Appointed Roles', n.d.

Kubo, S., 'An Exegesis of 1 Timothy 2:11–15 and its Implications', 1976

Larson, D. R., 'The Etiology of Homosexuality in English Medical Periodical Literature, 1965–75', 1976

'Homosexuality', 1983

Minutes of the General Conference Committee

Moore, R. J., 'Womanpower: The View from down Here', 1971

Nelson, R. M., 'Reverence for Life', Address to the General Conference of the Church of Jesus Christ of Latter-Day Saints, 6 April 1985

Neuffer, J., 'First Century Cultural Backgrounds in the Greco-Roman Empire', n.d.

Nies, R. D., 'Divorce and Remarriage', 1979

'North American Division Church Size and Membership Distribution', Review & Herald, 1983

'Objectives, Purposes and Beliefs', Seventh-day Adventist Kinship International, Inc.

Olsen, A. V., 'The Divorce Question', 1949

Pelt, J., 'The Soul, the Pill, and the Fetus', n.d.

'Population Sampling Report of the Seventh-day Adventists in the United States', Department of Education and Missionary Volunteer Department of the General Conference of Seventh-day Adventists, 1952

'A Proposed Policy for Marriage, Divorce and Remarriage – The Loma Linda University Church', various dates

'Report of the Committee on the Role of Women in the Church', 1985

'Report on Financial Statements 1981', Seventh-day Adventist World Service

Running, L. G., 'Study of the Role of Women in Israel, in the Background of the Contemporary Near East', 1973

'Survey of the Religious Issue (Role of Women) as Faced in Other Churches (Protestant, Roman Catholic, and Jewish Groups)', 1973

'Types of Role Available for Ordained Women in the Church', 1973

Schantz, B., 'The Development of Seventh-day Adventist Missionary Thought: A Contemporary Appraisal', Ph.D. Thesis, Fuller Theological Seminary, 1983

'Seminar on Genetic Engineering', Washington, DC, Department of Health, General Conference of Seventh-day Adventists, 1979

'The Spirit of Prophecy and Adultery, Divorce, Remarriage and Church Membership', Washington, DC: White Estate, 1975

Springett, R., 'The Bible and Homosexuality', n.d. [1985]

Staples, R. L., 'The Church and Polygamy in Sub-Saharan Africa', 1981

Stirling, B., 'Social Change and Women's Liberation: An Evaluation', 1973

'Society, Women and the Church', 1976

Süring, M., 'Reflections on the Ordination of Women', 1972

'Survey on the Role of Women in the Church', 1985

Syme, D. R., 'Program Feasibility Assessment – Kenya Private Sector Family Planning Project', 6 July 1983, commissioned by SDA World Service Inc., Washington, DC

Teel, C., 'Withdrawing Sect, Accommodating Church, Prophesying Remnant: Dilemmas in the Institutionalization of Adventism', 1980

Trenchard, W. C., 'Cleaving and Leaving: Marriage and Divorce in the Bible', n.d.

Vine, K. L., 'The Legal and Social Status of Women in the Pentateuch', 1976

Watts, K., 'The Role of Women in the Seventh-day Adventist Church', 1972

White, A. L., 'Marital Relations', 1962

Witzel, J., 'Compilation of Answers to Questions on Moral Issues Asked by Michael Pearson – Far Eastern Divison', 1981

Wood, M., 'Discrimination and the Adventist Woman Employee', n.d.

Yost, F. D., 'An Inquiry into the Role of Women in the SDA Church', 1977

Other sources

Morgan, J. L., 'A Sociological Analysis of Some Developments in the Moral Theology of the Church of England since 1900', Ph.D. Thesis, University of Oxford, 1976

Theobald, R., 'The Seventh-day Adventist Movement: A Sociological Study with Particular Reference to Great Britain', Ph.D. Thesis, University of London, 1979

BIBLIOGRAPHY

Published reports and ephemera

Adventist sources

Adventist Adoption and Family Services, n.d.

Annual Report 1983–4, Washington, DC: Adventist Development and Relief Agency International, 1984

Annual Statistical Report of Seventh-day Adventists, Washington, DC: General Conference of Seventh-day Adventists

Constitution, Bylaws and Working Policy, 1977 edn, General Conference of Seventh-day Adventists

Ethics Center, Loma Linda, Calif.: Loma Linda University for Christian Bioethics, n.d.

Guidelines Regarding Marriage and Divorce, Loma Linda University Church of Seventh-day Adventists, 1982

Pregnant?, Adventist Adoption Agency

Quest Learning Center – A Brief Look, Reading, Penn.: Quest, n.d.

SDA Kinship International Inc., Los Angeles: SDA Kinship International, Inc., 1983

Seventh-day Adventist Youth at the Mid-Century, Washington, DC: Review & Herald, 1951

Sexual Solitaire, Hollywood, Calif.: Wayout, 1971

Tel-Health, Florida Hospital, Orlando

Two of a Kind, Hollywood, Calif.: Wayout, 1977

Welcome to Adventist Contact, Takoma Park, Md.: Adventist Contact, 1977

Other sources

Abortion: An Ethical Discussion, London: Church Information Office, 1965

Causes of Unrest among the Women of the Church, Report Issued by the Special Committee of the General Council of the Presbyterian Church in the USA, 1927

Declaration on the Question of Admission of Women to the Ministerial Priesthood, 1977

The Family in Contemporary Society, London: SPCK, 1958

Homosexual Relationships: A Contribution to Discussion, London: Church Information Office, 1979

Justice and Non-Violence, Report of the General Board, Church of the Brethren Annual Conference, 1977

The Lambeth Conference: Encyclical Letter from the Bishops together with Reports and Resolutions, London: SPCK, 1908, 1920, 1930, 1948, 1958, 1968, 1978

327

BIBLIOGRAPHY

Marriage, Divorce and the Church, London: SPCK, 1971

The Problem of Homosexuality, London: Church Information Office, 1954

Putting Asunder, London: SPCK, 1966

Report of the Committee on Homosexual Offence and Prostitution, London: HMSO, 1957

Sexual Offenders and Social Punishment, London: Church Information Office, 1956

So Much in Common: Documents of Interest in the Conversations between the World Council of Churches and the Seventh-day Adventist Church, Geneva: World Council of Churches, 1973

Women in Ministry: A Study, London: Church Information Office, 1968

3 5282 00663 8889

Printed in the United States
134822LV00006B/24/P